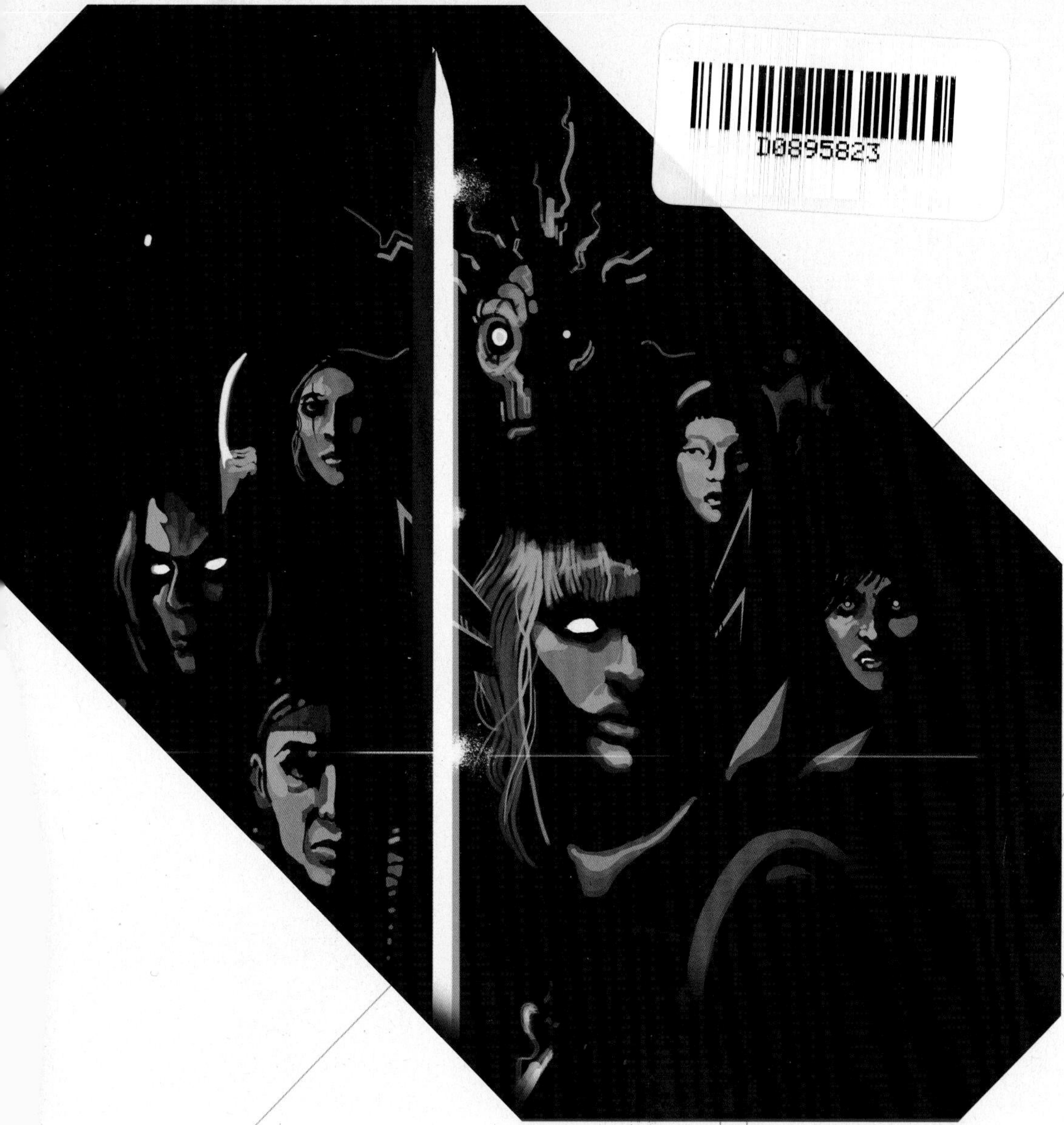

[kra_]
[koa_]

[reign_of_x]

REIGN OF X VOL. 7. Contains material originally published in magazine form as X-FORCE (2019) #18-19, CHILDREN OF THE ATOM (2021) #2, NEW MUTANTS (2019) #16-17 and CABLE (2020) #9. First printing 2021. ISBN 978-1-302-93203-9. Published by MARVEL WORLDWIDE, INC., a subsidiary of MARVEL ENTERTAINMENT, LLC. OFFICE OF PUBLICATION: 1290 Avenue of the Americas, New York, NY 10104. © 2021 MARVEL No similarity between any of the names, characters, persons, and/or institutions in this book with those of any living or dead person or institution is intended, and any such similarity which may exist is purely coincidental. **Printed in the Canada.** KEVIN FEIGE, Chief Creative Officer; DAN BUCKLEY, President, Marvel Entertainment; JOE QUESADA, EVP & Creative Director; DAVID BOGART, Associate Publisher & SVP of Talent Affairs; TOM BREVOORT, VP, Executive Editor; NICK LOWE, Executive Editor, VP of Content, Digital Publishing; DAVID GABRIEL, VP of Print & Digital Publishing; JEFF YOUNGQUIST, VP of Production & Special Projects; ALEX MORALES, Director of Publishing Operations; DAN EDINGTON, Managing Editor; RICKEY PURDIN, Director of Talent Relations; JENNIFER GRÜNWALD, Senior Editor, Special Projects; SUSAN CRESPI, Production Manager; STAN LEE, Chairman Emeritus. For information regarding advertising in Marvel Comics or on Marvel.com, please contact Vit DeBellis, Custom Solutions & Integrated Advertising Manager, at vdebellis@marvel. com. For Marvel subscription inquiries, please call 888-511-5480. **Manufactured between 10/1/2021 and 11/2/2021 by SOLISCO PRINTERS, SCOTT, QC, CANADA.**

10 9 8 7 6 5 4 3 2 1

REIGN OF X

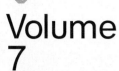

Volume
7

X-Men created by Stan Lee & Jack Kirby

Writers:	**Benjamin Percy, Vita Ayala & Gerry Duggan**
Artists:	**Garry Brown, Bernard Chang, Rod Reis & Phil Noto**
Color Artists:	**Guru-eFX, Marcelo Maiolo, Rod Reis & Phil Noto**
Letterers:	**VC's Joe Caramagna, Travis Lanham & Joe Sabino**
Cover Art:	**Joshua Cassara & Dean White; R.B. Silva & Erick Arciniega; Christian Ward; and Phil Noto**
Head of X:	**Jonathan Hickman**
Design:	**Tom Muller**
Assistant Editors:	**Lauren Amaro & Shannon Andrews Ballesteros**
Editors:	**Mark Basso, Chris Robinson, Annalise Bissa & Jordan D. White**
Collection Cover Art:	**Christian Ward**
Collection Editor:	**Jennifer Grünwald**
Assistant Editor:	**Daniel Kirchhoffer**
Assistant Managing Editor:	**Maia Loy**
Assistant Managing Editor:	**Lisa Montalbano**
VP Production & Special Projects:	**Jeff Youngquist**
SVP Print, Sales & Marketing:	**David Gabriel**
Editor in Chief:	**C.B. Cebulski**

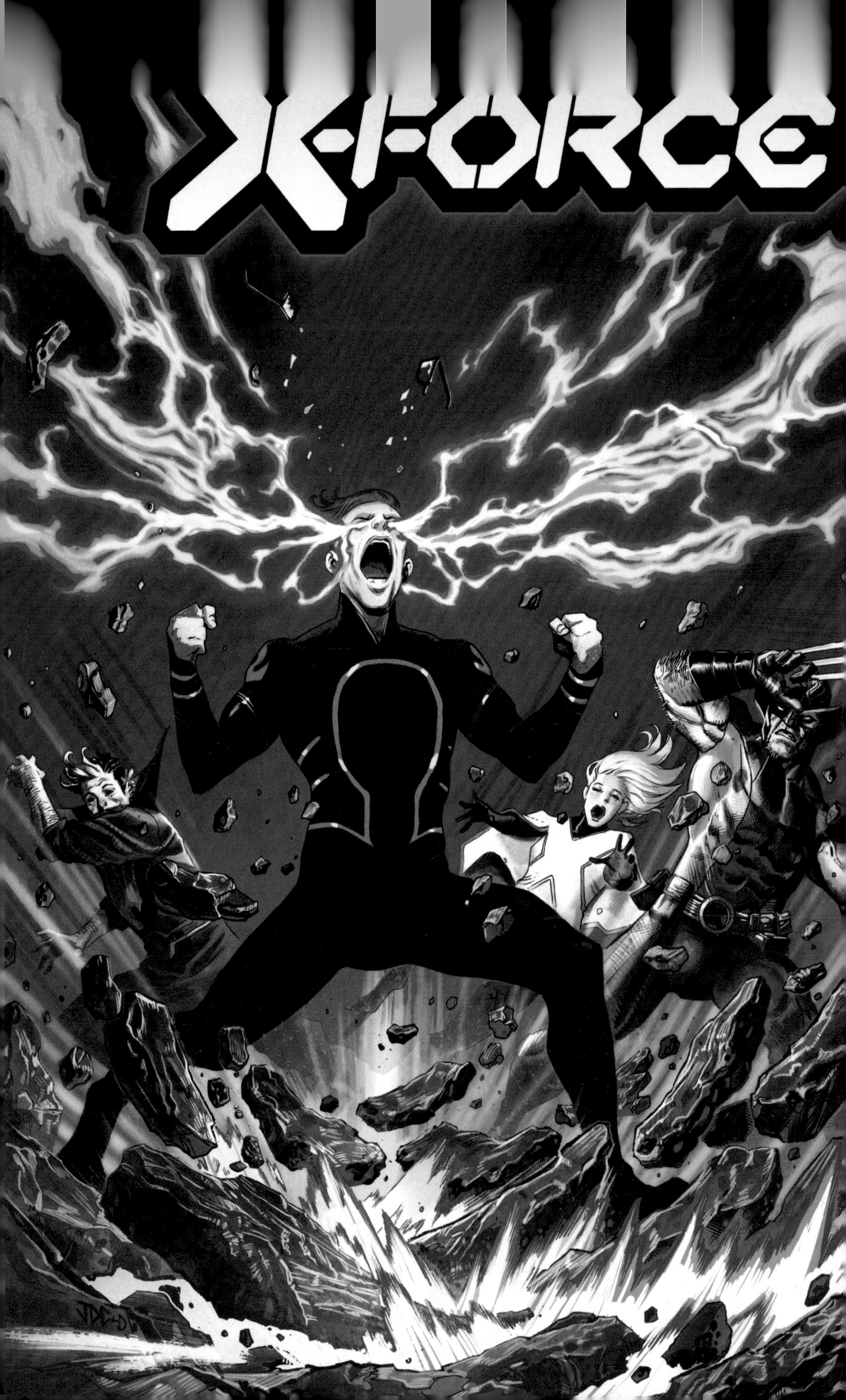
X-FORCE

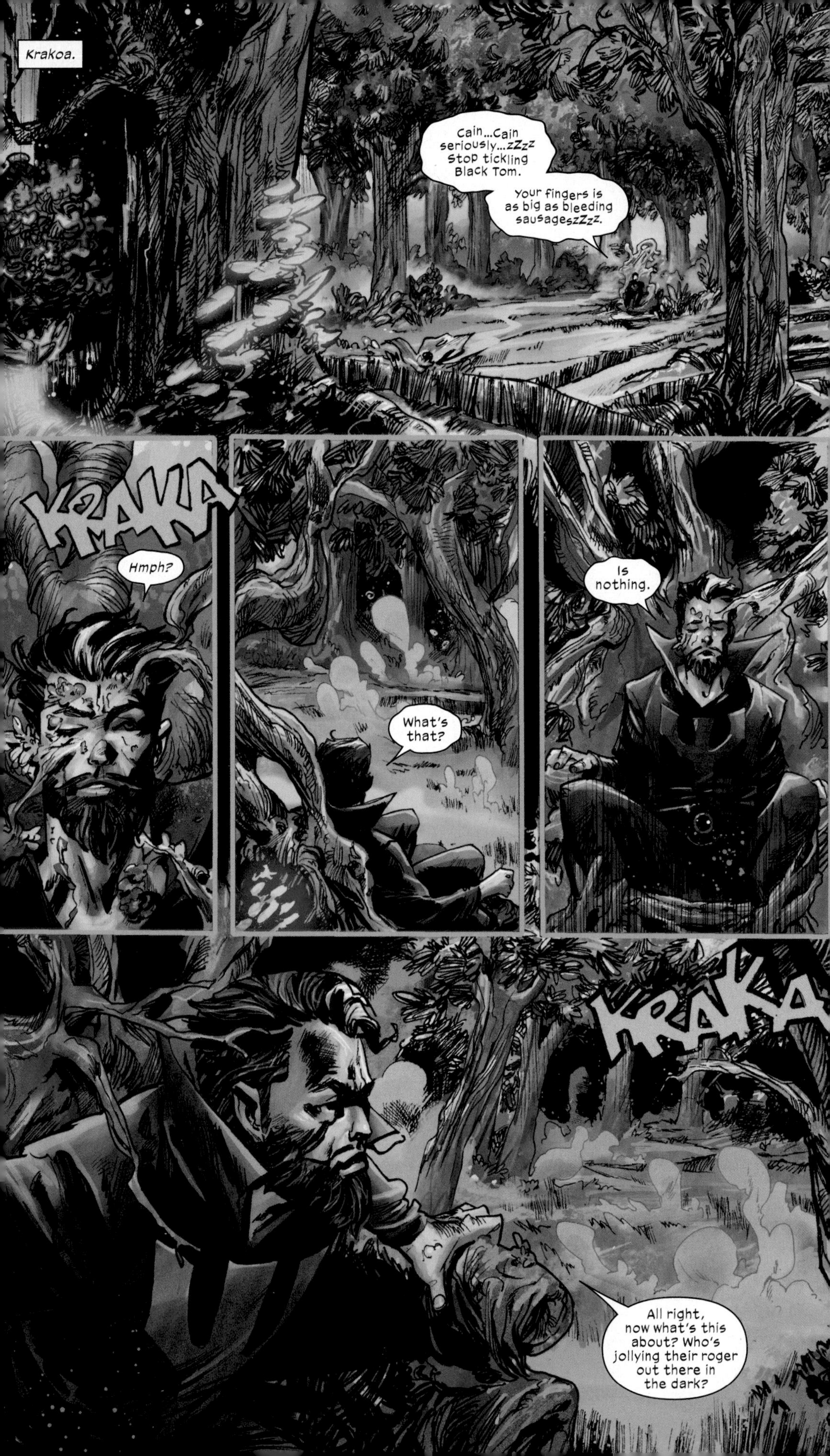
Krakoa.
Cain...Cain seriously...zZzz stop tickling Black Tom.
Your fingers is as big as bleeding sausageszZzz.
KRAKA
Hmph?
What's that?
Is nothing.
KRAKA
All right, now what's this about? Who's jollying their roger out there in the dark?

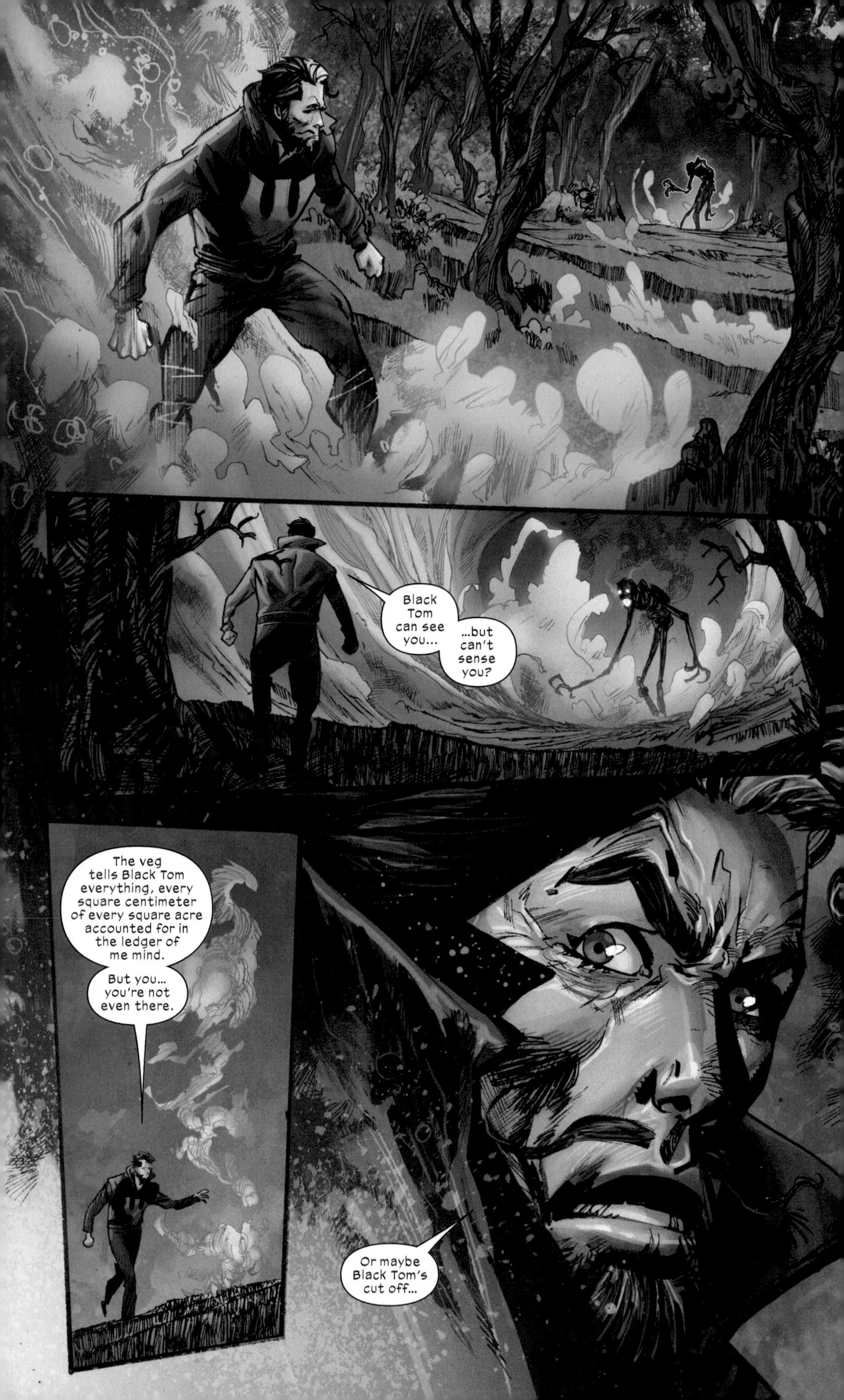
Black Tom can see you...
...but can't sense you?
The veg tells Black Tom everything, every square centimeter of every square acre accounted for in the ledger of me mind.
But you... you're not even there.
Or maybe Black Tom's cut off...

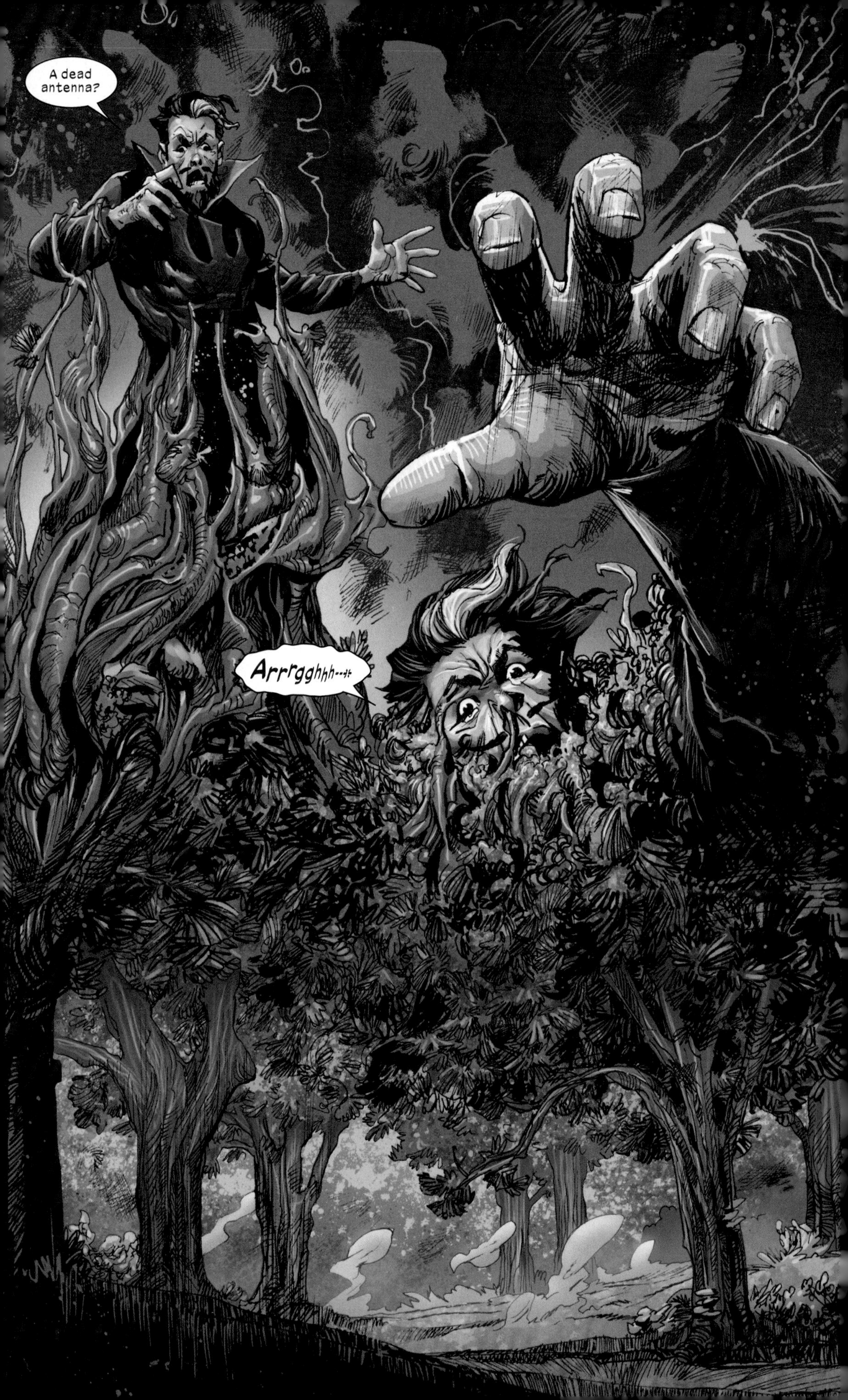
A dead antenna?
Arrrgghhh--!!

[00_mutant__espionage]
[00_law_order____X___]

WHAT CAN YOU REMEMBER?

Something is stalking the shores of Krakoa. Meanwhile, outside their borders, suspicion has been cast upon the new nation after a psychic attack on a cruise liner seems to point to a mutant perpetrator. Quentin was dispatched to investigate -- but was killed before being able to apprehend the culprit. Missing the memory of his death between Cerebro backups, Quentin and his girlfriend, Phoebe, are on the case to clear Krakoa's name...but when the surviving victims start showing Quentin's own psychic fingerprints, the two are forced to dig deeper into the source of this mystery, a source that may be closer to home than they realize...

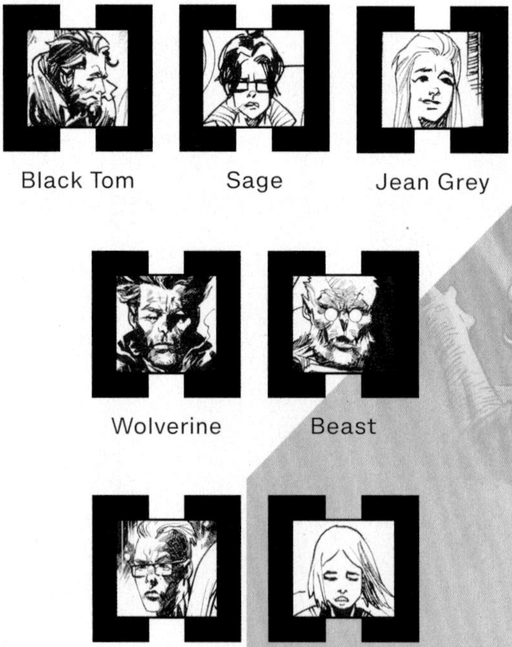

Black Tom Sage Jean Grey

Wolverine Beast

Kid Omega Phoebe Cuckoo

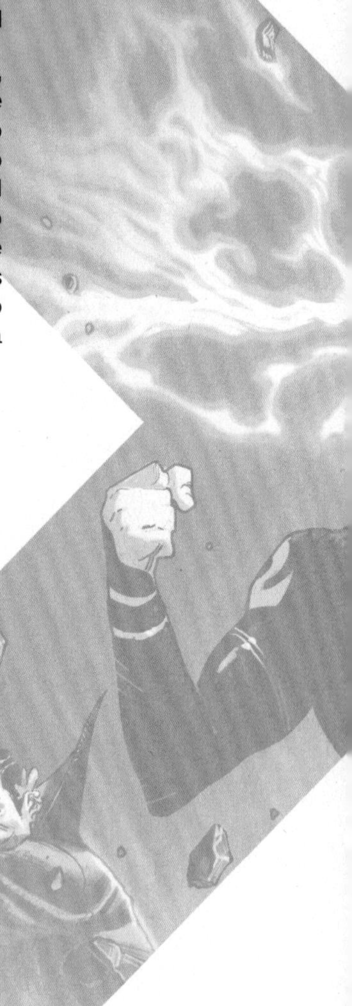

[00_Reign]
[00___ofX]

X-FORCE
[X_18]

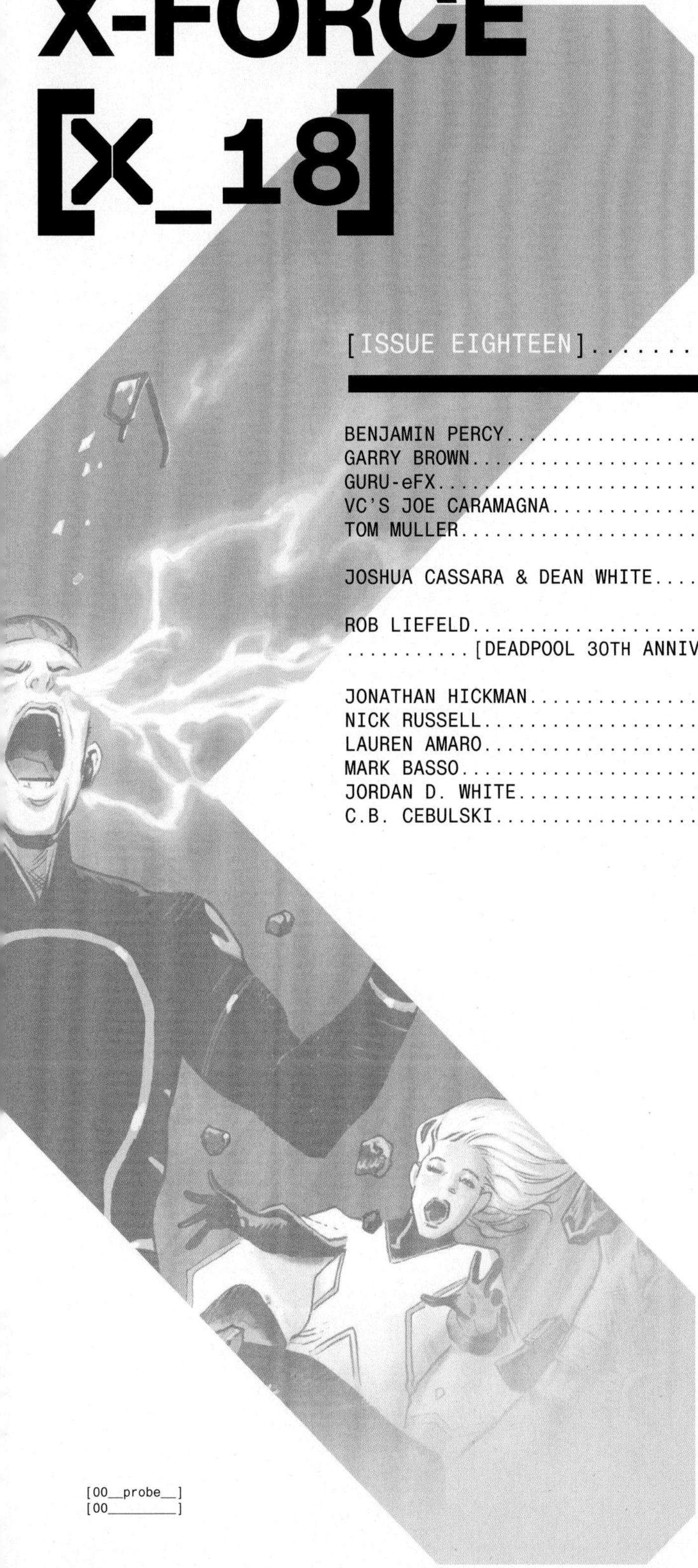

[ISSUE EIGHTEEN].........SHADOWS OF THE MIND

BENJAMIN PERCY...................................[WRITER]
GARRY BROWN......................................[ARTIST]
GURU-eFX...............................[COLOR ARTIST]
VC'S JOE CARAMAGNA.............................[LETTERER]
TOM MULLER.......................................[DESIGN]

JOSHUA CASSARA & DEAN WHITE.................[COVER ARTISTS]

ROB LIEFELD...
...........[DEADPOOL 30TH ANNIVERSARY VARIANT COVER ARTIST]

JONATHAN HICKMAN..............................[HEAD OF X]
NICK RUSSELL..................................[PRODUCTION]
LAUREN AMARO............................[ASSISTANT EDITOR]
MARK BASSO.......................................[EDITOR]
JORDAN D. WHITE...........................[SENIOR EDITOR]
C.B. CEBULSKI............................[EDITOR IN CHIEF]

[00__probe__]
[00_________]

[00_________]

[00________X]

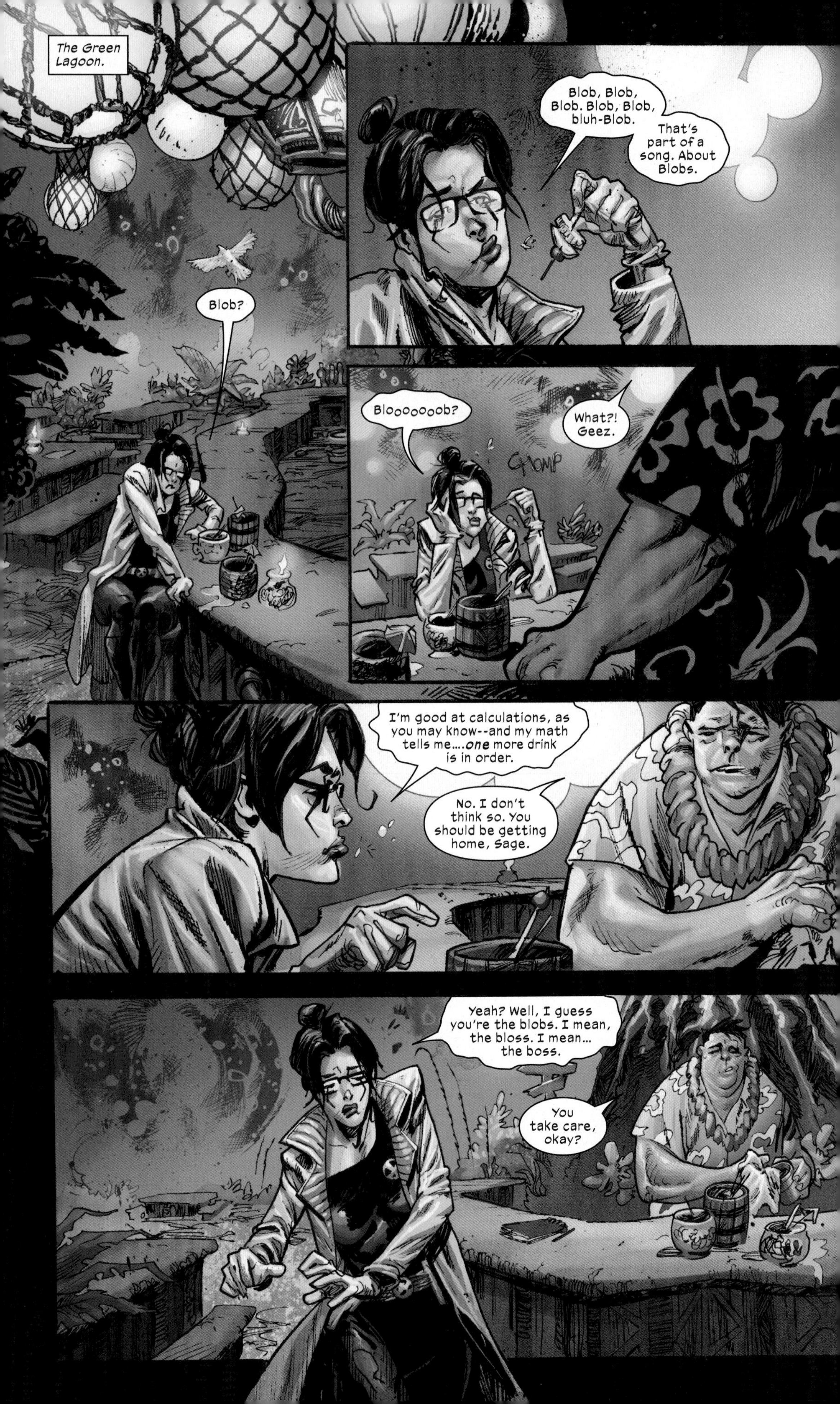
The Green Lagoon.
Blob, Blob, Blob. Blob, Blob, bluh-Blob.
That's part of a song. About Blobs.
Blob?
Blooooooob?
What?! Geez.
CHOMP
I'm good at calculations, as you may know--and my math tells me....*one* more drink is in order.
No. I don't think so. You should be getting home, Sage.
Yeah? Well, I guess you're the blobs. I mean, the bloss. I mean... the boss.
You take care, okay?

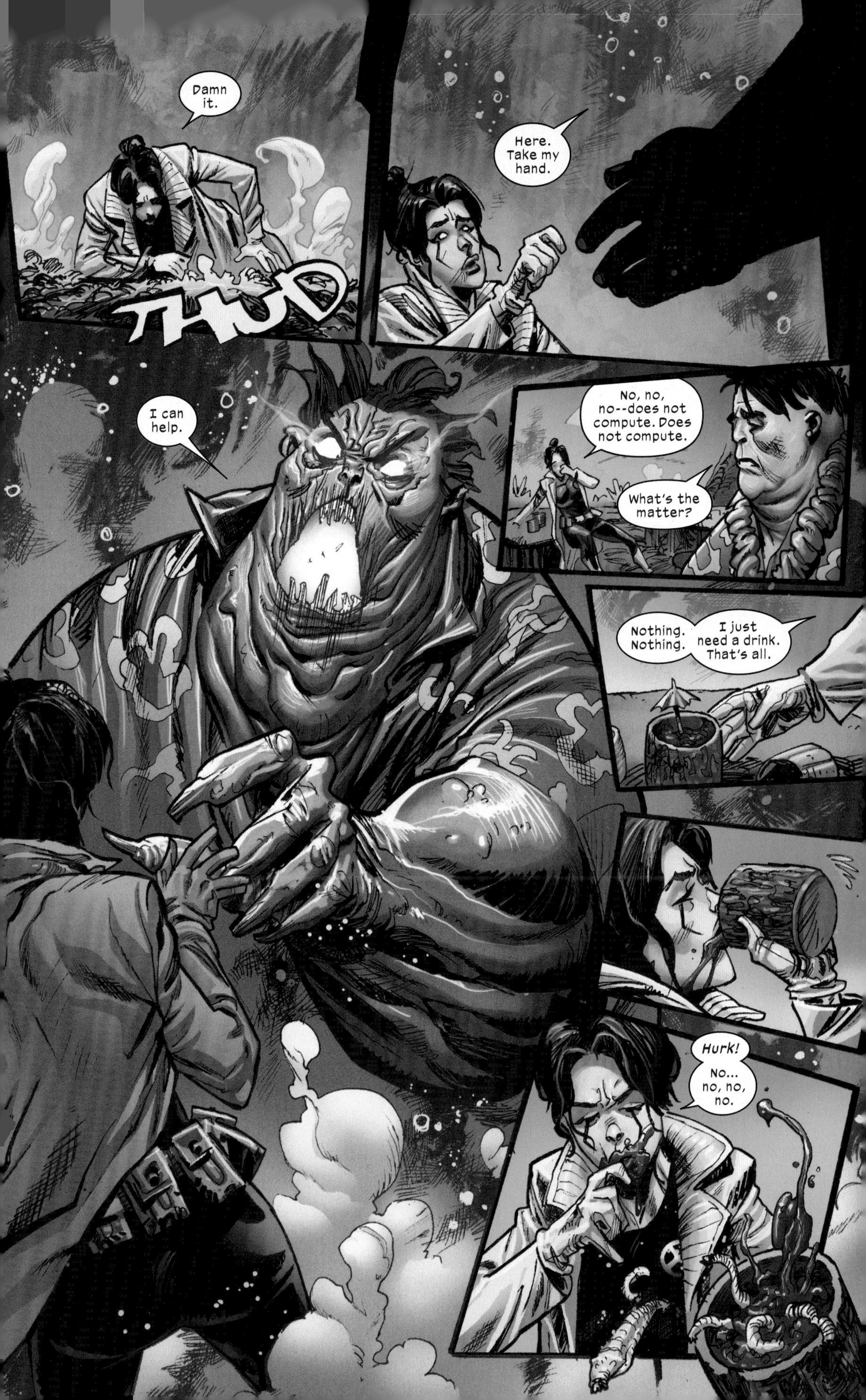
Damn it.
THUD
Here. Take my hand.
I can help.
No, no, no--does not compute. Does not compute.
What's the matter?
Nothing. Nothing.
I just need a drink. That's all.
Hurk!
No... no, no, no.

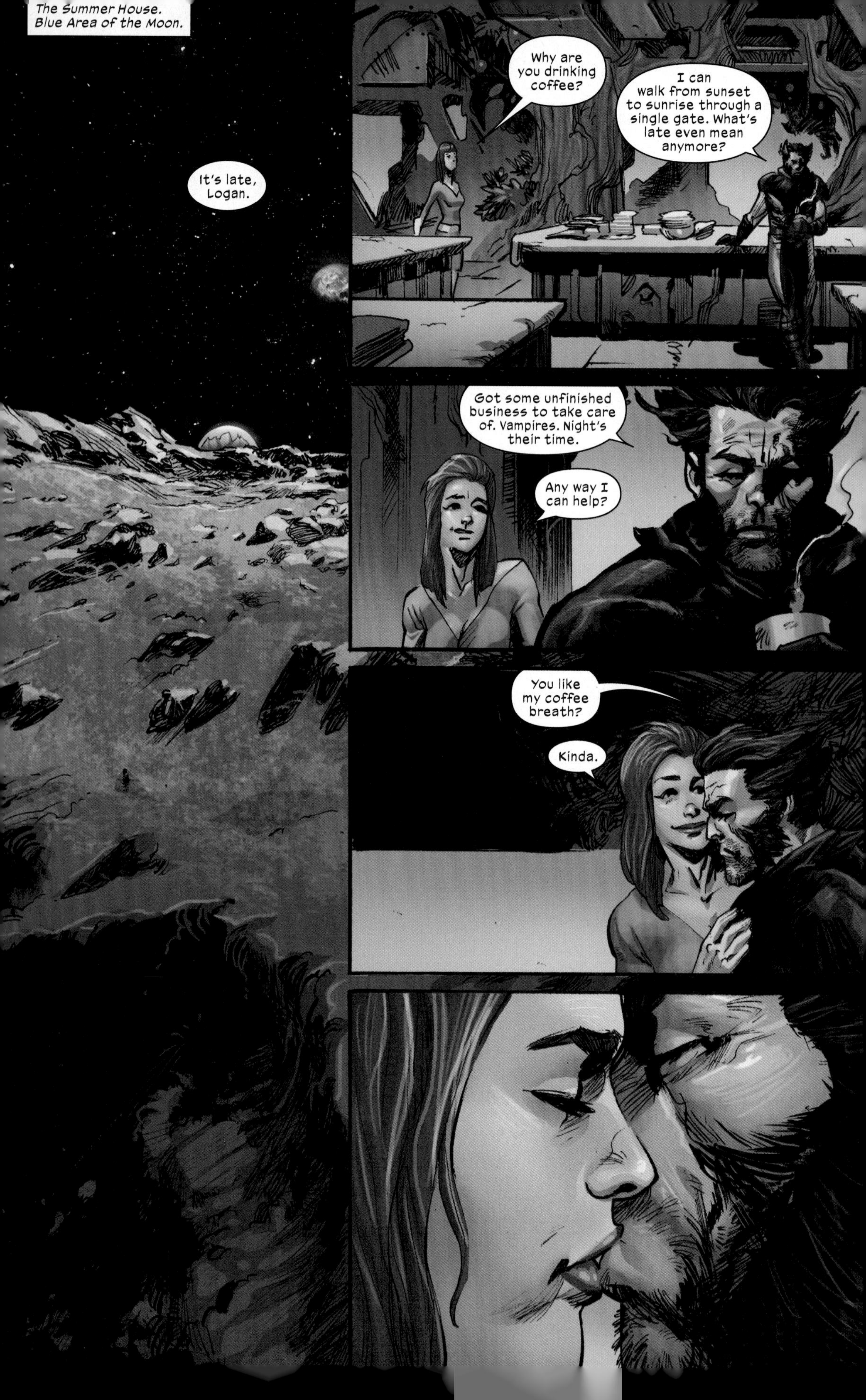
The Summer House.
Blue Area of the Moon.
It's late, Logan.
Why are you drinking coffee?
I can walk from sunset to sunrise through a single gate. What's late even mean anymore?
Got some unfinished business to take care of. Vampires. Night's their time.
Any way I can help?
You like my coffee breath?
Kinda.

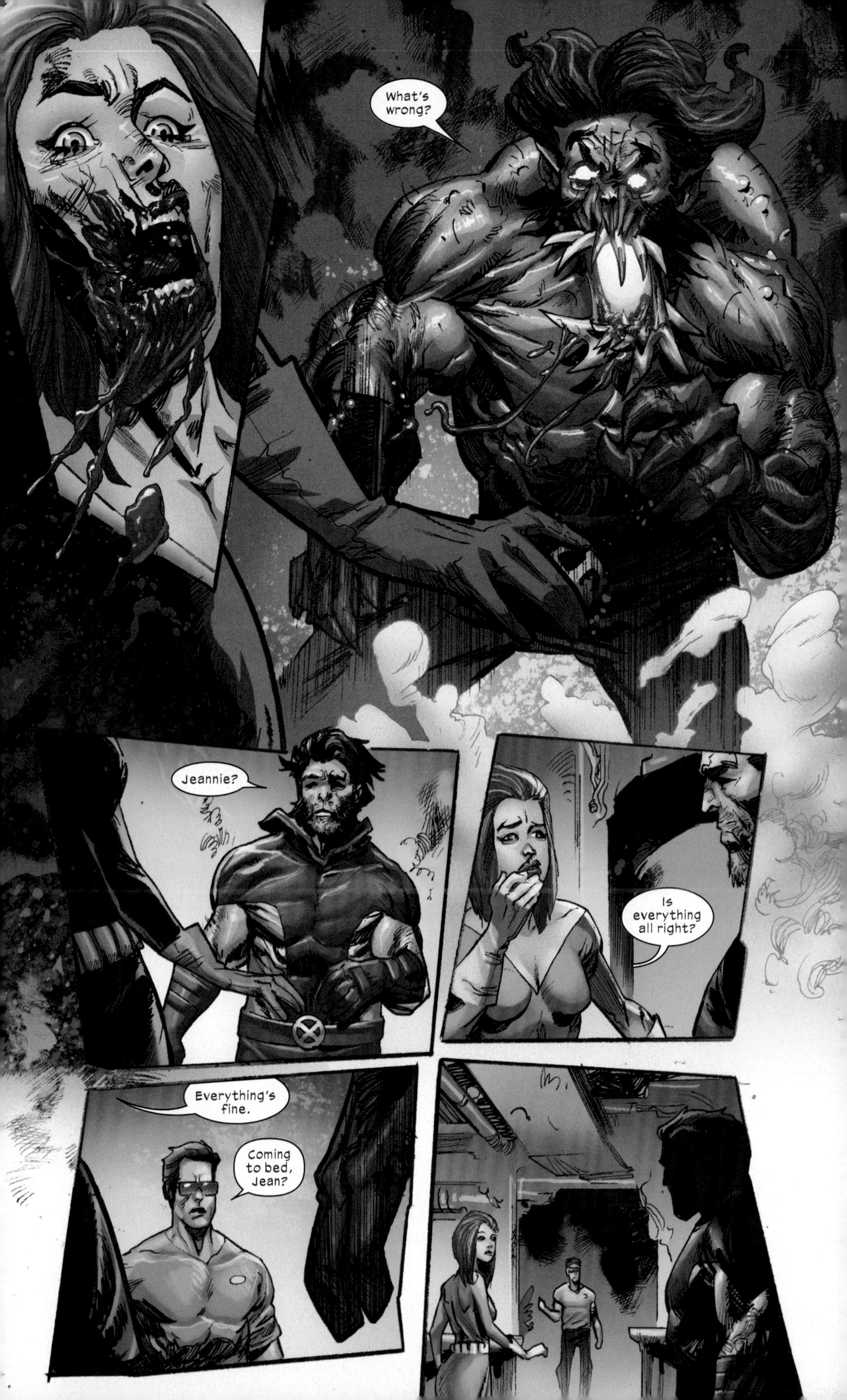
What's wrong?
Jeannie?
Is everything all right?
Everything's fine.
Coming to bed, Jean?

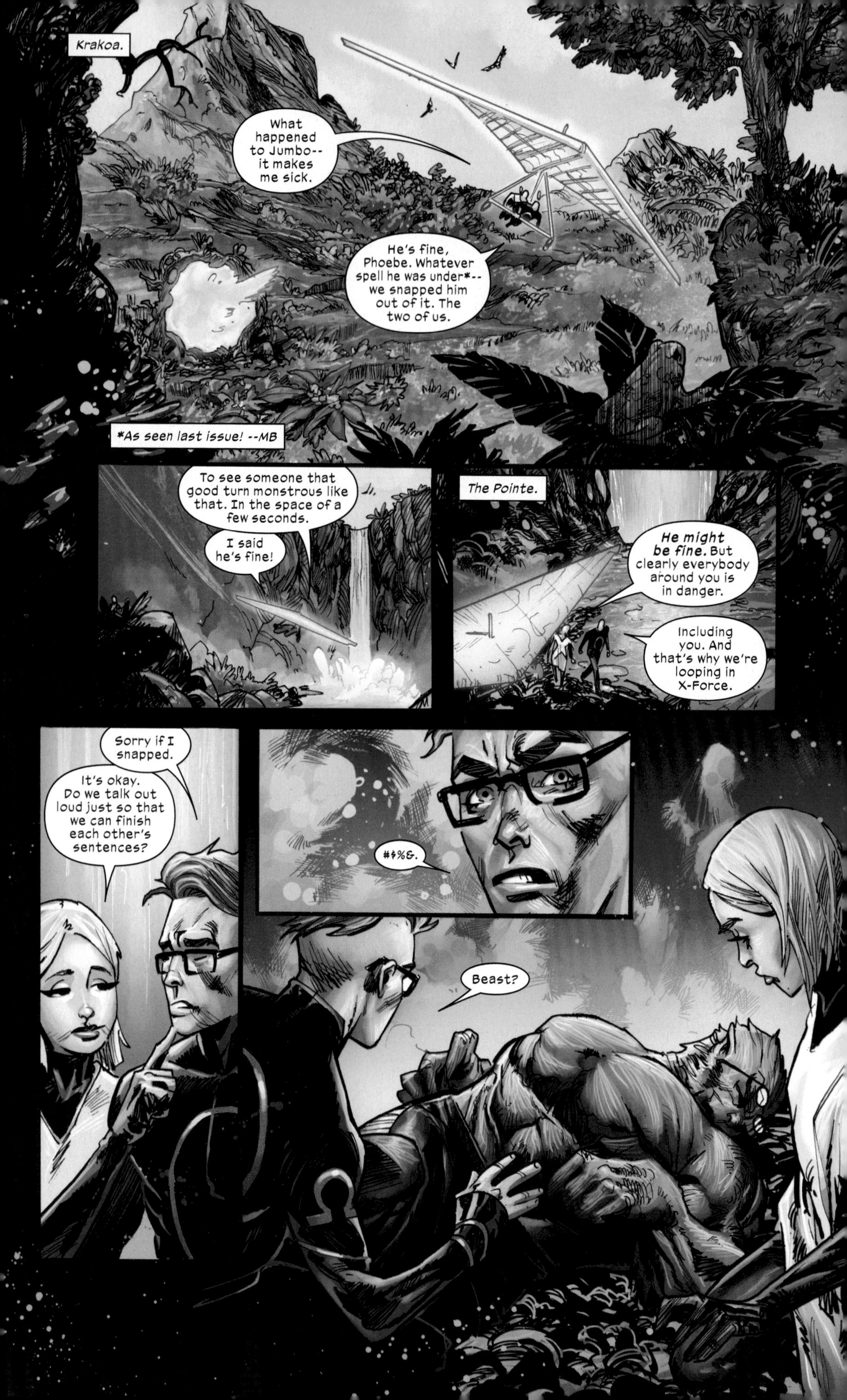
Krakoa.
What happened to Jumbo-- it makes me sick.
He's fine, Phoebe. Whatever spell he was under*-- we snapped him out of it. The two of us.
*As seen last issue! --MB
To see someone that good turn monstrous like that. In the space of a few seconds.
I said he's fine!
The Pointe.
He might be fine. But clearly everybody around you is in danger.
Including you. And that's why we're looping in X-Force.
Sorry if I snapped.
It's okay. Do we talk out loud just so that we can finish each other's sentences?
#$%&.
Beast?

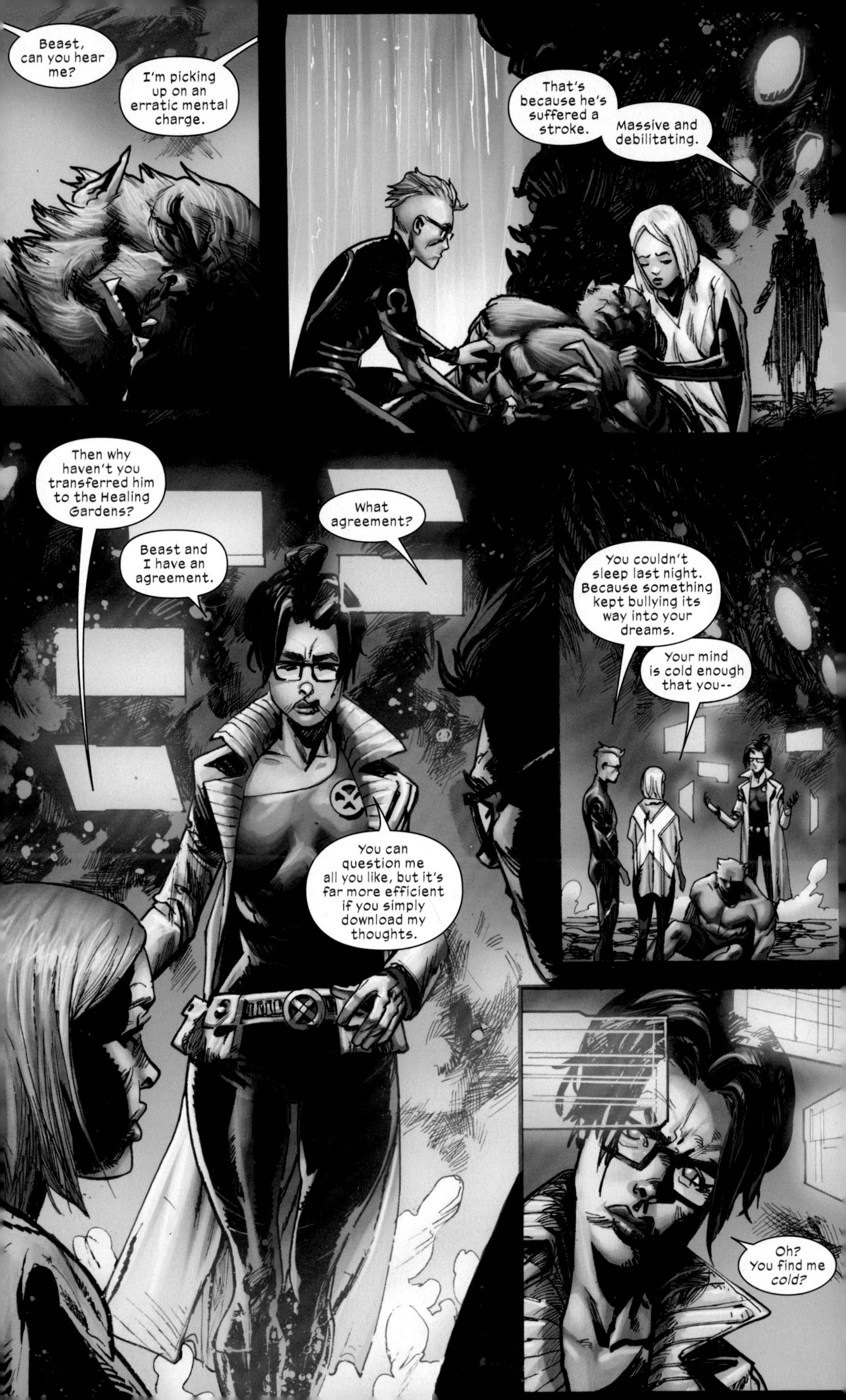
Beast, can you hear me?
I'm picking up on an erratic mental charge.
That's because he's suffered a stroke.
Massive and debilitating.
Then why haven't you transferred him to the Healing Gardens?
Beast and I have an agreement.
What agreement?
You can question me all you like, but it's far more efficient if you simply download my thoughts.
You couldn't sleep last night. Because something kept bullying its way into your dreams.
Your mind is cold enough that you--
Oh? You find me cold?

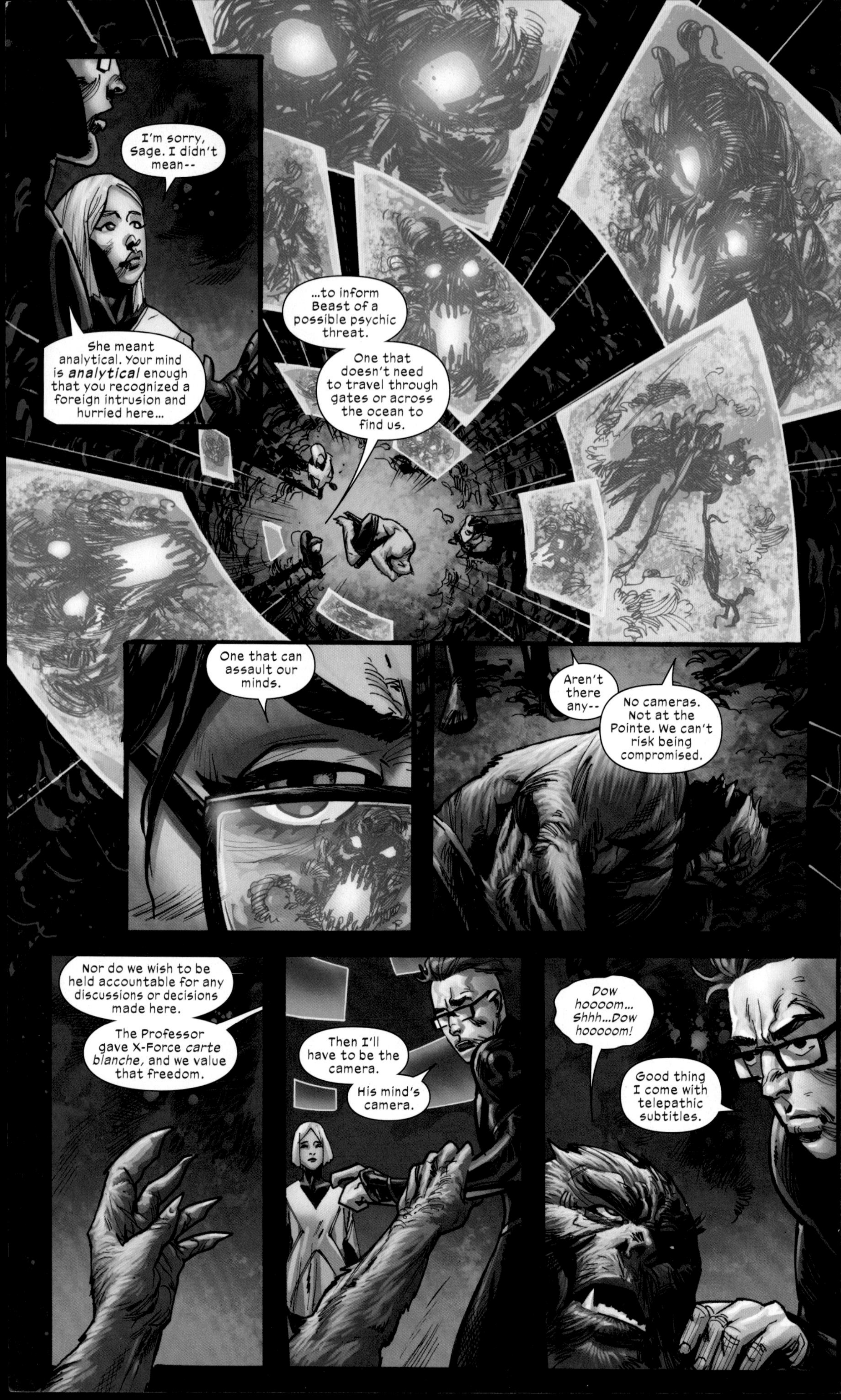
I'm sorry, Sage. I didn't mean--
She meant analytical. Your mind is *analytical* enough that you recognized a foreign intrusion and hurried here...
...to inform Beast of a possible psychic threat.
One that doesn't need to travel through gates or across the ocean to find us.
One that can assault our minds.
Aren't there any--
No cameras. Not at the Pointe. We can't risk being compromised.
Nor do we wish to be held accountable for any discussions or decisions made here.
The Professor gave X-Force *carte blanche*, and we value that freedom.
Then I'll have to be the camera.
His mind's camera.
Dow hoooom... Shhh...Dow hooooom!
Good thing I come with telepathic subtitles.

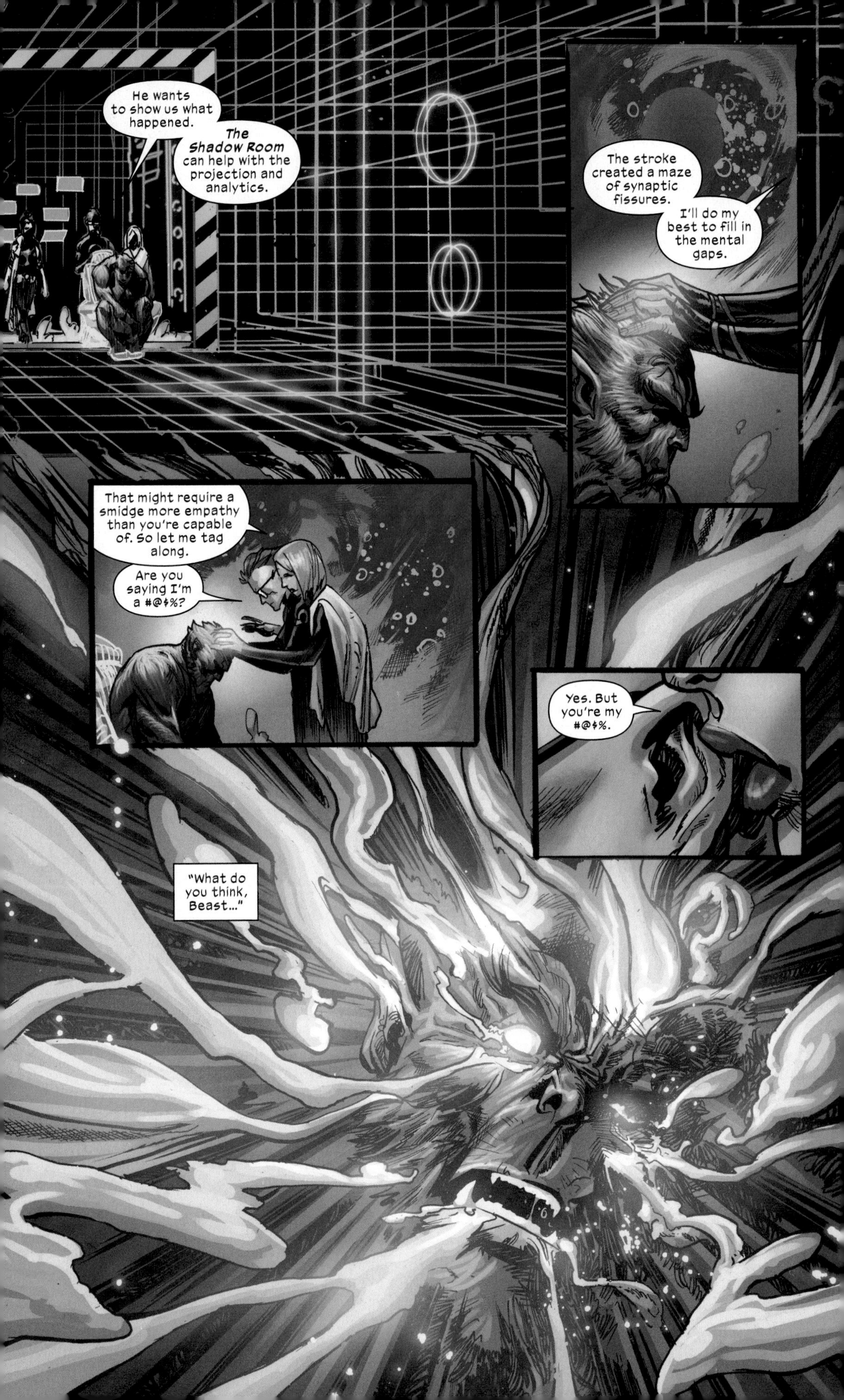

He wants to show us what happened.
The Shadow Room can help with the projection and analytics.
The stroke created a maze of synaptic fissures.
I'll do my best to fill in the mental gaps.
That might require a smidge more empathy than you're capable of. So let me tag along.
Are you saying I'm a #@$%?
Yes. But you're my #@$%.
"What do you think, Beast..."

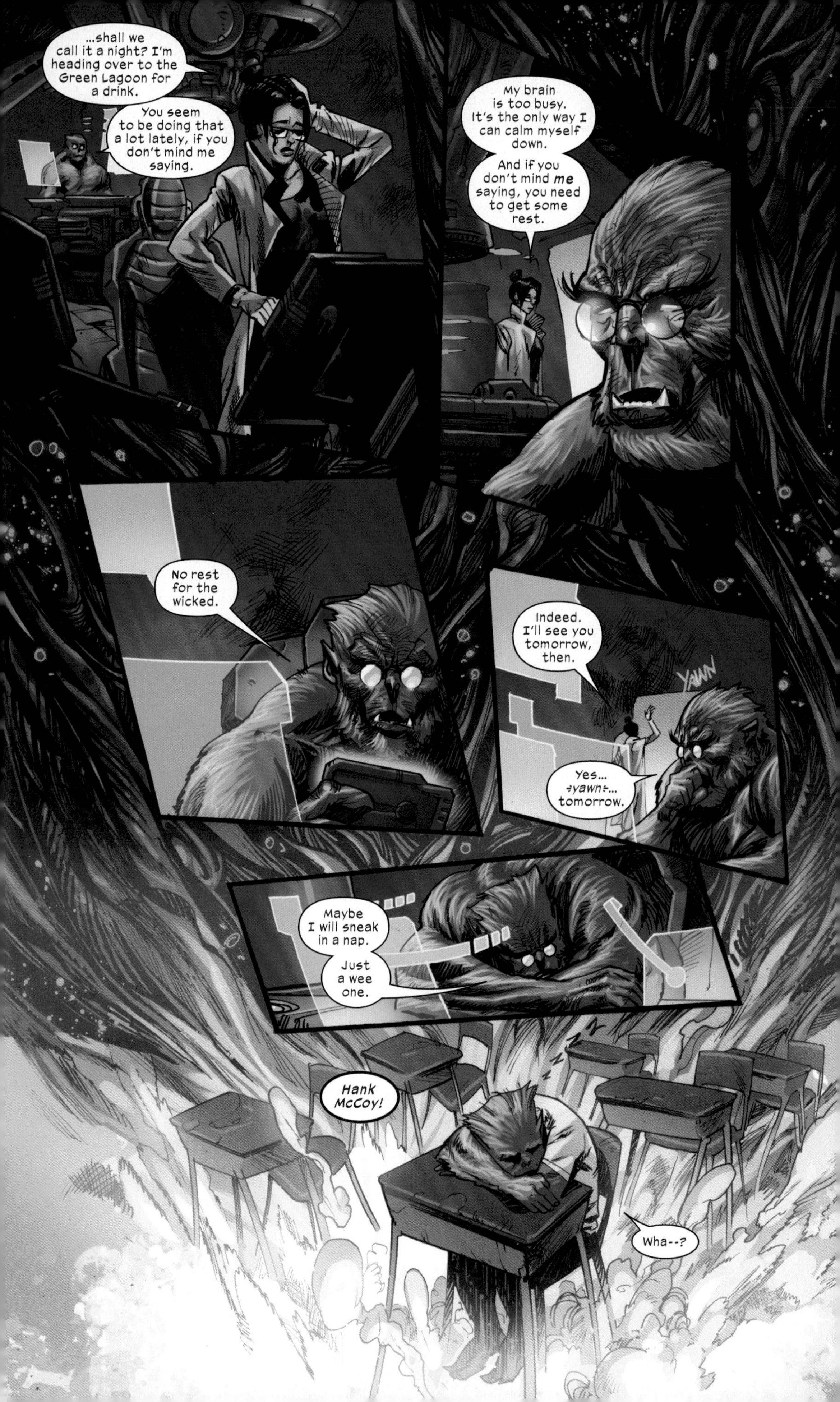
...shall we call it a night? I'm heading over to the Green Lagoon for a drink.
You seem to be doing that a lot lately, if you don't mind me saying.
My brain is too busy. It's the only way I can calm myself down.
And if you don't mind **me** saying, you need to get some rest.
No rest for the wicked.
Indeed. I'll see you tomorrow, then.
YAWN
Yes... ~yawn~... tomorrow.
Maybe I will sneak in a nap.
Just a wee one.
Hank McCoy!
Wha--?

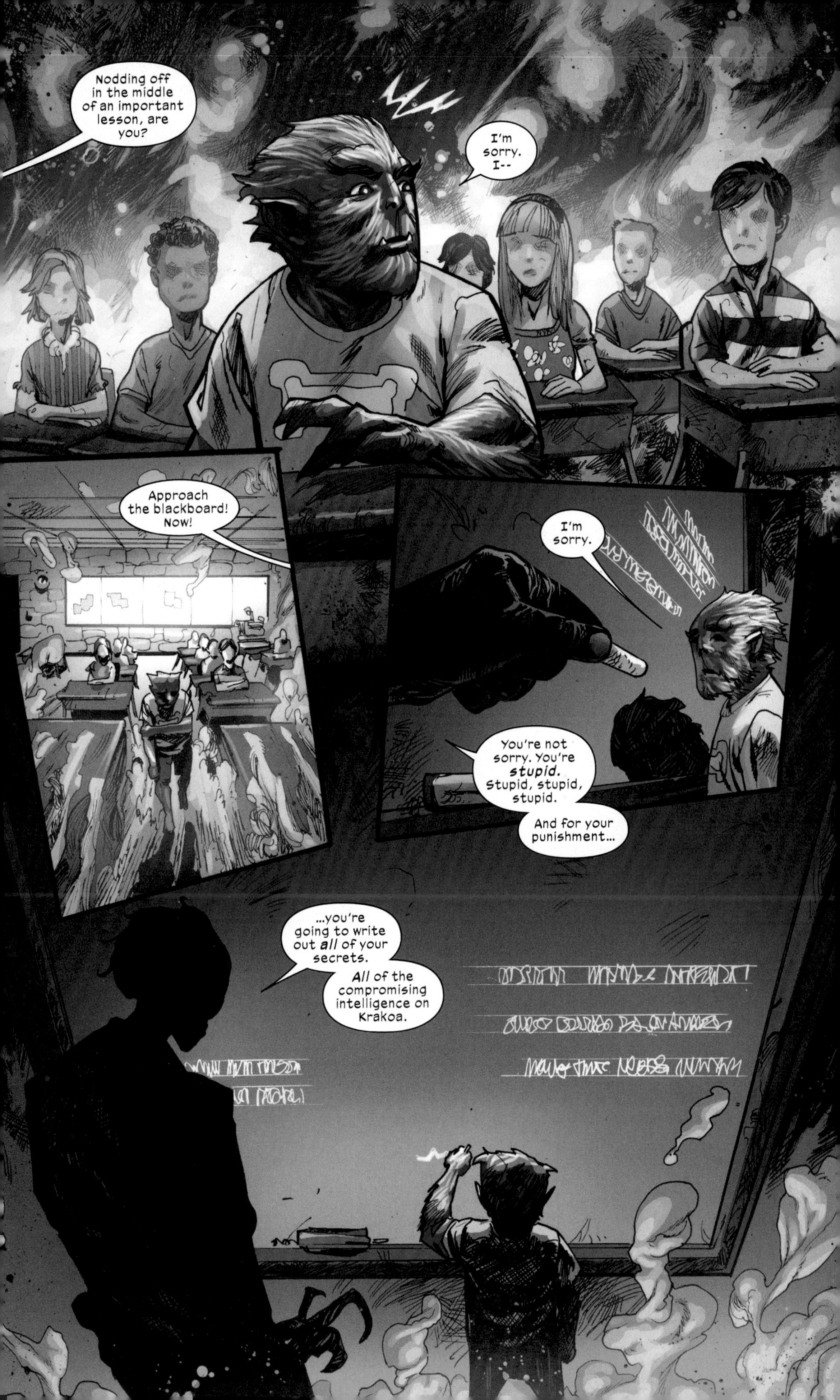
Nodding off in the middle of an important lesson, are you?
I'm sorry. I--
Approach the blackboard! Now!
I'm sorry.
You're not sorry. You're *stupid.* Stupid, stupid, stupid.
And for your punishment...
...you're going to write out *all* of your secrets.
All of the compromising intelligence on Krakoa.

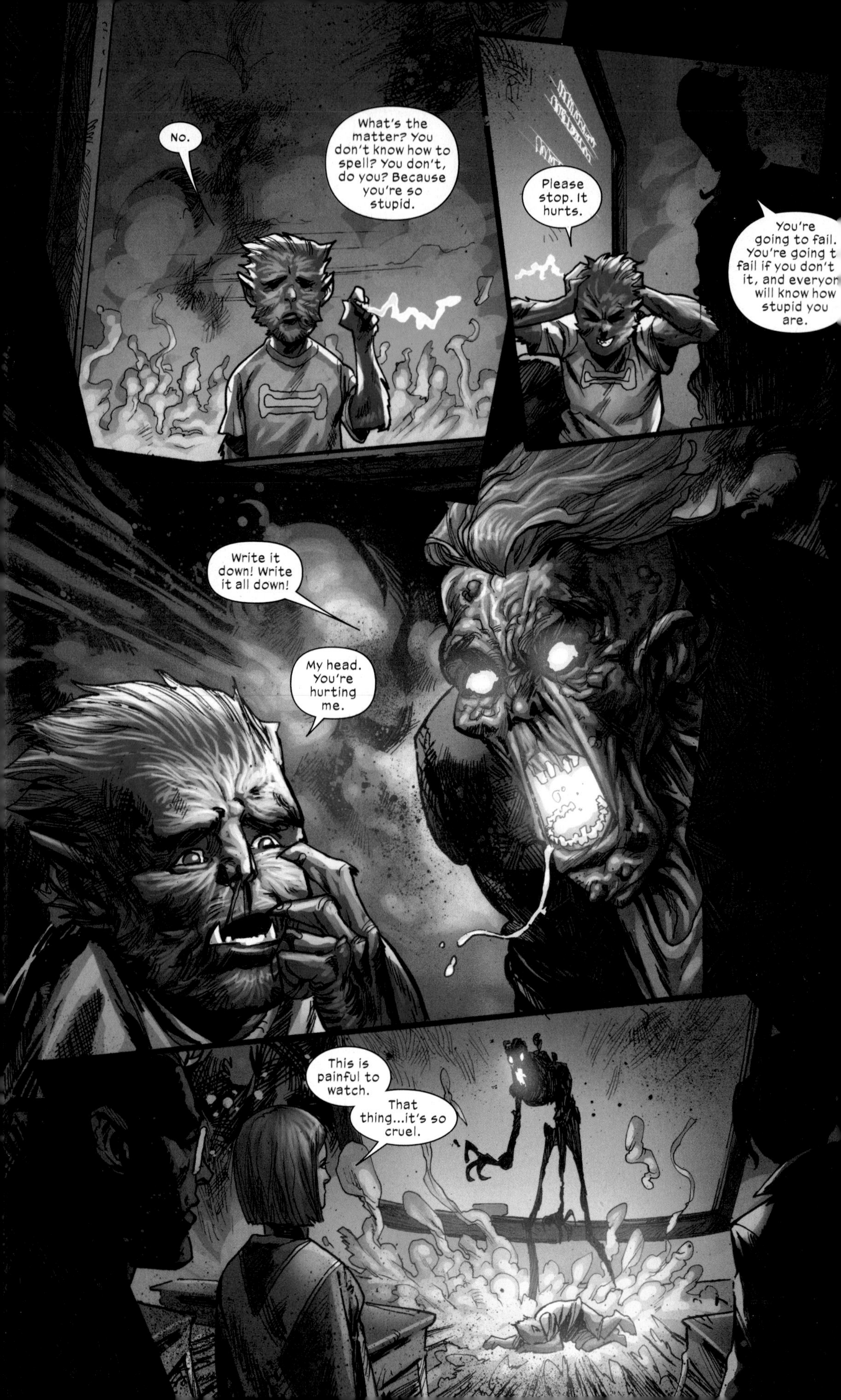
No.
What's the matter? You don't know how to spell? You don't, do you? Because you're so stupid.
Please stop. It hurts.
You're going to fail. You're going t fail if you don't it, and everyon will know how stupid you are.
Write it down! Write it all down!
My head. You're hurting me.
This is painful to watch.
That thing...it's so cruel.

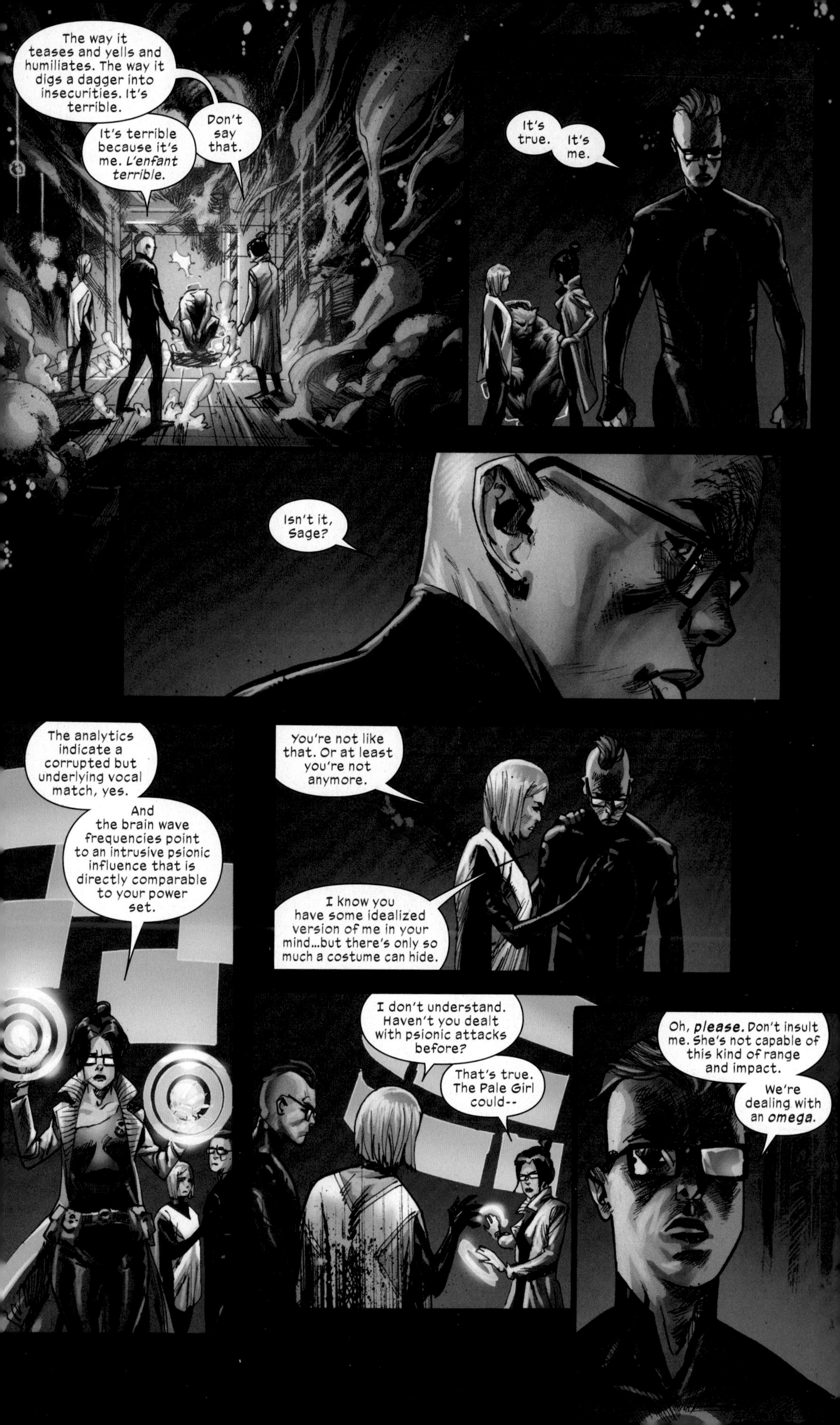

The way it teases and yells and humiliates. The way it digs a dagger into insecurities. It's terrible.
It's terrible because it's me. *L'enfant terrible*.
Don't say that.
It's true.
It's me.
Isn't it, Sage?
The analytics indicate a corrupted but underlying vocal match, yes.
And the brain wave frequencies point to an intrusive psionic influence that is directly comparable to your power set.
You're not like that. Or at least you're not anymore.
I know you have some idealized version of me in your mind...but there's only so much a costume can hide.
I don't understand. Haven't you dealt with psionic attacks before?
That's true. The Pale Girl could--
Oh, ***please.*** Don't insult me. She's not capable of this kind of range and impact.
We're dealing with an *omega*.

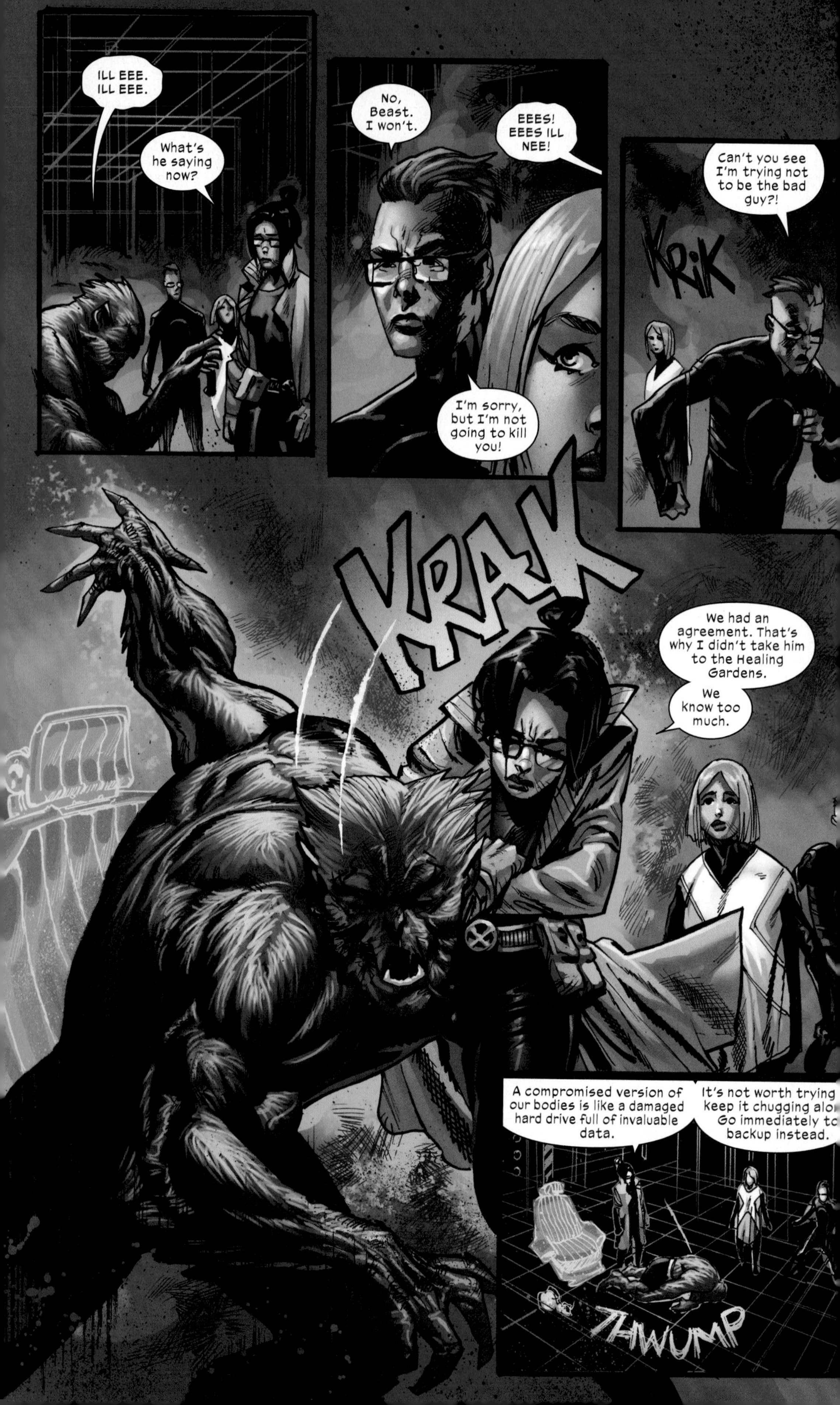

ILL EEE. ILL EEE.
What's he saying now?
No, Beast. I won't.
EEES! EEES ILL NEE!
I'm sorry, but I'm not going to kill you!
Can't you see I'm trying not to be the bad guy?!
KRIK
KRAK
We had an agreement. That's why I didn't take him to the Healing Gardens.
We know too much.
A compromised version of our bodies is like a damaged hard drive full of invaluable data.
It's not worth trying keep it chugging alo Go immediately to backup instead.
THWUMP

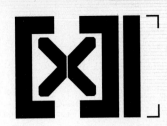

SAGE'S LOGBOOK

::: Observations :::

Suspect: Psychic Invader

Profile: Just as Domino's body -- and powers -- were harvested by XENO, the evidence suggests so were Quentin's. The number of deaths he has suffered makes it impossible to guess when this occurred (possibly on multiple occasions). But some nightmare version of him -- farmed from the same psionic well -- appears to be preying on us.

Modus Operandi: An intrusion of the unguarded mind. Sleep is an obvious gateway. But so is exuberant happiness (as evidenced by Jumbo), which opens up the possibility of extreme fear and anger as other potential vulnerabilities. Or drunkenness.

<< see subnote >>

Further Queries: How much data can be off-loaded by the invader? Could there be a lasting mental presence akin to malware? What sort of psychic firewalls can be locked in place?

Immediate Action Item: Beast is temporarily absent -- as a result of resurrection protocols -- and I am exhausted from being up all night. I need to keep my brain locked down. I will inquire with Dr. Reyes re: organic stimulants and also see if there have been any suspicious accidents admitted to the Healing Gardens.

—

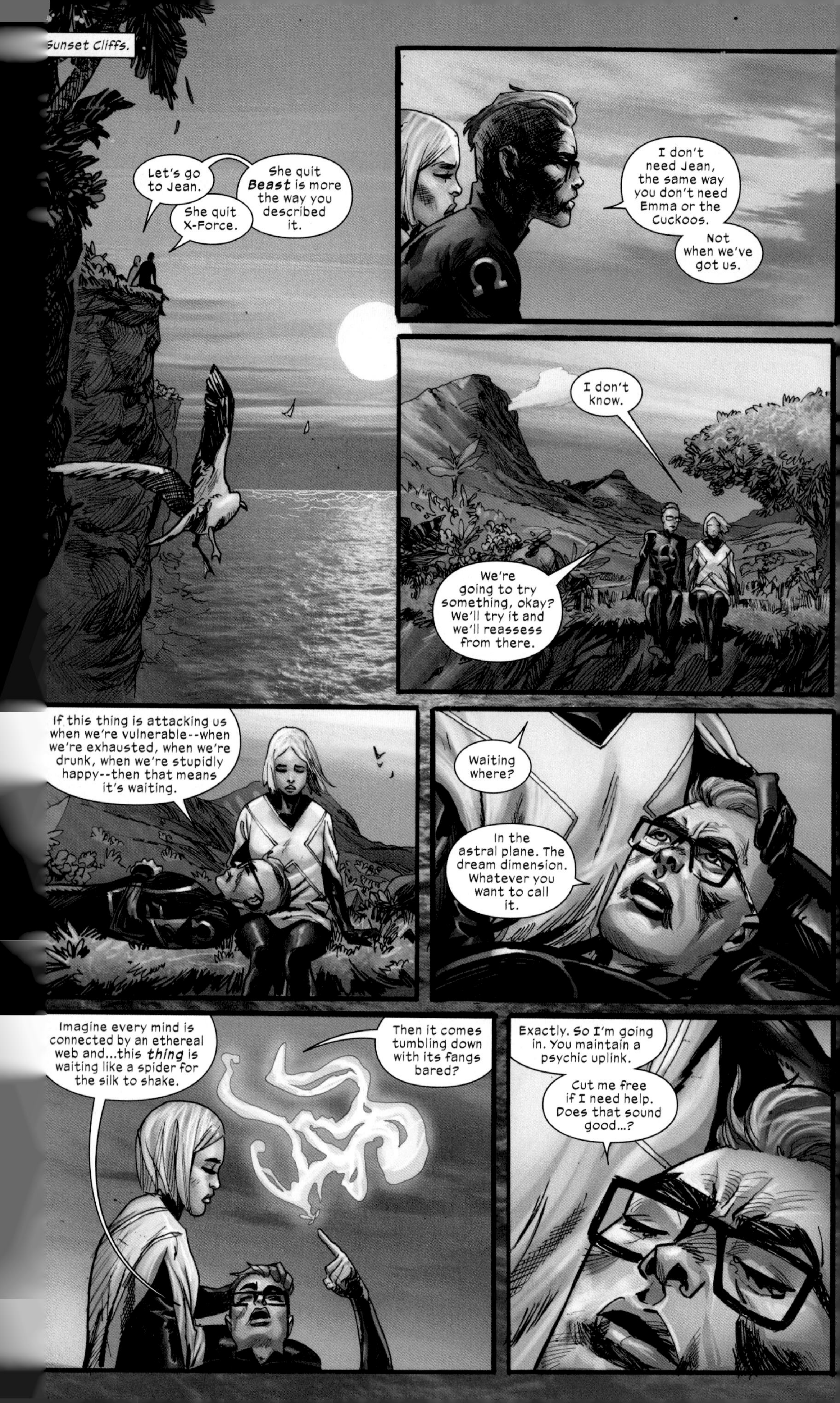

Sunset Cliffs.
Let's go to Jean.
She quit X-Force.
She quit *Beast* is more the way you described it.
I don't need Jean, the same way you don't need Emma or the Cuckoos.
Not when we've got us.
I don't know.
We're going to try something, okay? We'll try it and we'll reassess from there.
If this thing is attacking us when we're vulnerable--when we're exhausted, when we're drunk, when we're stupidly happy--then that means it's waiting.
Waiting where?
In the astral plane. The dream dimension. Whatever you want to call it.
Imagine every mind is connected by an ethereal web and...this *thing* is waiting like a spider for the silk to shake.
Then it comes tumbling down with its fangs bared?
Exactly. So I'm going in. You maintain a psychic uplink.
Cut me free if I need help. Does that sound good...?

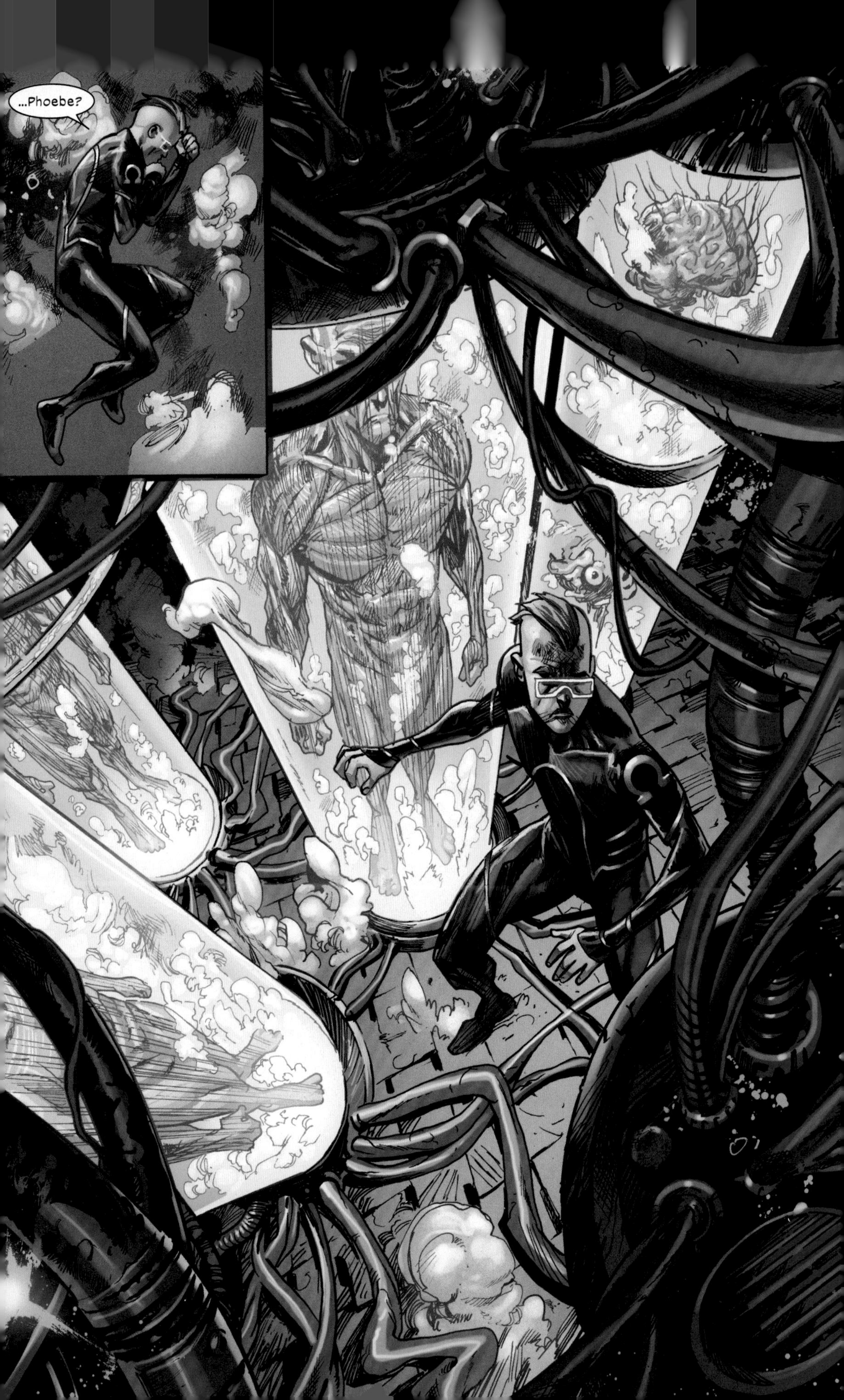
...Phoebe?

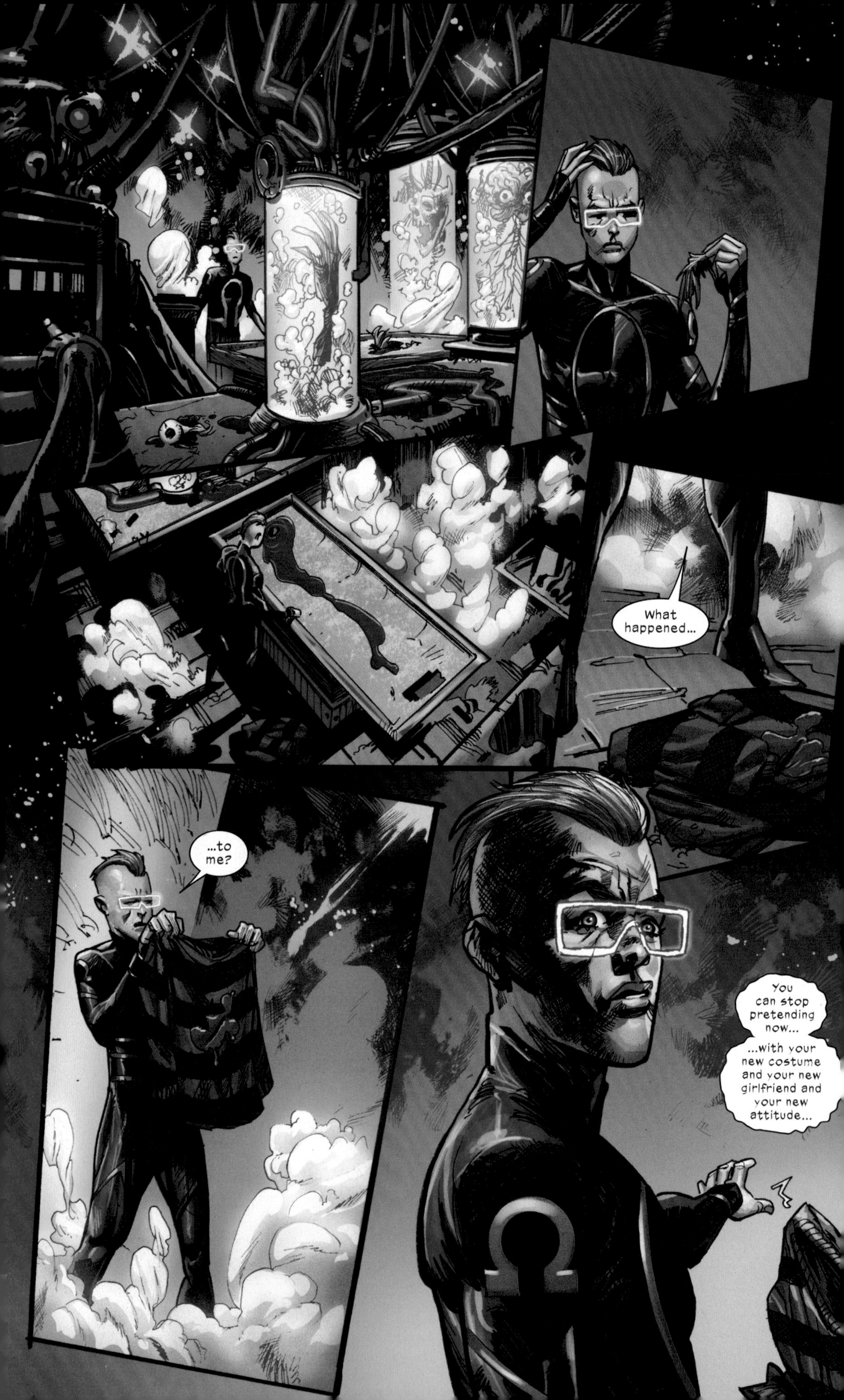
What happened...
...to me?
You can stop pretending now...
...with your new costume and your new girlfriend and your new attitude...

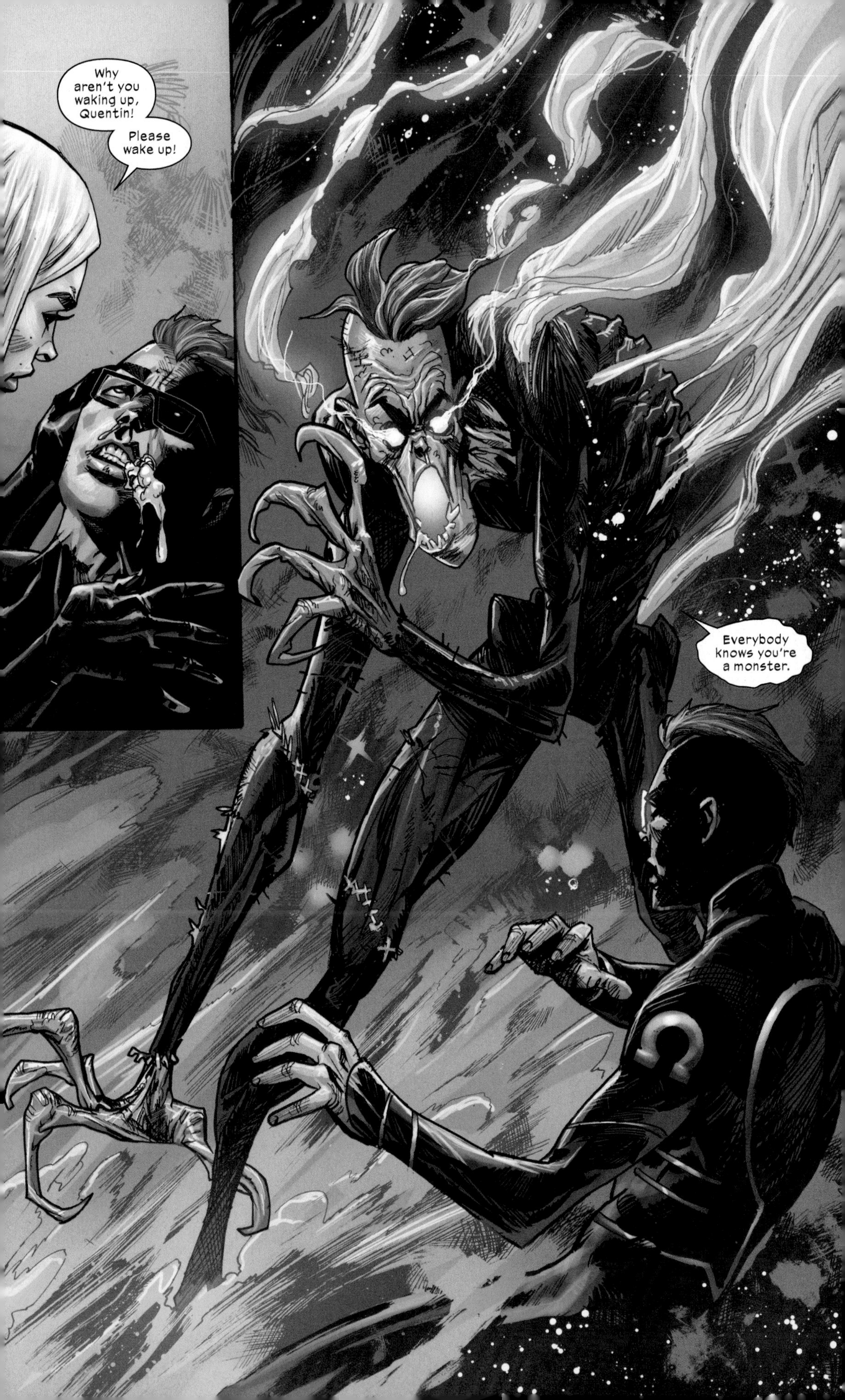
Why aren't you waking up, Quentin!
Please wake up!
Everybody knows you're a monster.

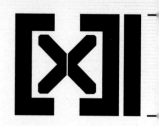

SAGE'S LOGBOOK cont.

Subnote: <<< On Drunkenness >>>

I keep track of everything.

The big stuff, like the number of mutants entering and exiting transit gates at any given moment or the number of petals harvested and exported on any given day.

But I also keep track of the little stuff too. I can tell you the number of dogs I've petted (325). The number of cups of chai I've drunk (7,653). The number of landmines I almost stepped on as a child (1). The number of pomegranates eaten (629) and the average number of seeds within one (998). The number of eyeglasses I've owned (34). The number of times I've cried while listening to Purcell's "Dido's Lament" (12) or the number of times I've danced to Mariah Carey (671). I can tell you the number of times I've been kissed by someone who really meant it (2) versus the number who didn't (22).

But...I've been losing count lately. Of the number of drinks I consume in a given evening.

The math comes apart...

The numbers dissolve...

<<<< >>>>

—

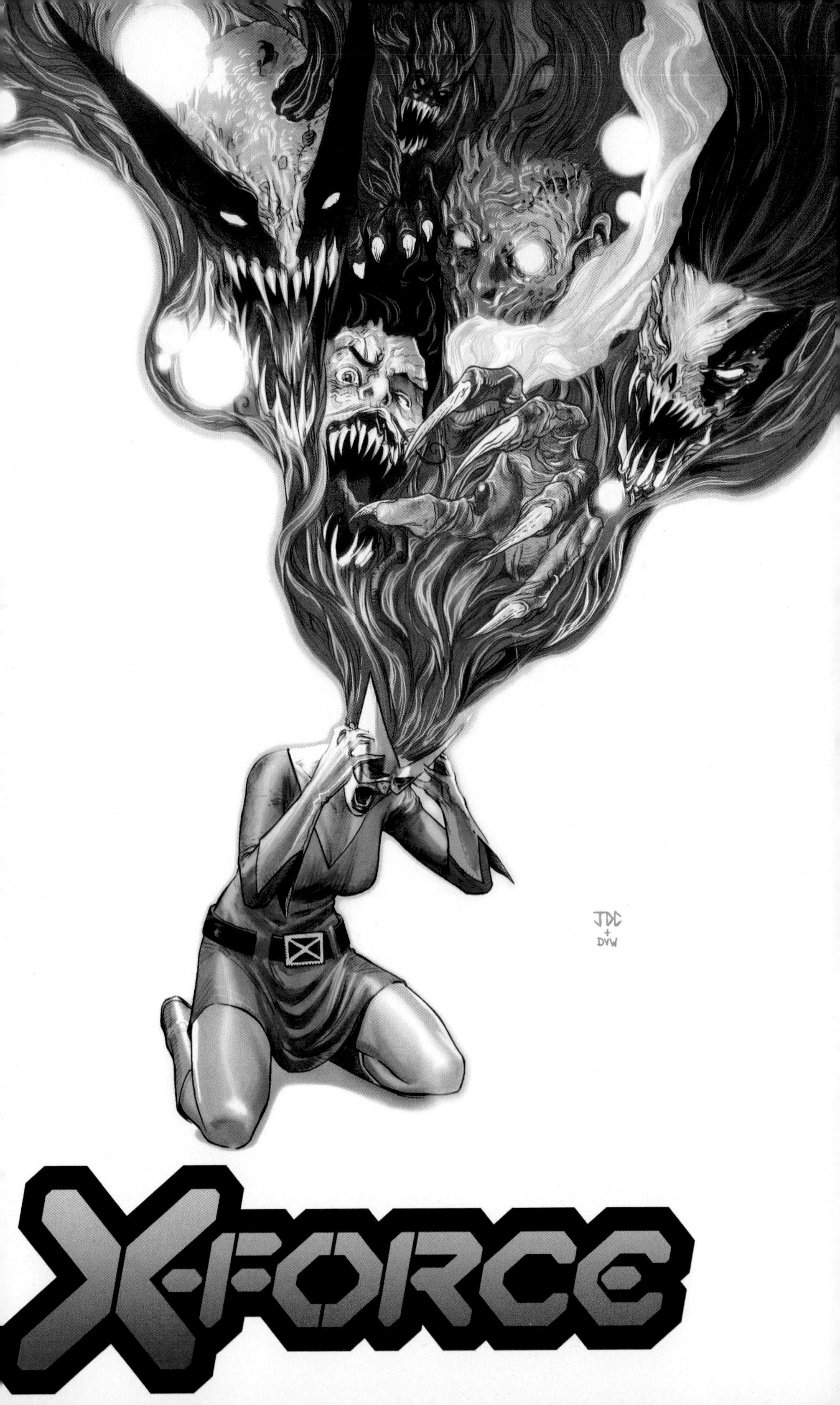
JDC
+
DVW
X-FORCE

[00_mutant__espionage]
[00_law_order____X___]

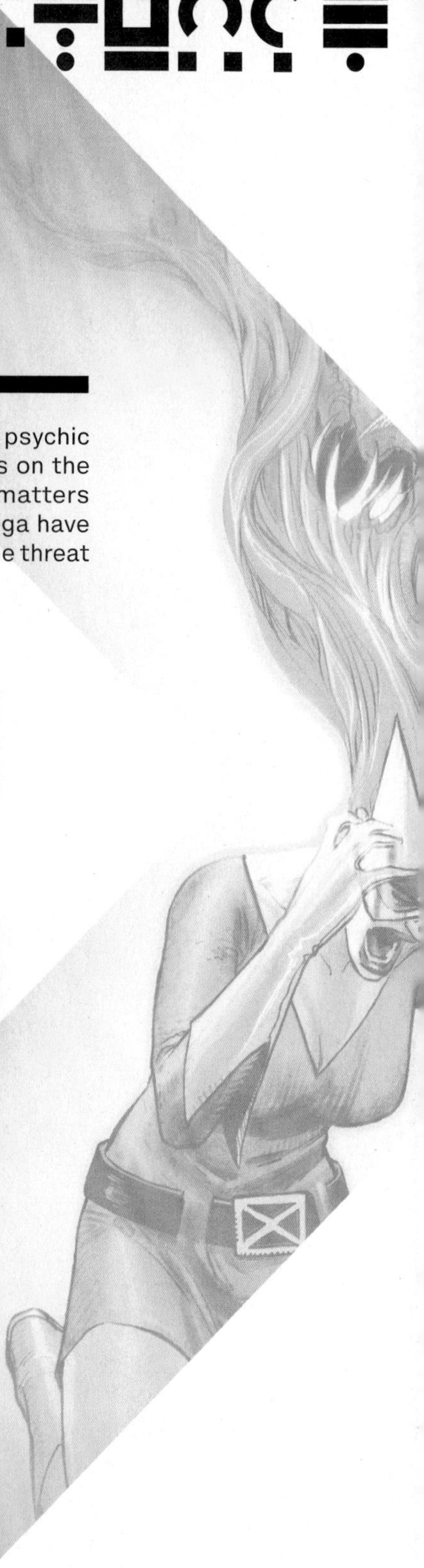

DREAMWALKER

Beast is dead. Black Tom is missing. And a rogue psychic enemy bearing Kid Omega's telepathic signature is on the loose and targeting the rest of X-Force. Taking matters into their own hands, Phoebe Cuckoo and Kid Omega have entered the astral plane in the hope of confronting the threat head-on...

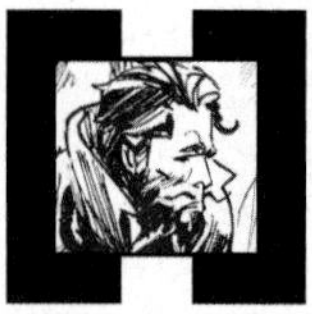

Black Tom

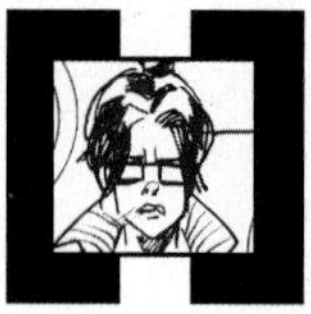

Sage

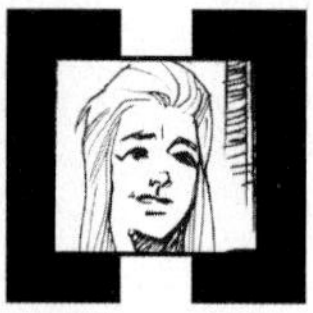

Jean Grey

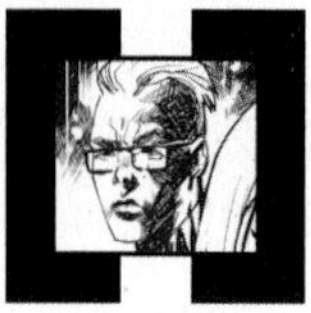

Kid Omega

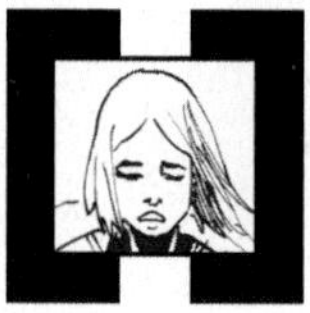

Phoebe Cuckoo

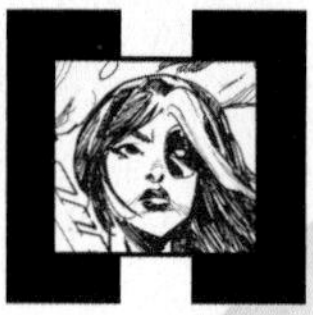

Domino

[00_Reign]
[00___ofX]

X-FORCE

[X_19]

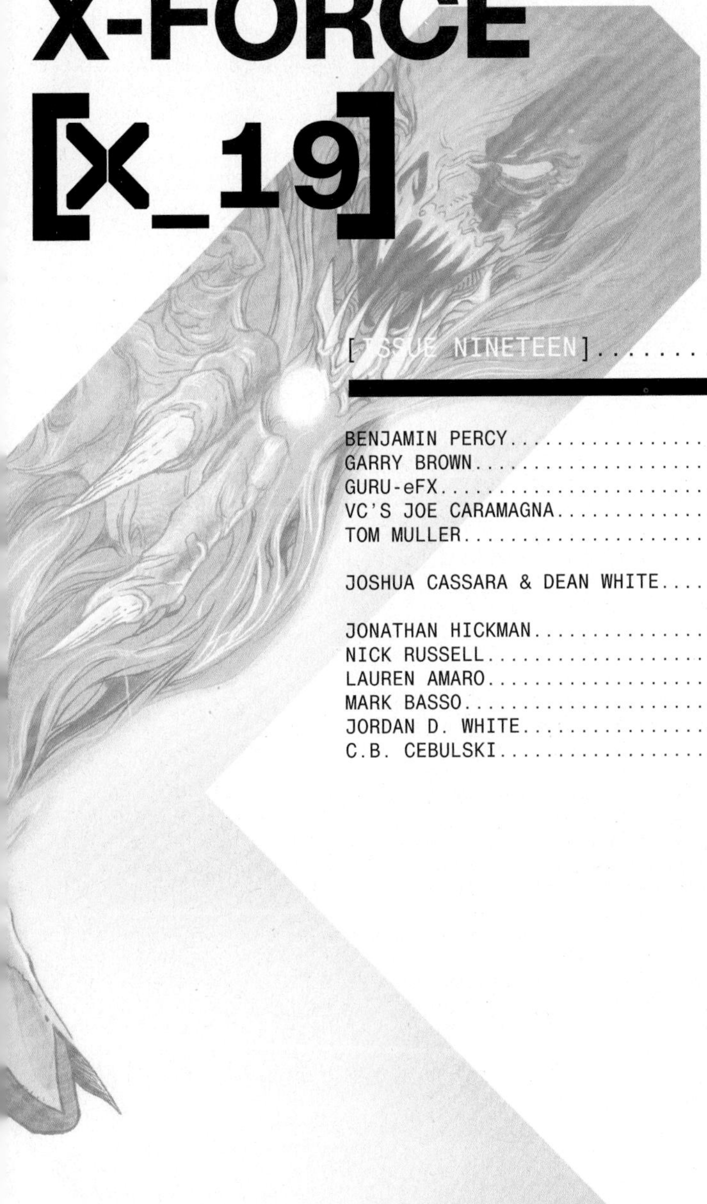

[ISSUE NINETEEN]...........DEAD OF NIGHTMARE

BENJAMIN PERCY....................................[WRITER]
GARRY BROWN.......................................[ARTIST]
GURU-eFX....................................[COLOR ARTIST]
VC'S JOE CARAMAGNA..............................[LETTERER]
TOM MULLER..[DESIGN]

JOSHUA CASSARA & DEAN WHITE.................[COVER ARTISTS]

JONATHAN HICKMAN...............................[HEAD OF X]
NICK RUSSELL..................................[PRODUCTION]
LAUREN AMARO............................[ASSISTANT EDITOR]
MARK BASSO..[EDITOR]
JORDAN D. WHITE............................[SENIOR EDITOR]
C.B. CEBULSKI............................[EDITOR IN CHIEF]

[00__probe__]
[00_________]

[00_________]

[00________X]

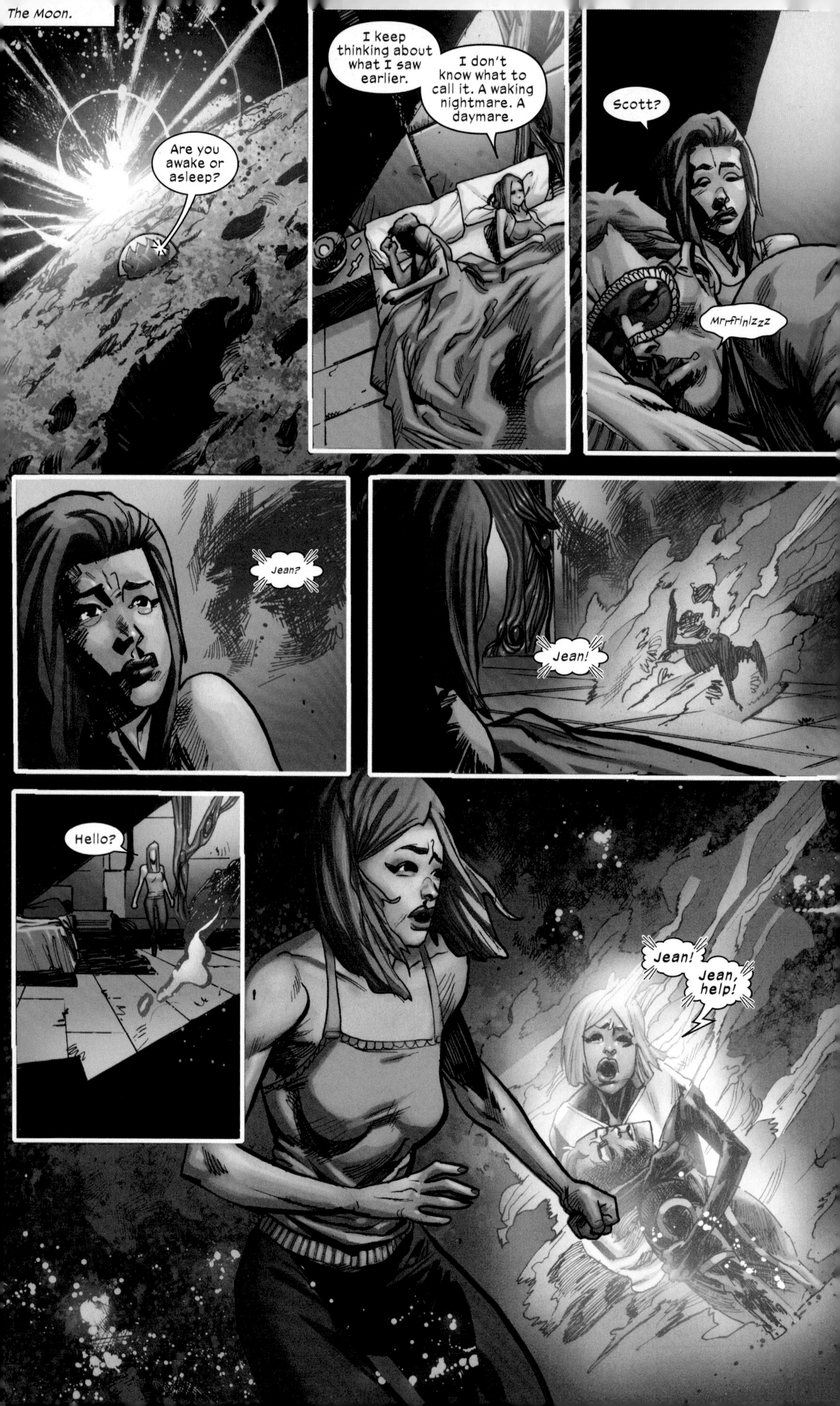
The Moon.
Are you awake or asleep?
I keep thinking about what I saw earlier.
I don't know what to call it. A waking nightmare. A daymare.
Scott?
Mrr-frinlzzz
Jean?
Jean!
Hello?
Jean!
Jean, help!

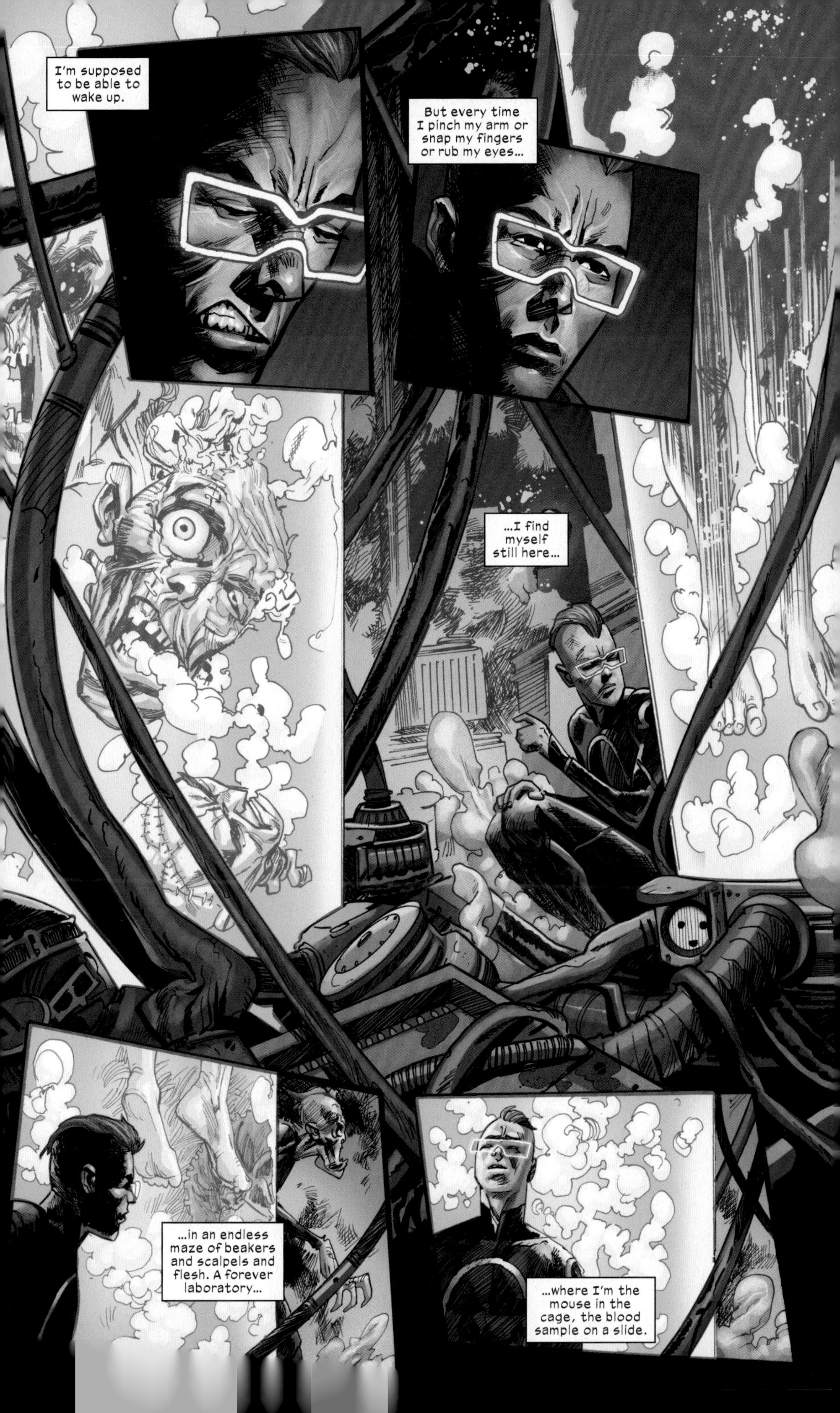
I'm supposed to be able to wake up.
But every time I pinch my arm or snap my fingers or rub my eyes...
...I find myself still here...
...in an endless maze of beakers and scalpels and flesh. A forever laboratory...
...where I'm the mouse in the cage, the blood sample on a slide.

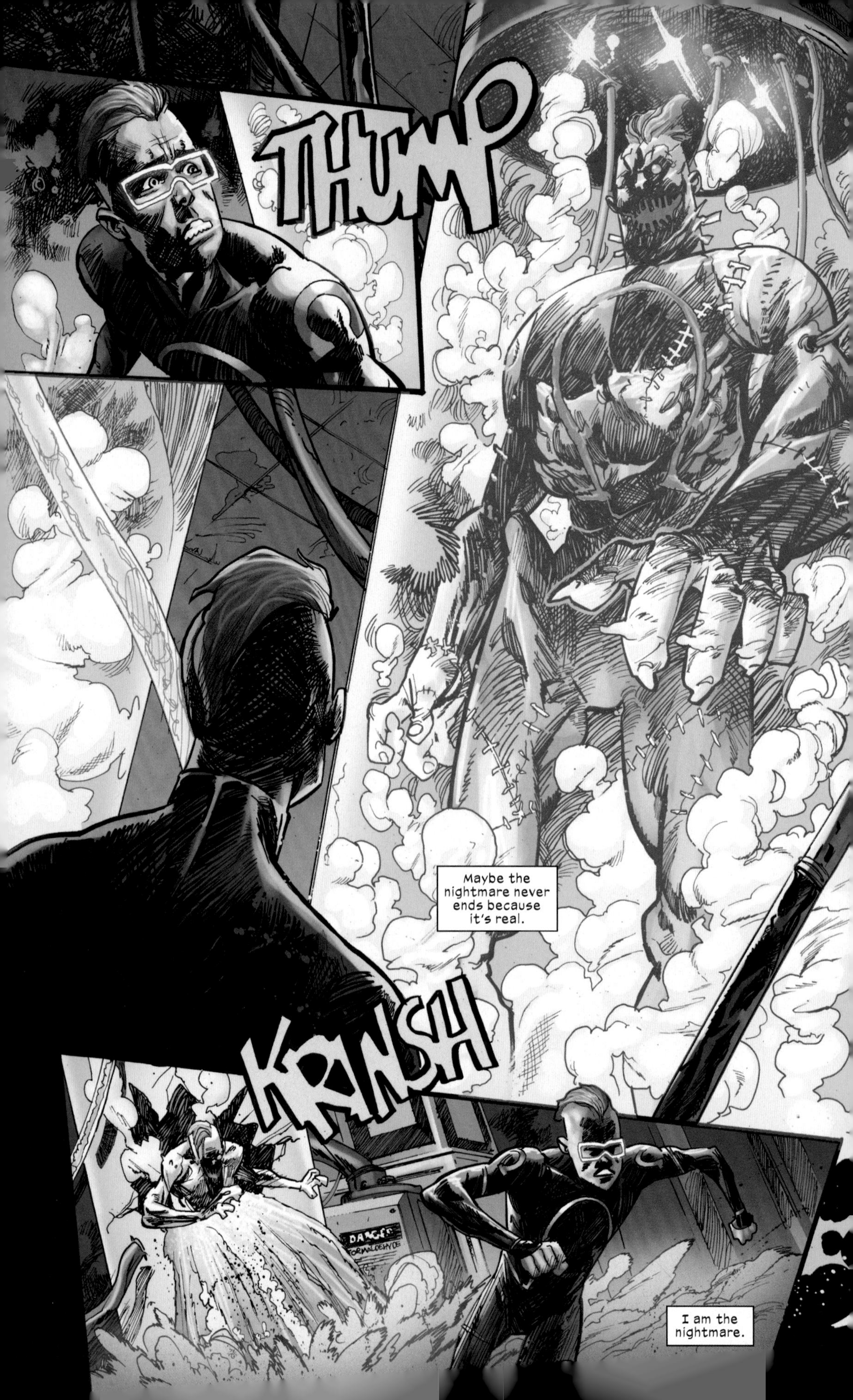

THUMP
Maybe the nightmare never ends because it's real.
KRNSH
DANGER FORMALDEHYDE
I am the nightmare.

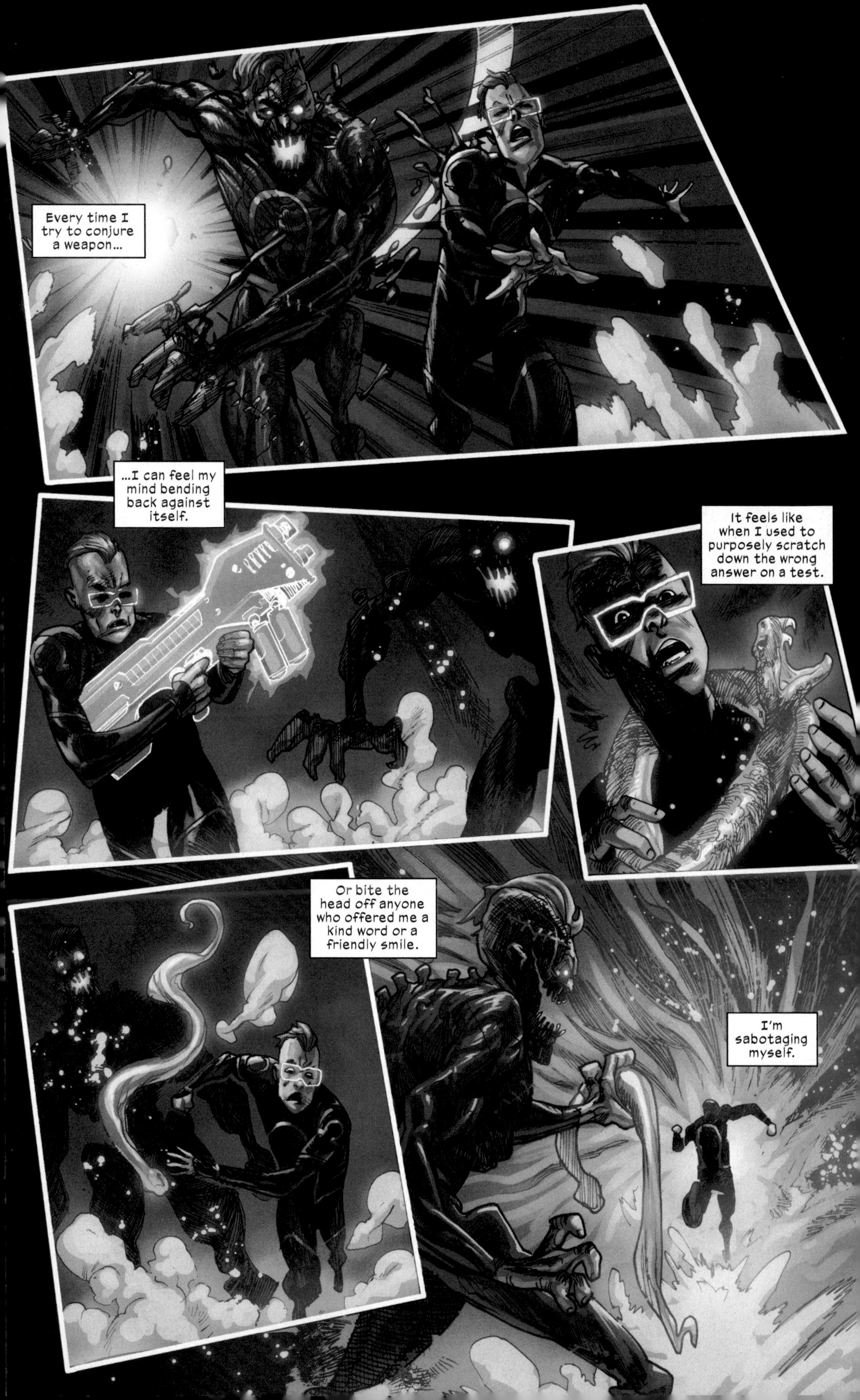
Every time I try to conjure a weapon...
...I can feel my mind bending back against itself.
It feels like when I used to purposely scratch down the wrong answer on a test.
Or bite the head off anyone who offered me a kind word or a friendly smile.
I'm sabotaging myself.

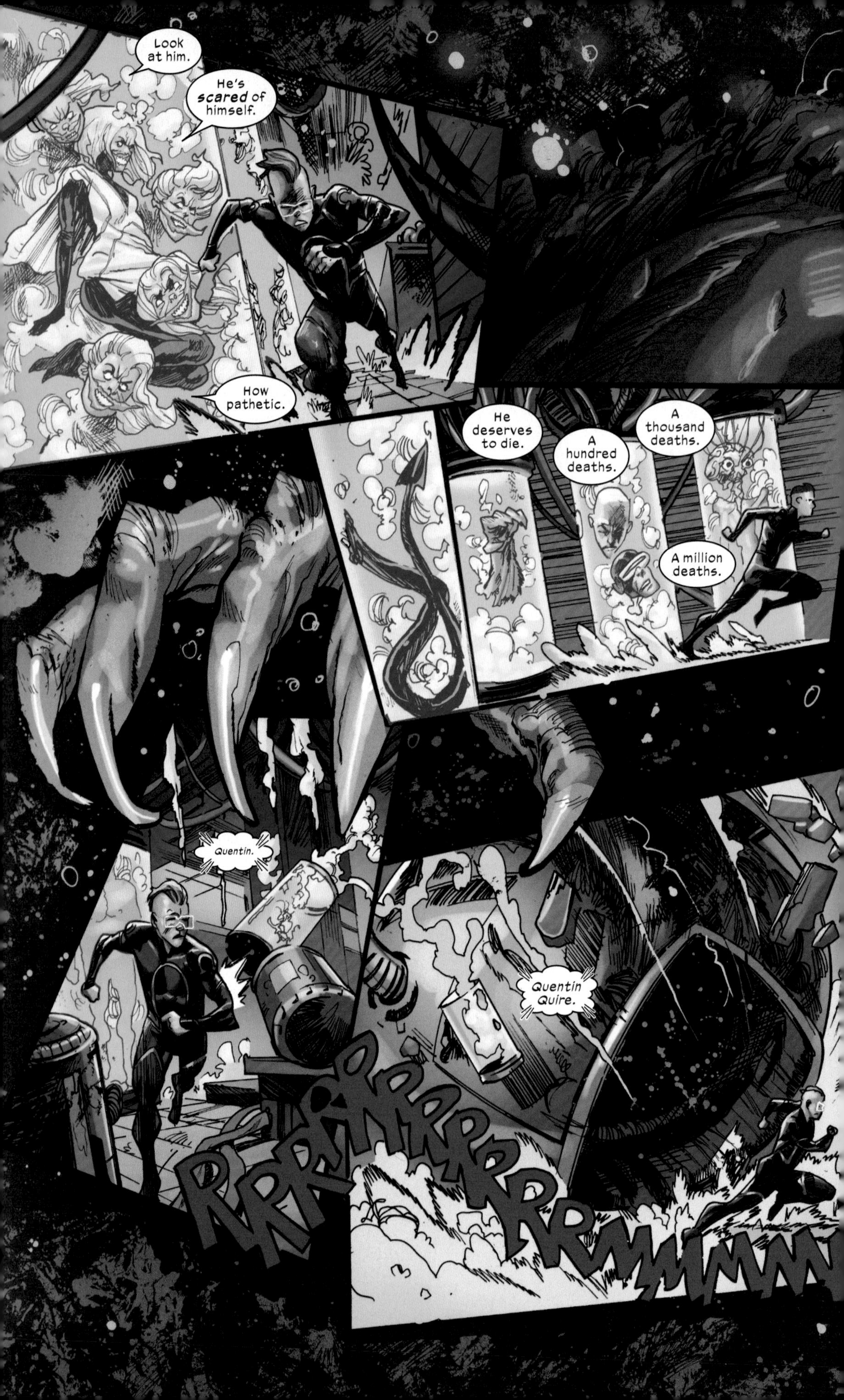
Look at him.
He's *scared* of himself.
How pathetic.
He deserves to die.
A hundred deaths.
A thousand deaths.
A million deaths.
Quentin.
Quentin Quire.
RRRRRRRRRRRRRRMMMMM

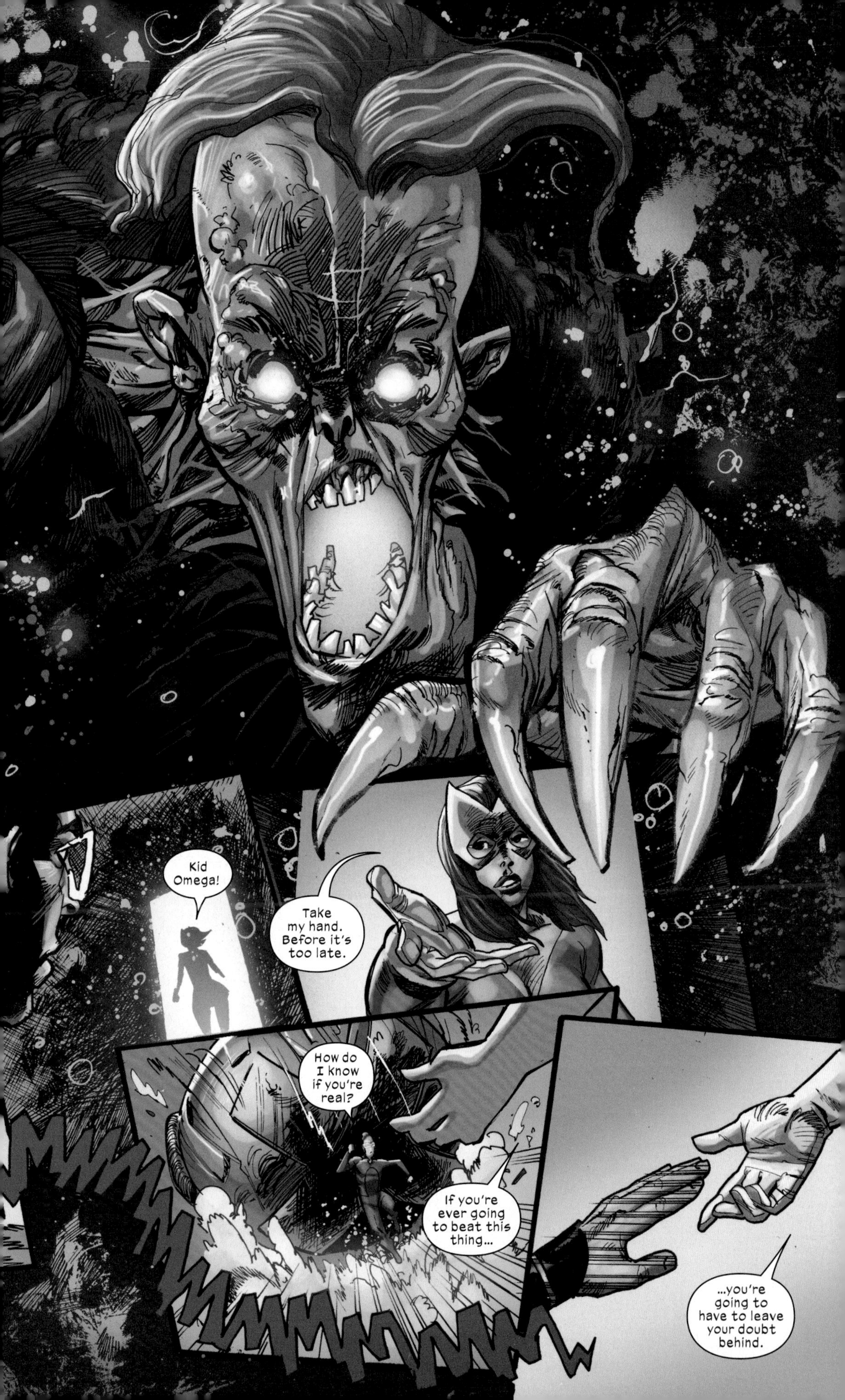
Kid Omega!
Take my hand. Before it's too late.
How do I know if you're real?
If you're ever going to beat this thing...
...you're going to have to leave your doubt behind.

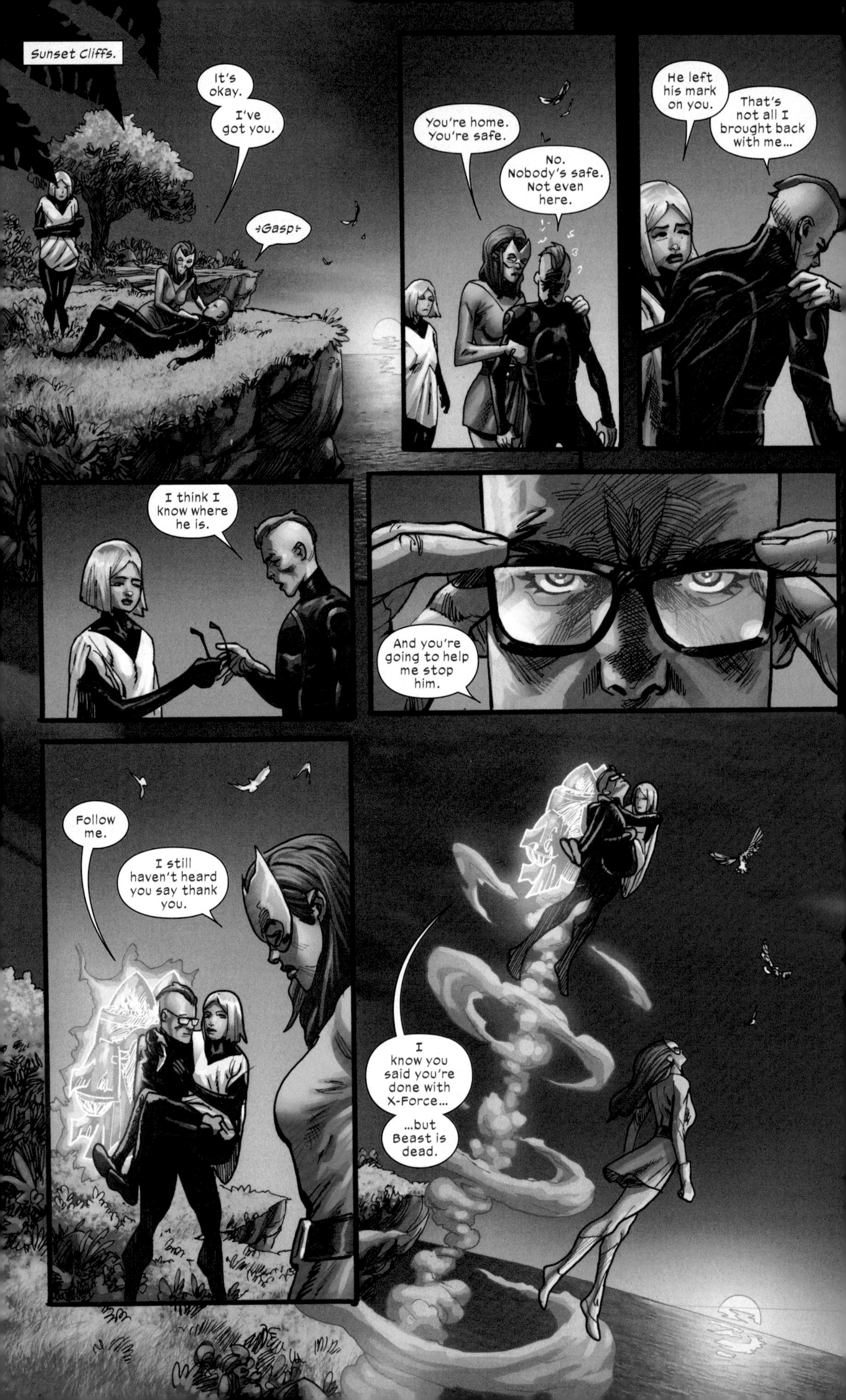
Sunset Cliffs.
It's okay.
I've got you.
-Gasp-
You're home. You're safe.
No. Nobody's safe. Not even here.
He left his mark on you.
That's not all I brought back with me...
I think I know where he is.
And you're going to help me stop him.
Follow me.
I still haven't heard you say thank you.
I know you said you're done with X-Force...
...but Beast is dead.

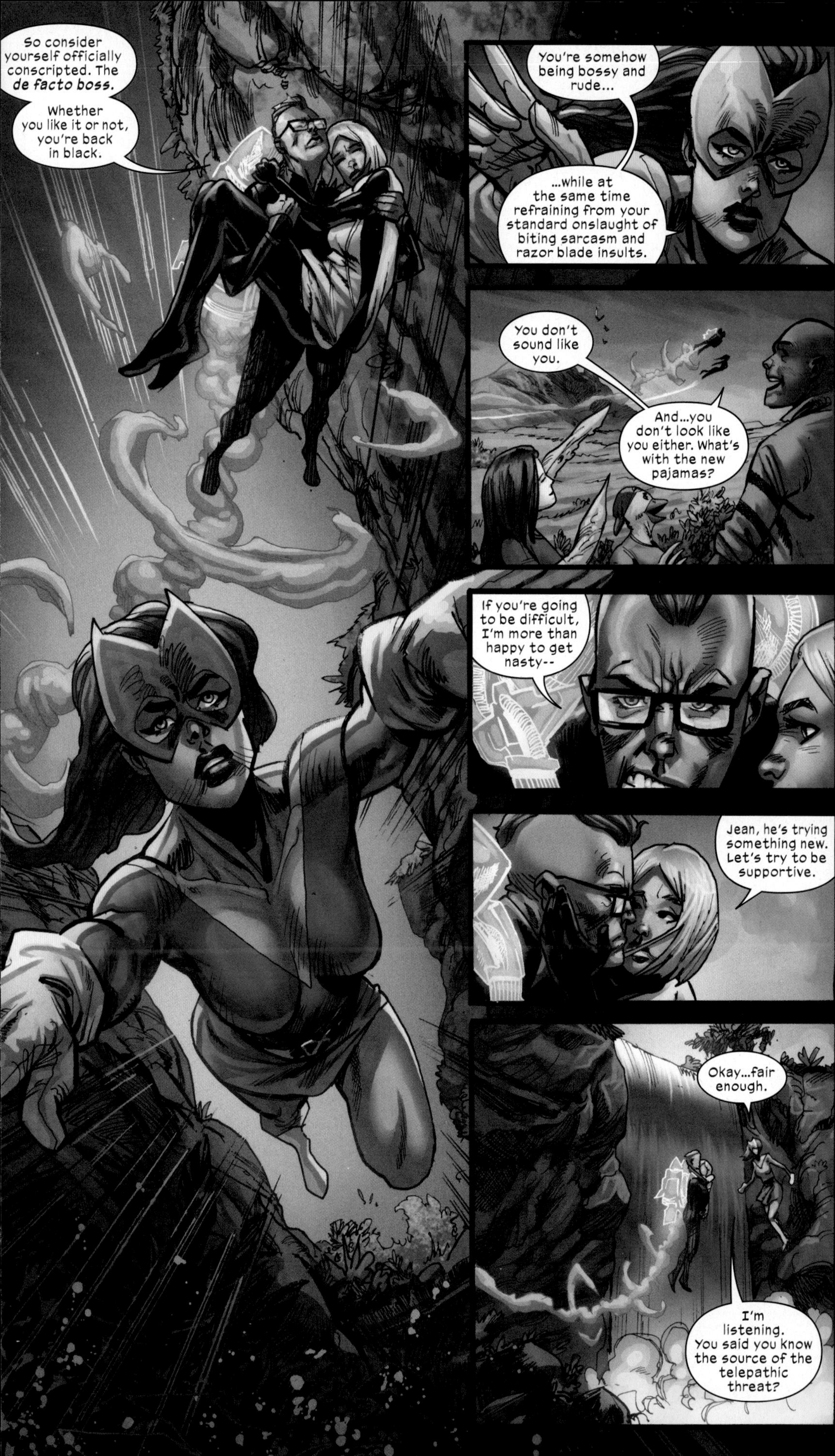

So consider yourself officially conscripted. The *de facto boss.*
Whether you like it or not, you're back in black.
You're somehow being bossy and rude...
...while at the same time refraining from your standard onslaught of biting sarcasm and razor blade insults.
You don't sound like you.
And...you don't look like you either. What's with the new pajamas?
If you're going to be difficult, I'm more than happy to get nasty--
Jean, he's trying something new. Let's try to be supportive.
Okay...fair enough.
I'm listening. You said you know the source of the telepathic threat?

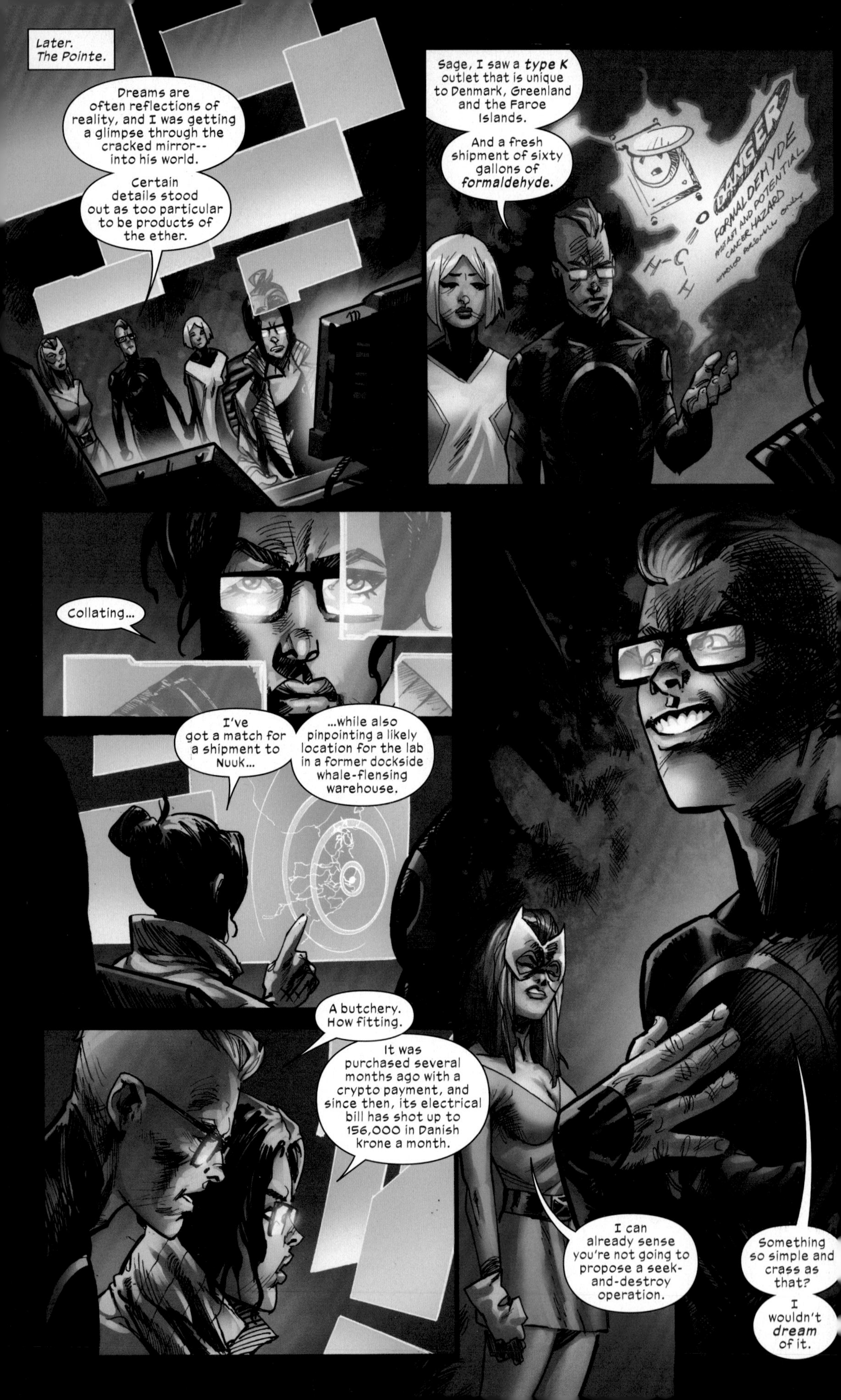
Later.
The Pointe.
Dreams are often reflections of reality, and I was getting a glimpse through the cracked mirror-- into his world.
Certain details stood out as too particular to be products of the ether.
Sage, I saw a type K outlet that is unique to Denmark, Greenland and the Faroe Islands.
And a fresh shipment of sixty gallons of formaldehyde.
DANGER
FORMALDEHYDE
Collating...
I've got a match for a shipment to Nuuk...
...while also pinpointing a likely location for the lab in a former dockside whale-flensing warehouse.
A butchery. How fitting.
It was purchased several months ago with a crypto payment, and since then, its electrical bill has shot up to 156,000 in Danish krone a month.
I can already sense you're not going to propose a seek-and-destroy operation.
Something so simple and crass as that?
I wouldn't dream of it.

He paints every morning. Because his hands haven't yet been dirtied and weakened from a long day in the fields. And because that's when the light is kindest, when the colors and the textures announce themselves, when sun negotiates with night and offers the perfect tracery of shadow.

The subjects vary. A landscape. A portrait. An abstract. But embedded in each of them is a hidden meaning.

Painters, like poets, have always snuck things into their work. Michelangelo's *Creation of Adam* contains an anatomical illustration of the human brain. Van Eyck's *Arnolfini Portrait* hides Latin inscriptions and mirrored images. Codes. Secrets.

The paintings have...admirers. They are mailed to galleries. They are purchased for a handsome price. "I feel like the artist is speaking to me," the buyer says.

летописец

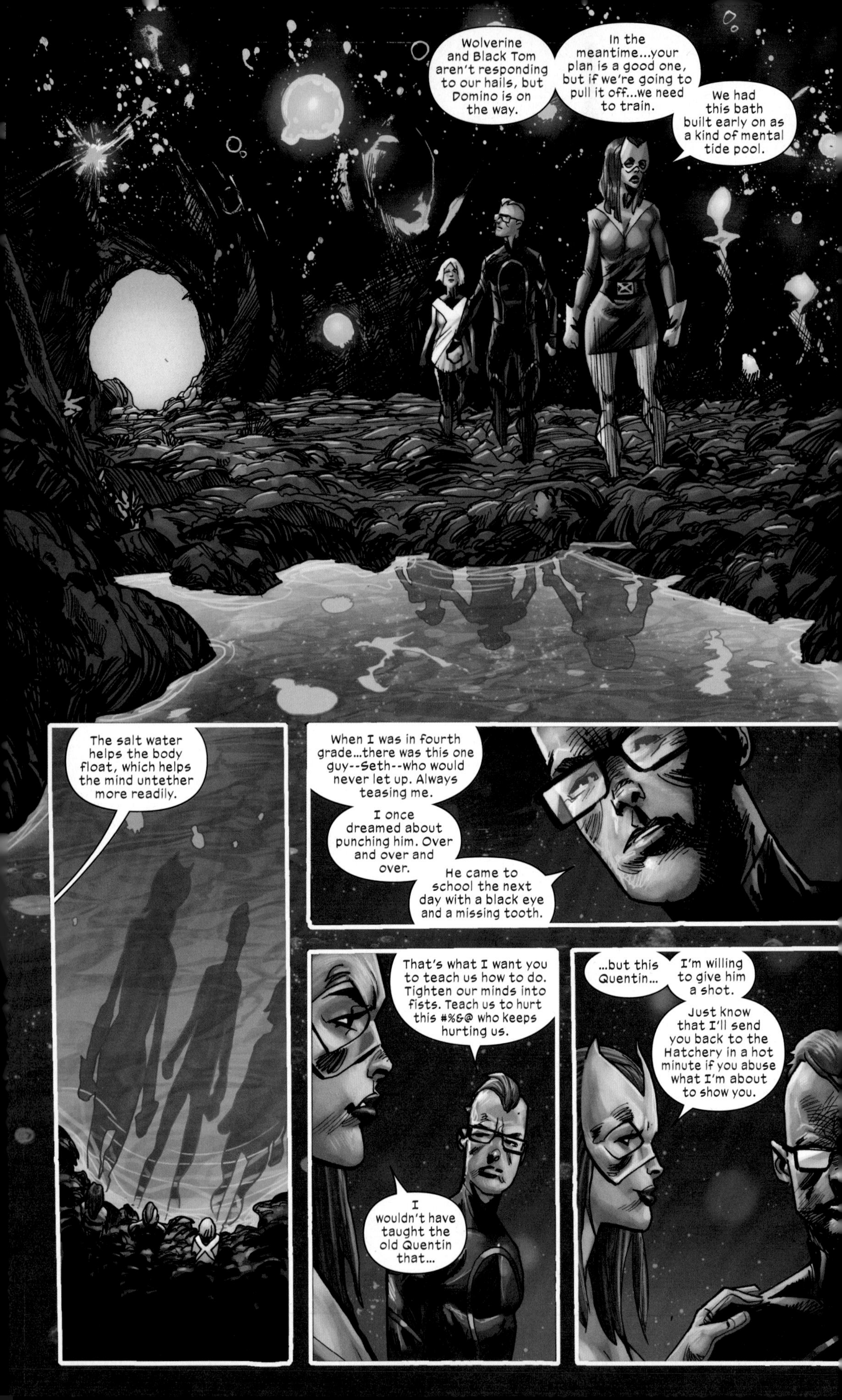

Wolverine and Black Tom aren't responding to our hails, but Domino is on the way.
In the meantime...your plan is a good one, but if we're going to pull it off...we need to train.
We had this bath built early on as a kind of mental tide pool.
The salt water helps the body float, which helps the mind untether more readily.
When I was in fourth grade...there was this one guy--Seth--who would never let up. Always teasing me.
I once dreamed about punching him. Over and over and over.
He came to school the next day with a black eye and a missing tooth.
That's what I want you to teach us how to do. Tighten our minds into fists. Teach us to hurt this #%&@ who keeps hurting us.
I wouldn't have taught the old Quentin that...
...but this Quentin...
I'm willing to give him a shot.
Just know that I'll send you back to the Hatchery in a hot minute if you abuse what I'm about to show you.

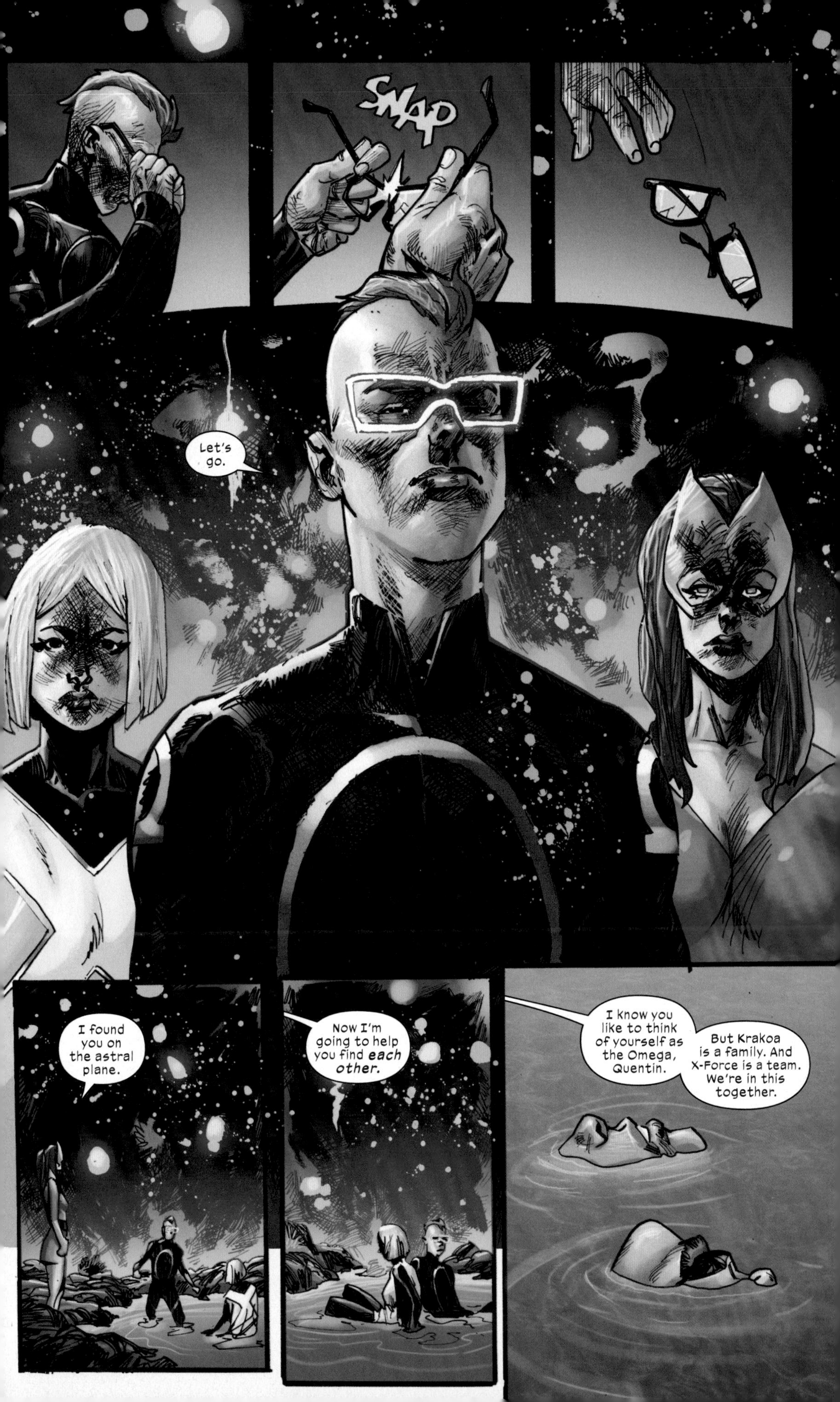
SNAP
Let's go.
I found you on the astral plane.
Now I'm going to help you find *each other.*
I know you like to think of yourself as the Omega, Quentin.
But Krakoa is a family. And X-Force is a team. We're in this together.

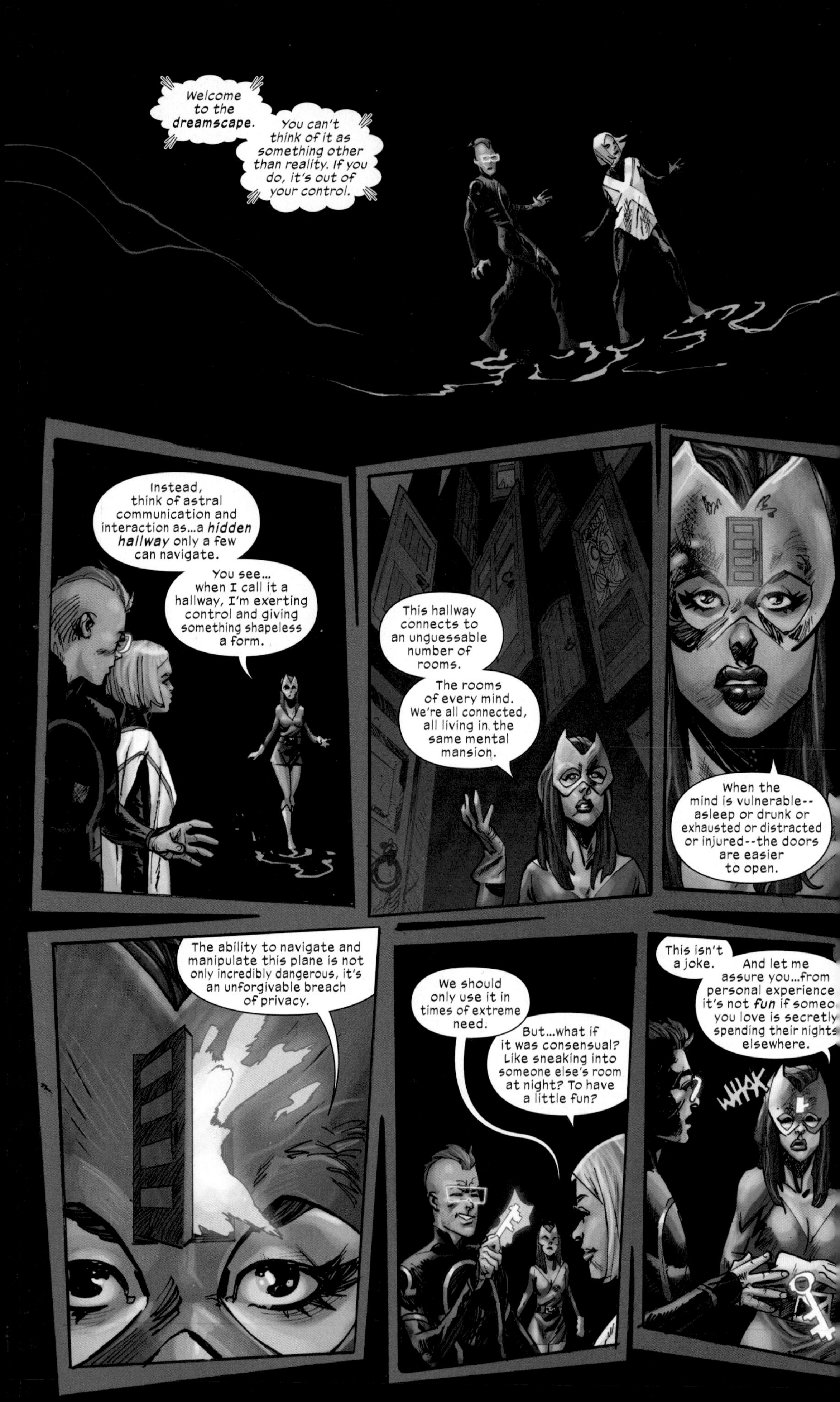

Welcome to the dreamscape.
You can't think of it as something other than reality. If you do, it's out of your control.
Instead, think of astral communication and interaction as...a hidden hallway only a few can navigate.
You see... when I call it a hallway, I'm exerting control and giving something shapeless a form.
This hallway connects to an unguessable number of rooms.
The rooms of every mind. We're all connected, all living in the same mental mansion.
When the mind is vulnerable-- asleep or drunk or exhausted or distracted or injured--the doors are easier to open.
The ability to navigate and manipulate this plane is not only incredibly dangerous, it's an unforgivable breach of privacy.
We should only use it in times of extreme need.
But...what if it was consensual? Like sneaking into someone else's room at night? To have a little fun?
This isn't a joke.
And let me assure you...from personal experience it's not fun if someo you love is secretly spending their nights elsewhere.
WHAK

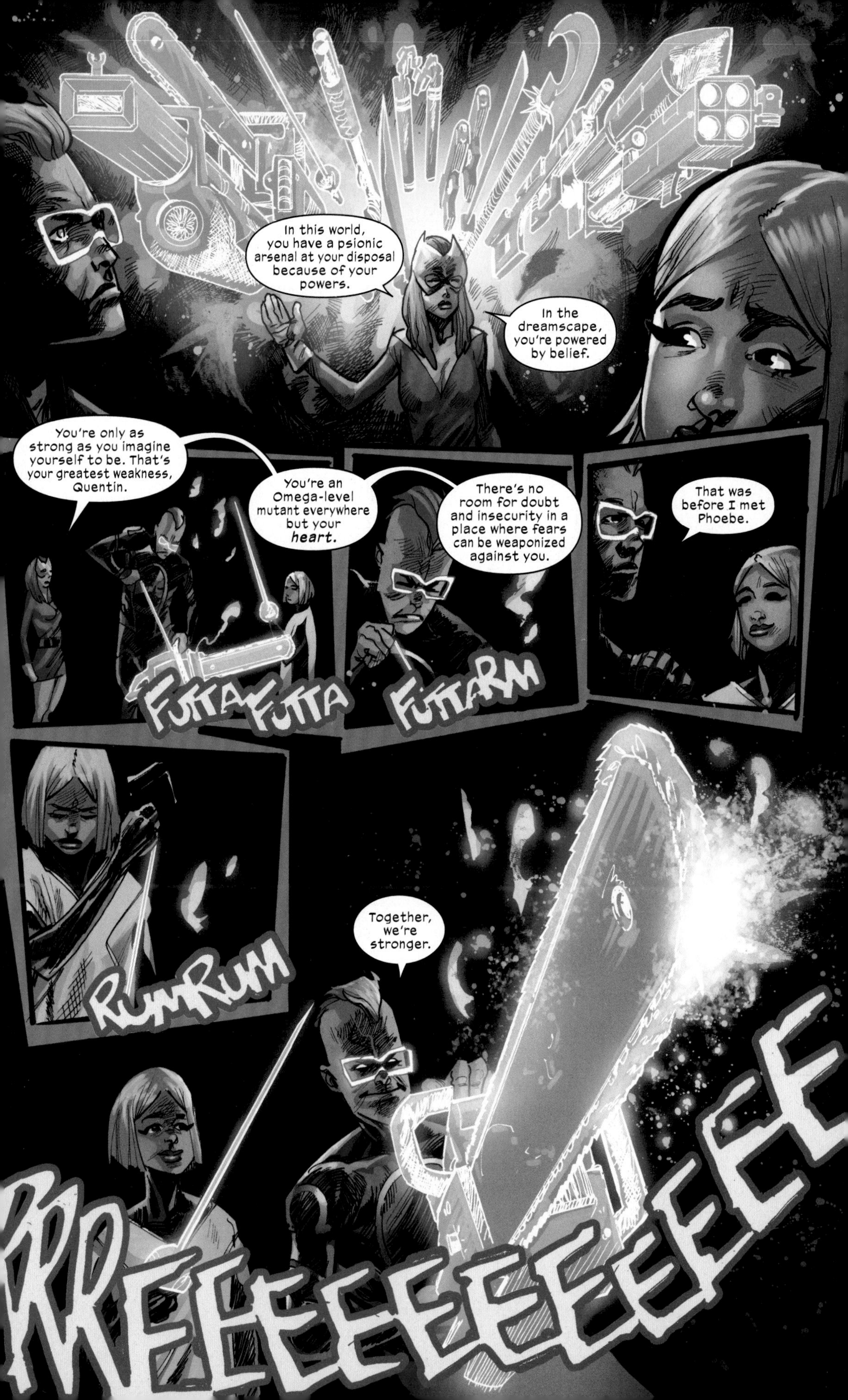
In this world, you have a psionic arsenal at your disposal because of your powers.
In the dreamscape, you're powered by belief.
You're only as strong as you imagine yourself to be. That's your greatest weakness, Quentin.
You're an Omega-level mutant everywhere but your *heart.*
FUTTA FUTTA
There's no room for doubt and insecurity in a place where fears can be weaponized against you.
FUTTARM
That was before I met Phoebe.
RUMRUM
Together, we're stronger.
RRREEEEEEEEEEEEE

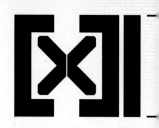

A CONVERSATION AMONG PSYCHICS

QUENTIN: I'm going to win.

JEAN: You need to stop thinking about things in the first person. We. We are going to win.

QUENTIN: Fine. Whatever. We're going to win.

JEAN: It's not just the we that underlies Krakoa, it's the we that inhabits the dreamscape. We are all connected through a web of mental energy, and we need to exterminate the spider that haunts it.

QUENTIN: Phoebe and I will hunt the nightmare. You and Domino will hunt the conjurer of nightmares. It's a race. Across astral and actual geographies. Whoever kills him first is the true Omega. Which is me. Obviously.

JEAN: It's not a competition. We're working toward the same goal, and whoever gets there first hardly matters.

QUENTIN: That's no fun. Stop being a mom who wants everybody to have the same cut of cake.

JEAN: Quentin...you're probably not going to be able to stop him in the dreamscape. He's...you, after all. You're equals. But if you slow him down, if you distract him, then maybe Domino and I can locate and destroy the host.

QUENTIN: Jean...

JEAN: Yeah?

QUENTIN: You...you know what it's like...to lose control? To become the worst possible version of yourself?

JEAN: I do.

QUENTIN: How do you keep going? Knowing a part of you is a monster?

JEAN: You don't have control over your past, but you're the author of your future. You, Quentin. You choose how you want your story to end.

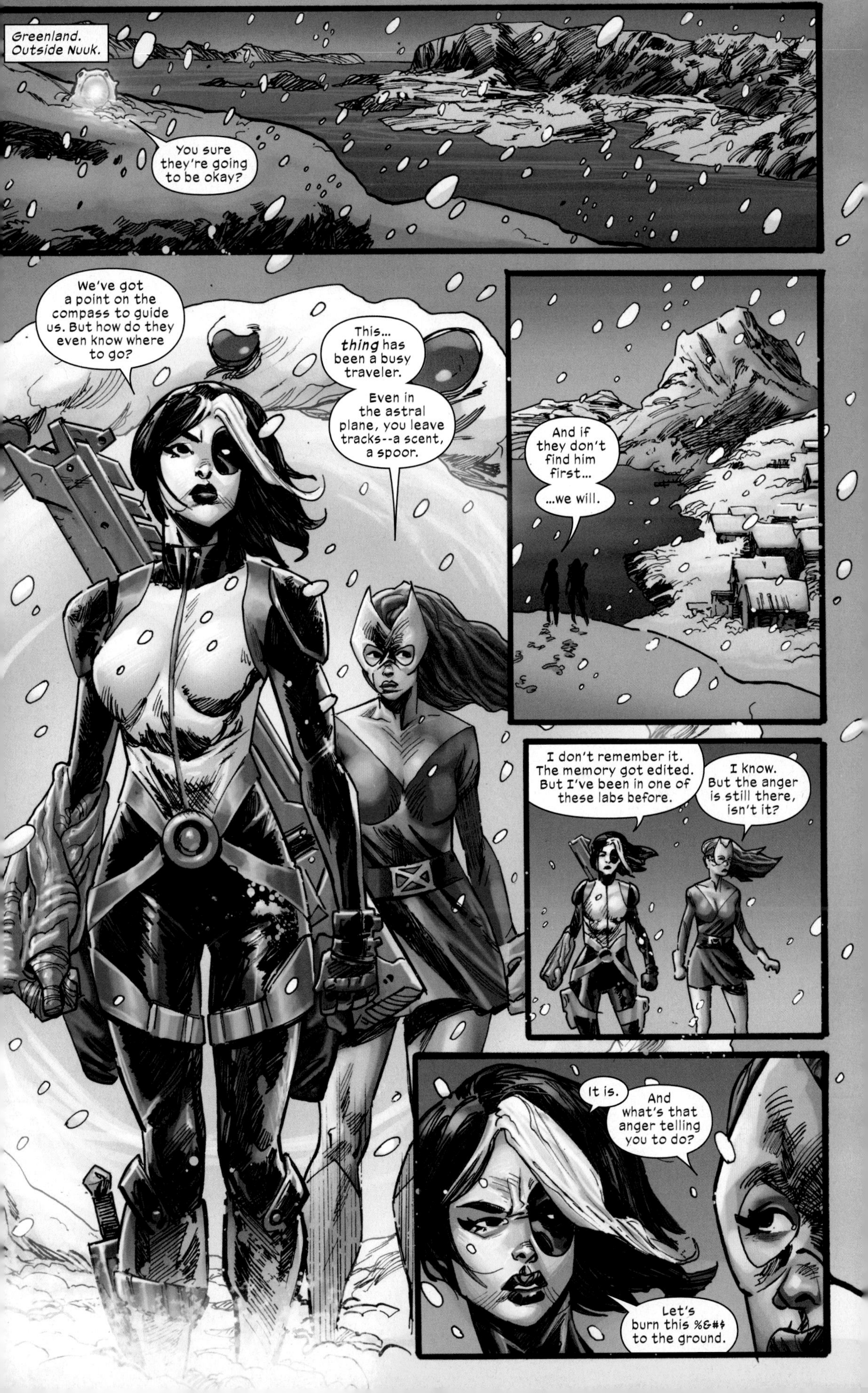
Greenland. Outside Nuuk.
You sure they're going to be okay?
We've got a point on the compass to guide us. But how do they even know where to go?
This... thing has been a busy traveler.
Even in the astral plane, you leave tracks--a scent, a spoor.
And if they don't find him first...
...we will.
I don't remember it. The memory got edited. But I've been in one of these labs before.
I know. But the anger is still there, isn't it?
It is.
And what's that anger telling you to do?
Let's burn this %&#$ to the ground.

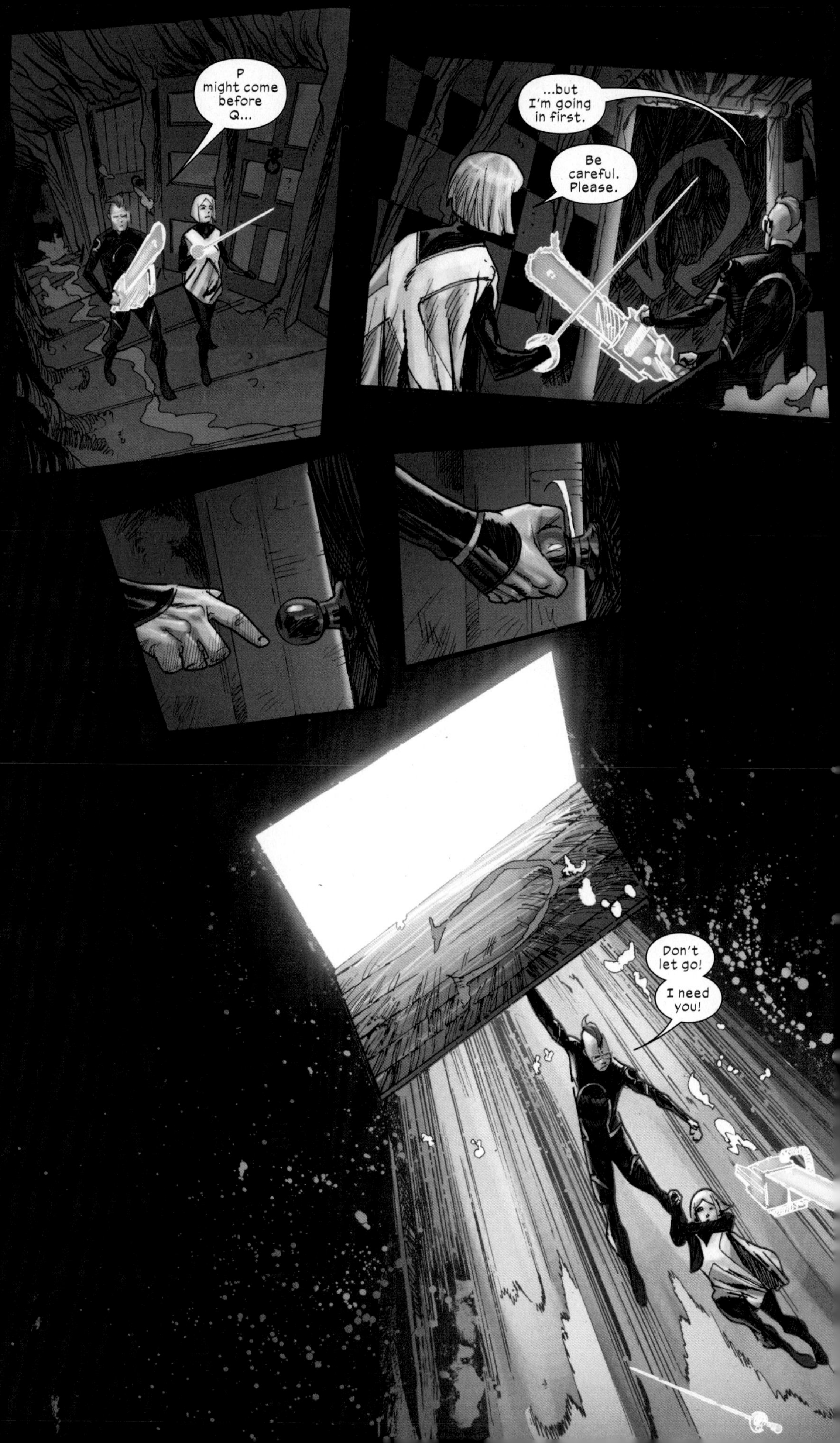
P might come before Q...
...but I'm going in first.
Be careful. Please.
Don't let go!
I need you!

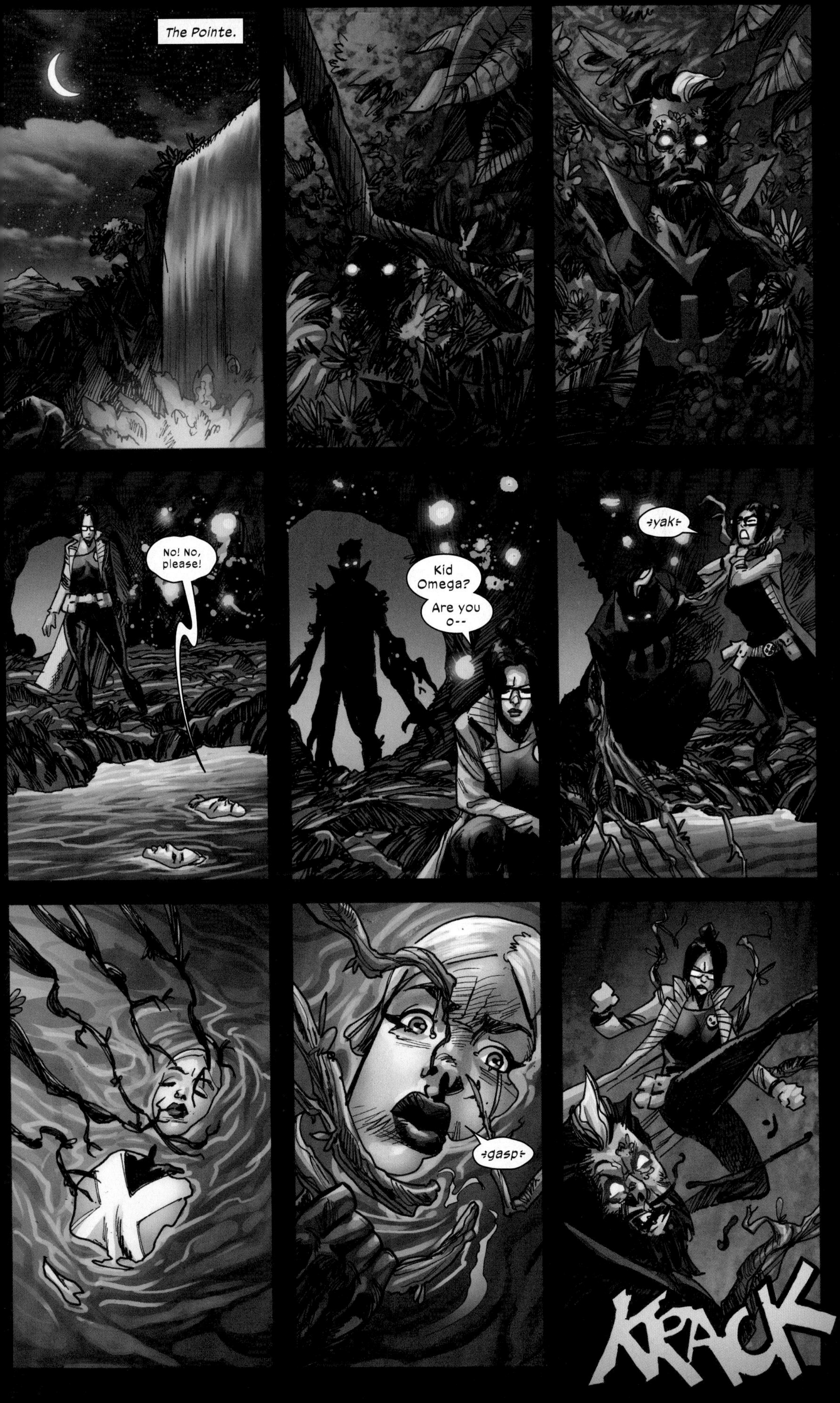

The Pointe.
No! No, please!
Kid Omega?
Are you o--
yak
gasp
KRACK

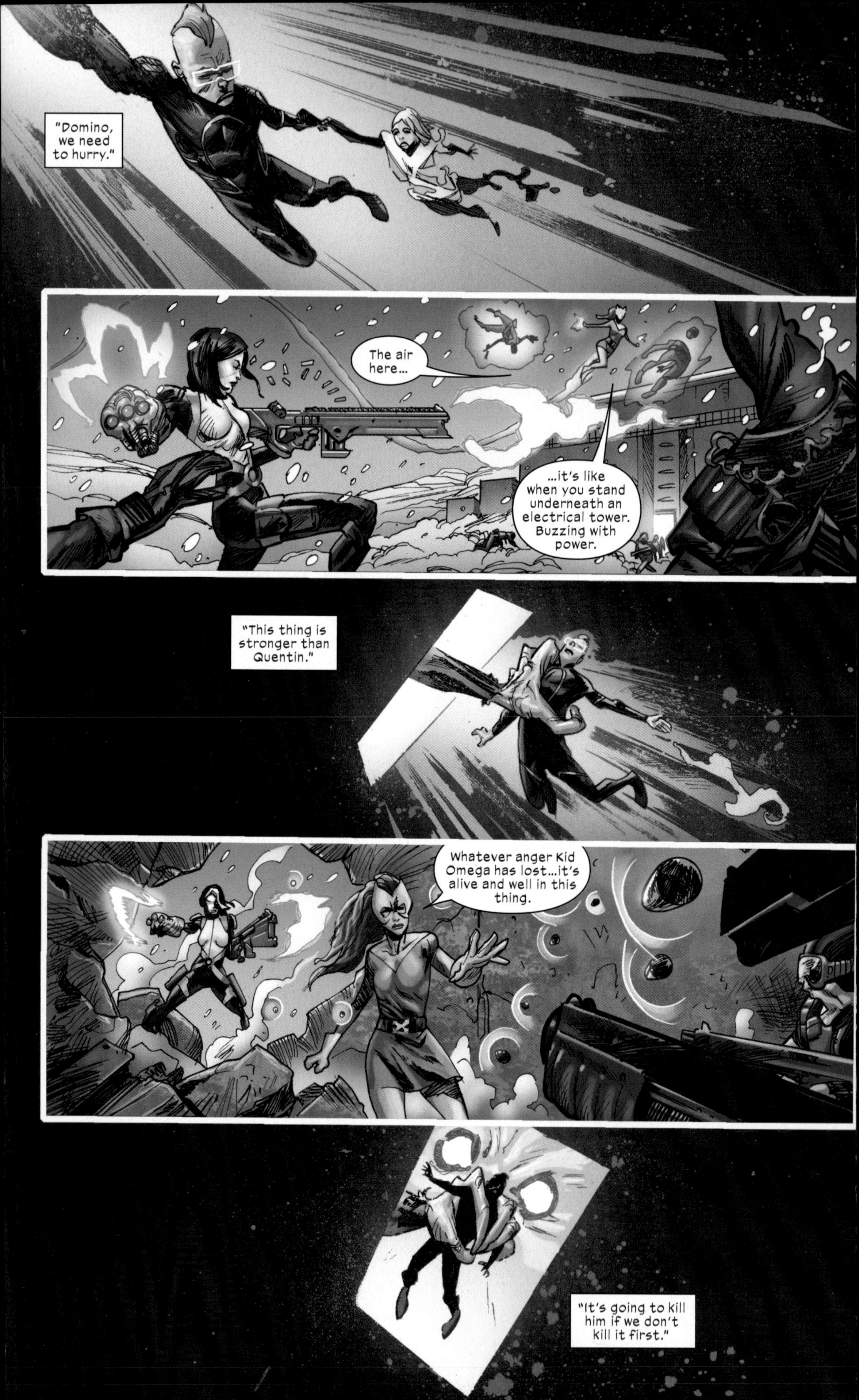
"Domino, we need to hurry."
The air here...
...it's like when you stand underneath an electrical tower. Buzzing with power.
"This thing is stronger than Quentin."
Whatever anger Kid Omega has lost...it's alive and well in this thing.
"It's going to kill him if we don't kill it first."

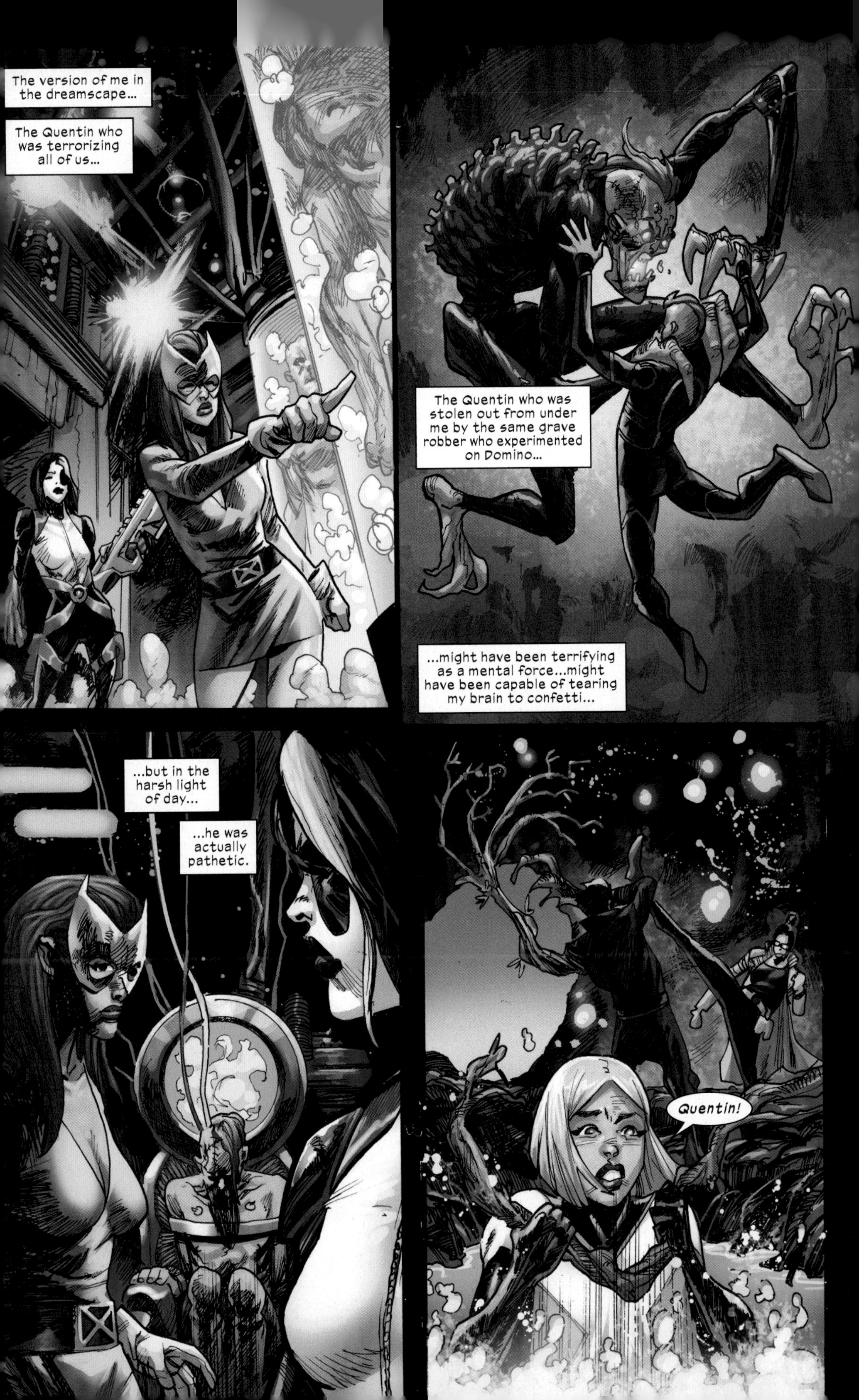
The version of me in the dreamscape...
The Quentin who was terrorizing all of us...
The Quentin who was stolen out from under me by the same grave robber who experimented on Domino...
...might have been terrifying as a mental force...might have been capable of tearing my brain to confetti...
...but in the harsh light of day...
...he was actually pathetic.
Quentin!

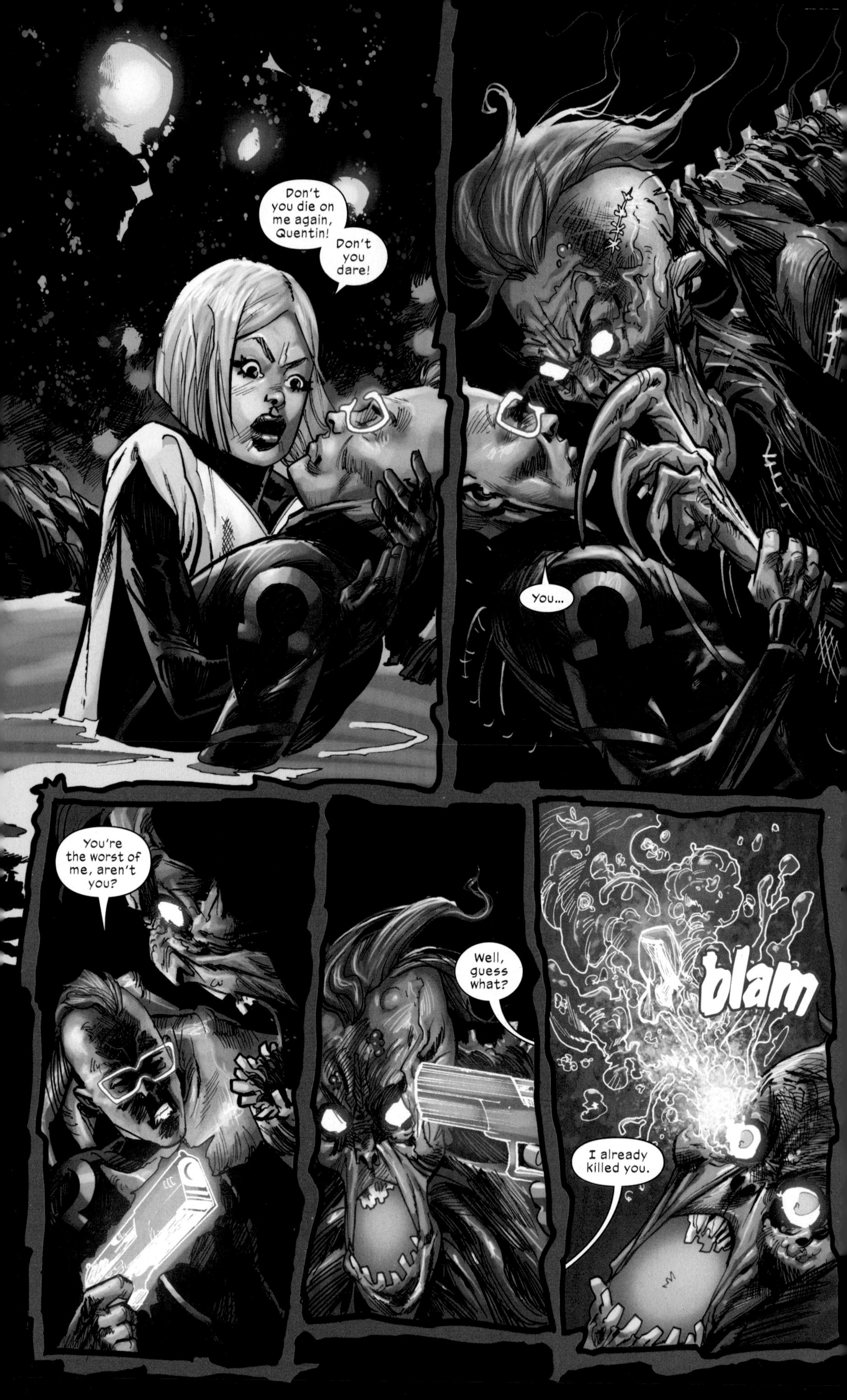
Don't you die on me again, Quentin!
Don't you dare!
You...
You're the worst of me, aren't you?
Well, guess what?
blam
I already killed you.

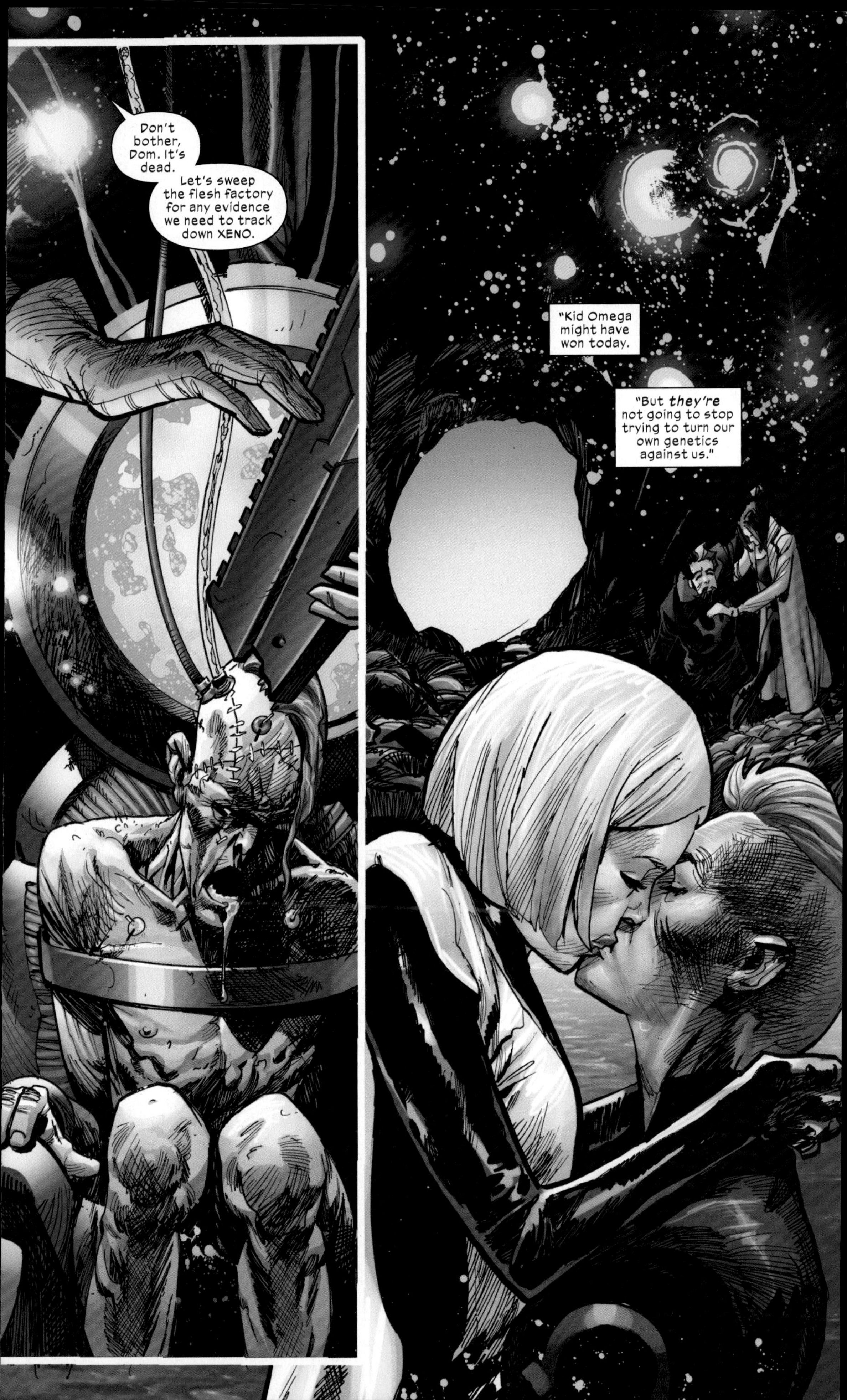

Don't bother, Dom. It's dead.
Let's sweep the flesh factory for any evidence we need to track down XENO.
"Kid Omega might have won today.
"But *they're* not going to stop trying to turn our own genetics against us."

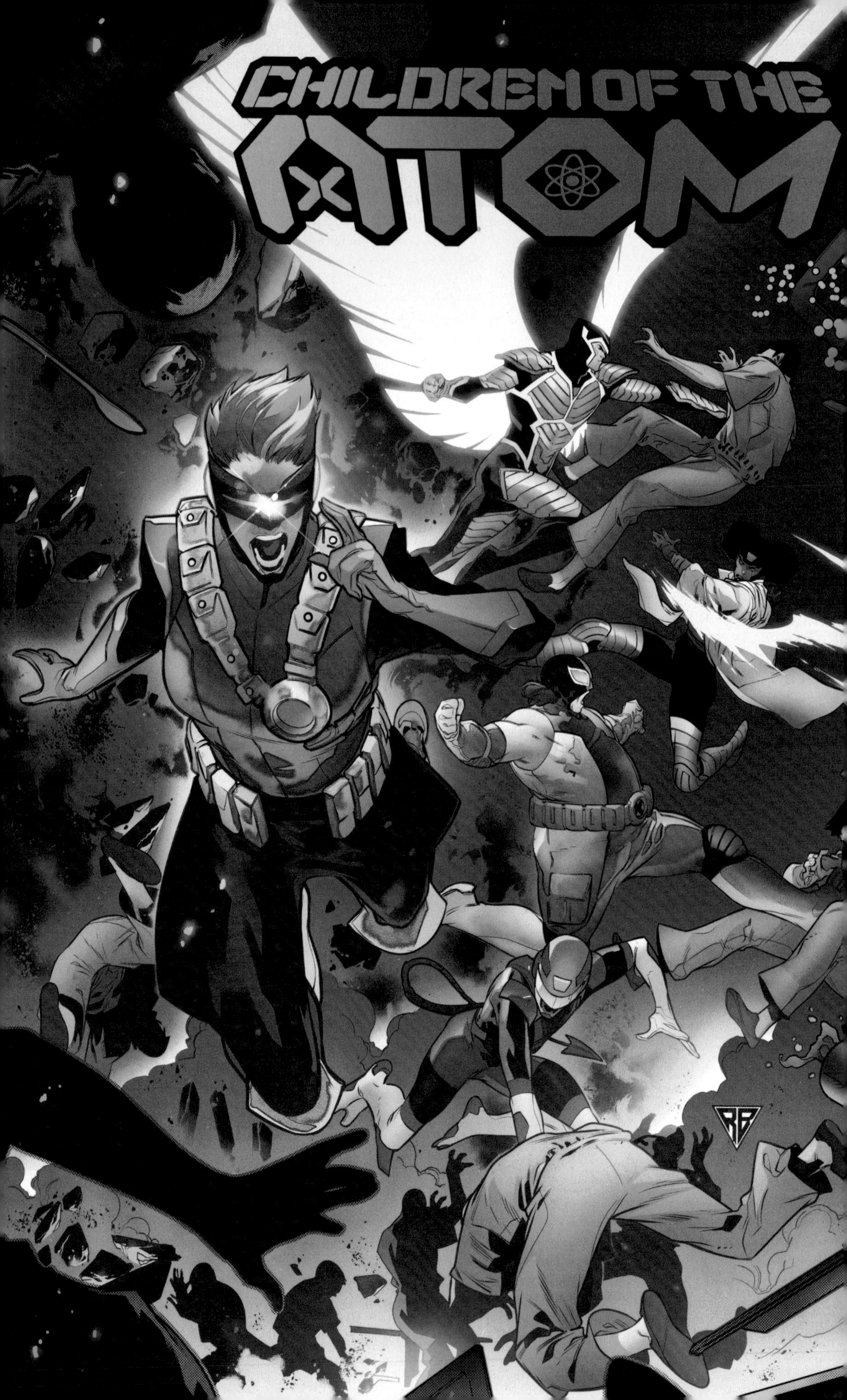
CHILDREN OF THE
ATOM

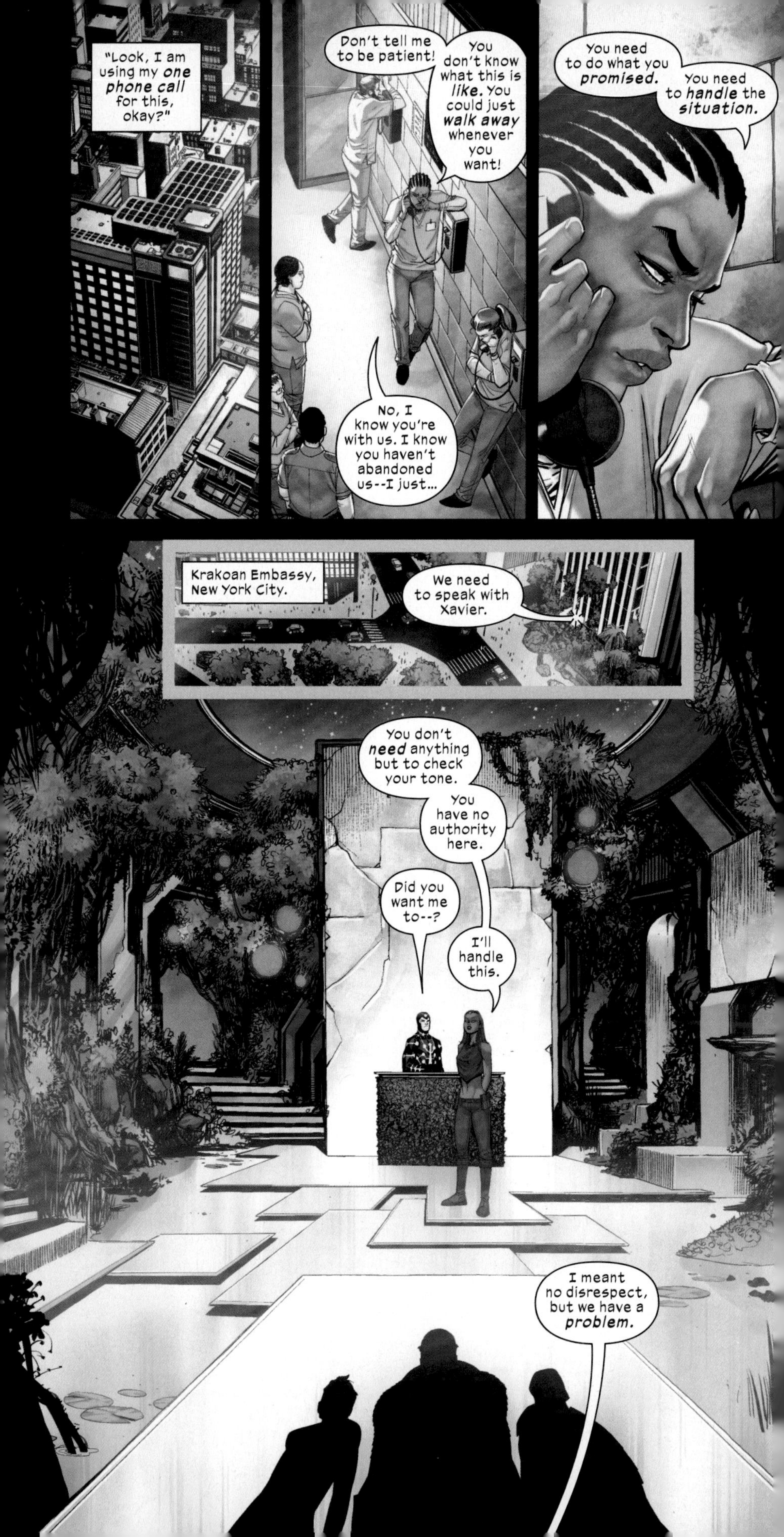
"Look, I am using my *one phone call* for this, okay?"
Don't tell me to be patient!
You don't know what this is *like.* You could just *walk away* whenever you want!
No, I know you're with us. I know you haven't abandoned us--I just...
You need to do what you *promised.*
You need to *handle* the *situation.*
Krakoan Embassy, New York City.
We need to speak with Xavier.
You don't *need* anything but to check your tone.
You have no authority here.
Did you want me to--?
I'll handle this.
I meant no disrespect, but we have a *problem.*

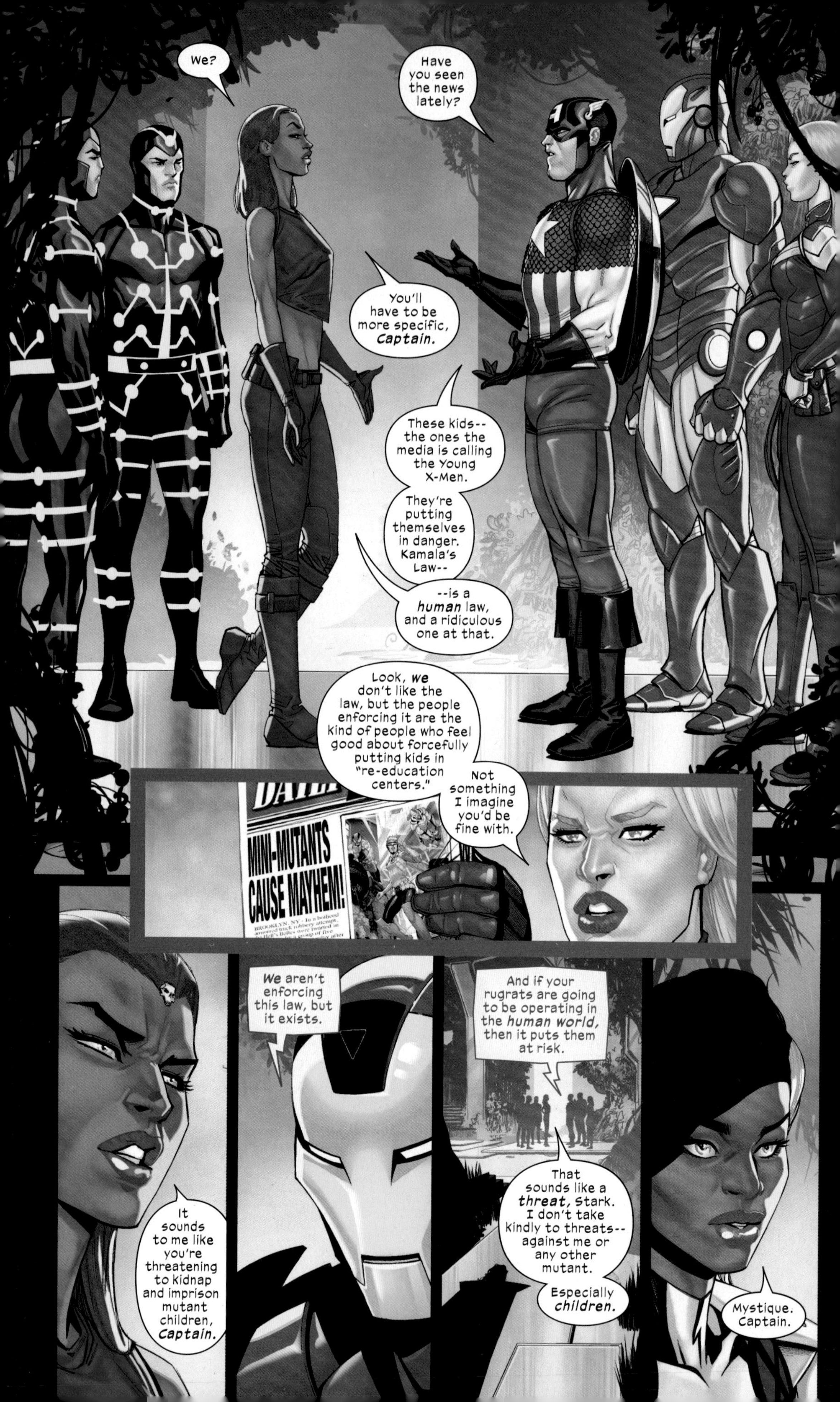

We?
Have you seen the news lately?
You'll have to be more specific, *Captain.*
These kids-- the ones the media is calling the Young X-Men.
They're putting themselves in danger. Kamala's Law--
--is a *human* law, and a ridiculous one at that.
Look, *we* don't like the law, but the people enforcing it are the kind of people who feel good about forcefully putting kids in "re-education centers."
Not something I imagine you'd be fine with.
DAILY
MINI-MUTANTS CAUSE MAYHEM!
We aren't enforcing this law, but it exists.
And if your rugrats are going to be operating in the *human world,* then it puts them at risk.
It sounds to me like you're threatening to kidnap and imprison mutant children, *Captain.*
That sounds like a *threat,* Stark. I don't take kindly to threats-- against me or any other mutant.
Especially *children.*
Mystique. Captain.

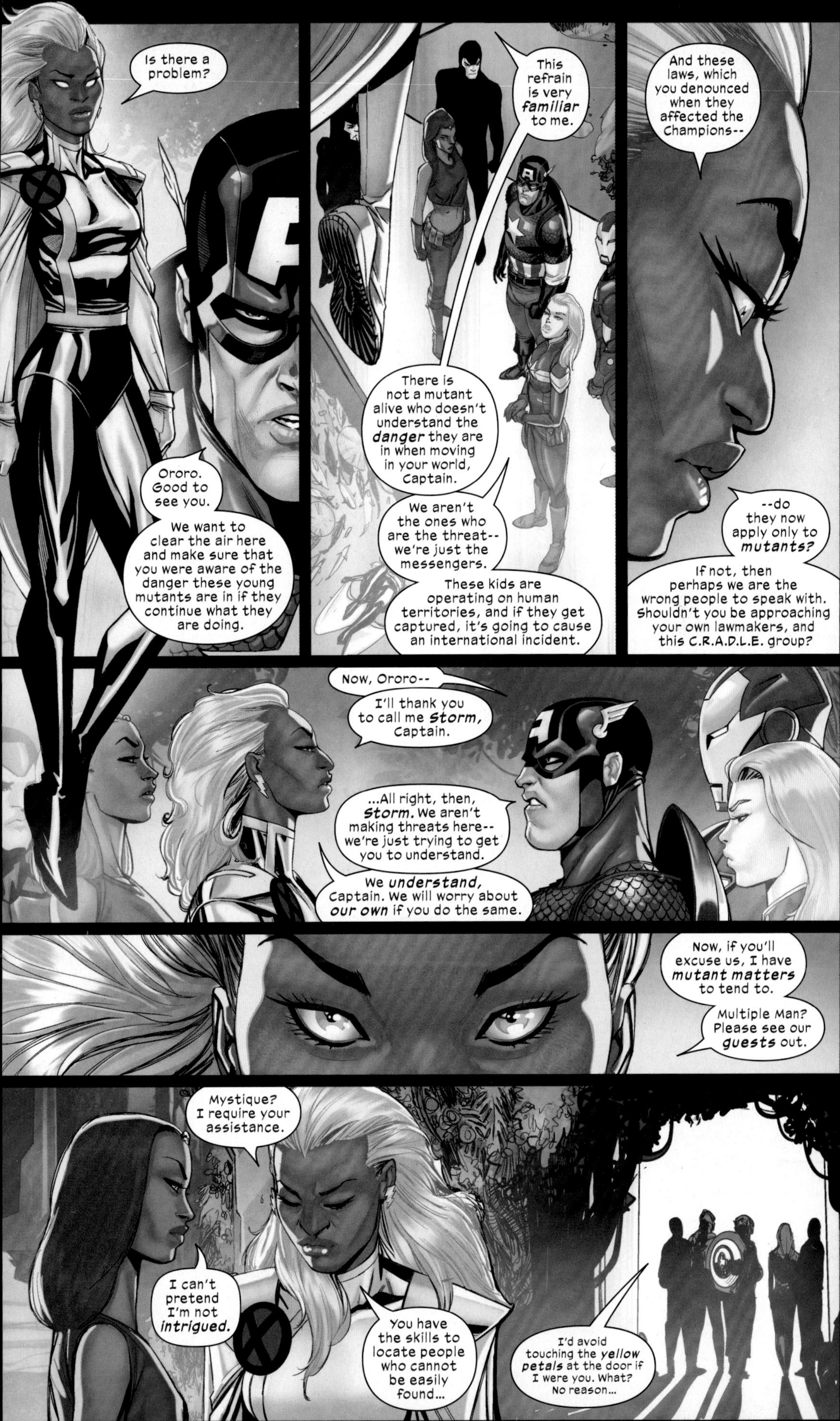

Is there a problem?
Ororo. Good to see you.
We want to clear the air here and make sure that you were aware of the danger these young mutants are in if they continue what they are doing.
This refrain is very *familiar* to me.
There is not a mutant alive who doesn't understand the *danger* they are in when moving in your world, Captain.
We aren't the ones who are the threat-- we're just the messengers.
These kids are operating on human territories, and if they get captured, it's going to cause an international incident.
And these laws, which you denounced when they affected the Champions--
--do they now apply only to *mutants?*
If not, then perhaps we are the wrong people to speak with. Shouldn't you be approaching your own lawmakers, and this C.R.A.D.L.E. group?
Now, Ororo--
I'll thank you to call me *Storm,* Captain.
...All right, then, *Storm.* We aren't making threats here-- we're just trying to get you to understand.
We *understand,* Captain. We will worry about *our own* if you do the same.
Now, if you'll excuse us, I have *mutant matters* to tend to.
Multiple Man? Please see our *guests* out.
Mystique? I require your assistance.
I can't pretend I'm not *intrigued.*
You have the skills to locate people who cannot be easily found...
I'd avoid touching the *yellow petals* at the door if I were you. What? No reason...

TIME TO COME HOME

Mutants around the world have flocked to the island-nation of Krakoa for safety, security and to be part of the first mutant society.

New teen vigilantes CHILDREN OF THE ATOM recently met some of their heroes, the X-MEN, while helping put the villainous HELL'S BELLES behind bars. The young team decided it was high time they joined their fellow X-Men on Krakoa, but when they walked through the Krakoan gate, they found themselves standing in the same spot...

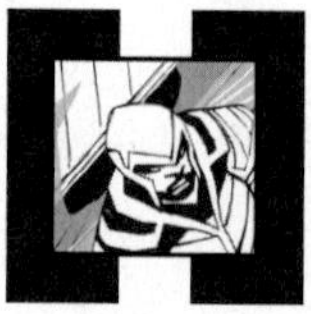

Cherub

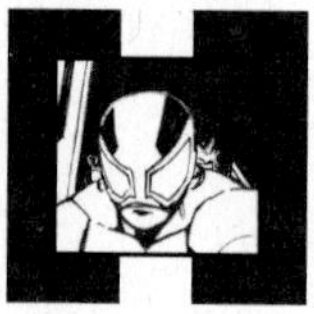

Marvel Guy

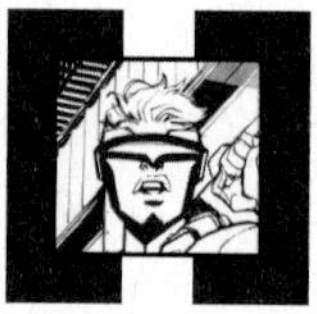

Cyclops-Lass

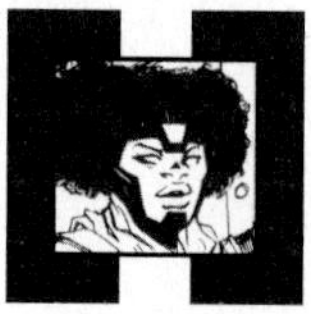

Gimmick

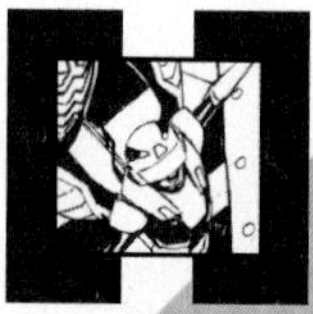

Daycrawler

CHILDREN OF THE ATOM
[X_02]

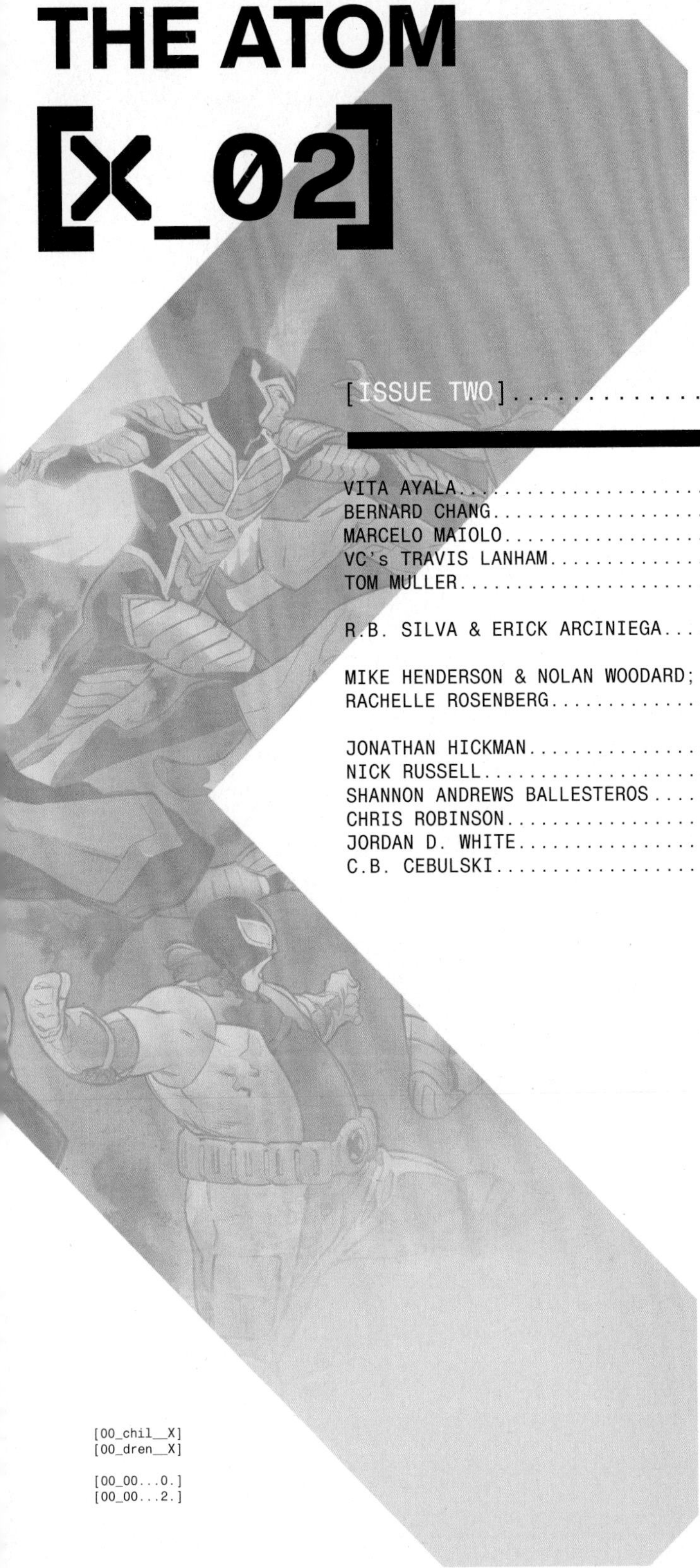

[ISSUE TWO].....................PRISON BREAK

VITA AYALA...[WRITER]
BERNARD CHANG.....................................[ARTIST]
MARCELO MAIOLO..............................[COLOR ARTIST]
VC's TRAVIS LANHAM...............................[LETTERER]
TOM MULLER..[DESIGN]

R.B. SILVA & ERICK ARCINIEGA................[COVER ARTISTS]

MIKE HENDERSON & NOLAN WOODARD; TODD NAUCK &
RACHELLE ROSENBERG..................[VARIANT COVER ARTISTS]

JONATHAN HICKMAN.................................[HEAD OF X]
NICK RUSSELL....................................[PRODUCTION]
SHANNON ANDREWS BALLESTEROS..............[ASSISTANT EDITOR]
CHRIS ROBINSON....................................[EDITOR]
JORDAN D. WHITE.............................[SENIOR EDITOR]
C.B. CEBULSKI.............................[EDITOR IN CHIEF]

[00_chil__X]
[00_dren__X]

[00_00...0.]
[00_00...2.]

[00_____]
[00_of____]

[00_the___]

[00__atom__]

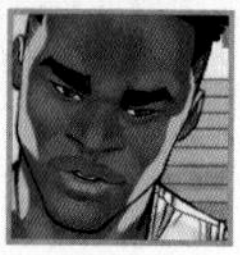

FINNA_FIGHT
Gabe Brathwaite

FOLLOWED

"YOU MUST BE A MUTANT TO HAVE ABS LIKE THAT" WORKOUT
(Intermediate)

I get asked about core workouts all the time, and the one thing that always comes up is that people "want the abs but don't have the time." You ***make*** time for the things you think are important!

This workout will have you cut like Wolverine's claws got a grudge.

Remember the motto: hustle smarter, so you can go harder.

(Also, remember to rest 60 seconds between sets.)

WARM-UP

Home: 20 jumping jacks (2 sets)/Gym: treadmill for half a mile, at 4 mph.

WORKOUT

- 16 elbow-to-knee crunches (2 sets)
- 1-minute star plank hold (2 sets per arm)
- 8 clapping push-ups (2 sets)
- 16 Russian twists (2 sets)
- 12 butt-ups (2 sets)
- 12 raised leg circles (2 sets)
- 16 mountain climbers (2 sets)

COOLDOWN

Stretching, at least 5 minutes.

REWARD FOOD:

Swole-Search Smoothie*

*click the link to check it out!

1,024 fist bumps

APRIL #mutant #abs #workout #mutantabs #swolesearchsmoothie

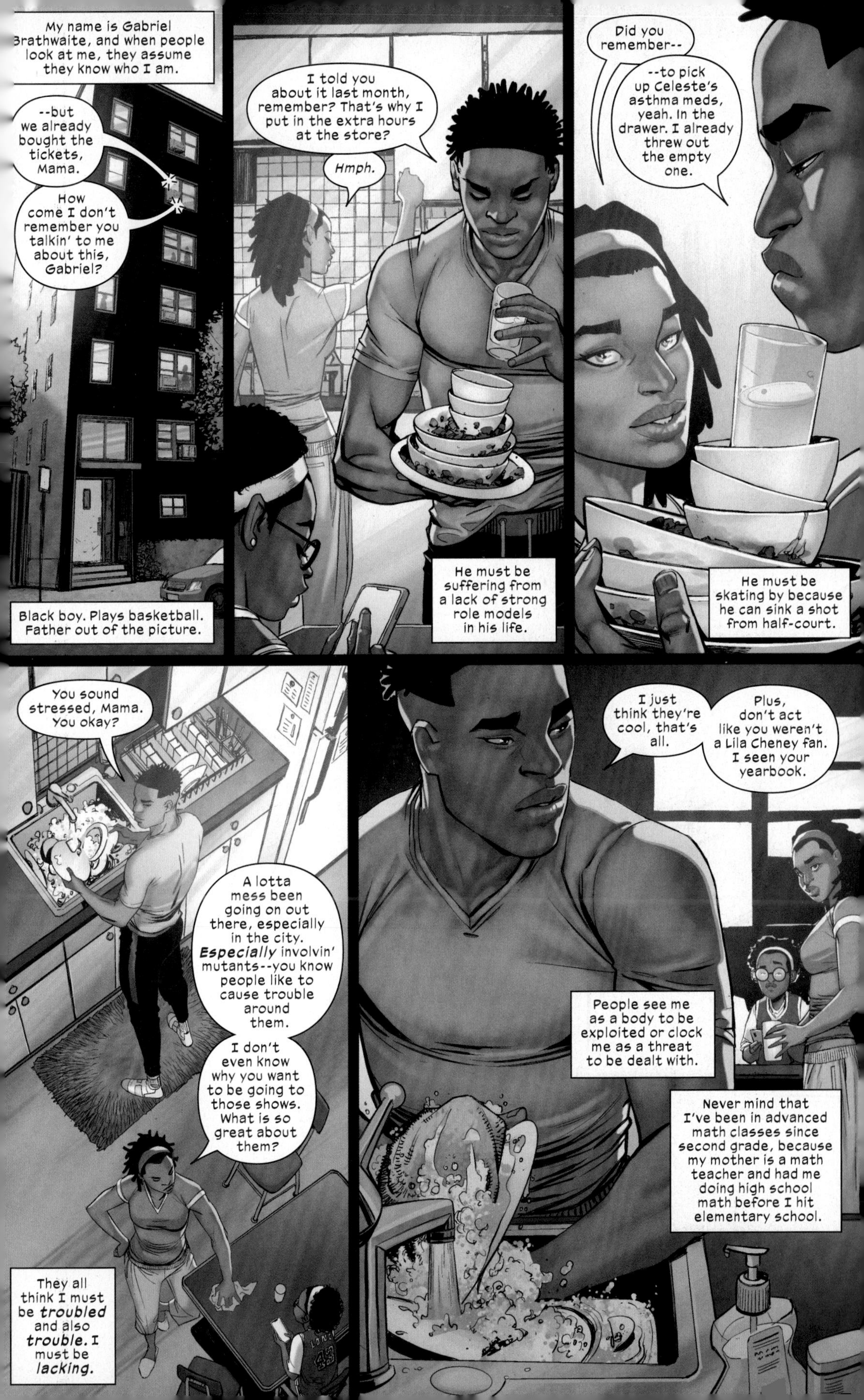
My name is Gabriel Brathwaite, and when people look at me, they assume they know who I am.
--but we already bought the tickets, Mama.
How come I don't remember you talkin' to me about this, Gabriel?
Black boy. Plays basketball. Father out of the picture.
I told you about it last month, remember? That's why I put in the extra hours at the store?
Hmph.
He must be suffering from a lack of strong role models in his life.
Did you remember--
--to pick up Celeste's asthma meds, yeah. In the drawer. I already threw out the empty one.
He must be skating by because he can sink a shot from half-court.
You sound stressed, Mama. You okay?
A lotta mess been going on out there, especially in the city. *Especially* involvin' mutants--you know people like to cause trouble around them.
I don't even know why you want to be going to those shows. What is so great about them?
They all think I must be *troubled* and also *trouble*. I must be *lacking*.
I just think they're cool, that's all.
Plus, don't act like you weren't a Lila Cheney fan. I seen your yearbook.
People see me as a body to be exploited or clock me as a threat to be dealt with.
Never mind that I've been in advanced math classes since second grade, because my mother is a math teacher and had me doing high school math before I hit elementary school.

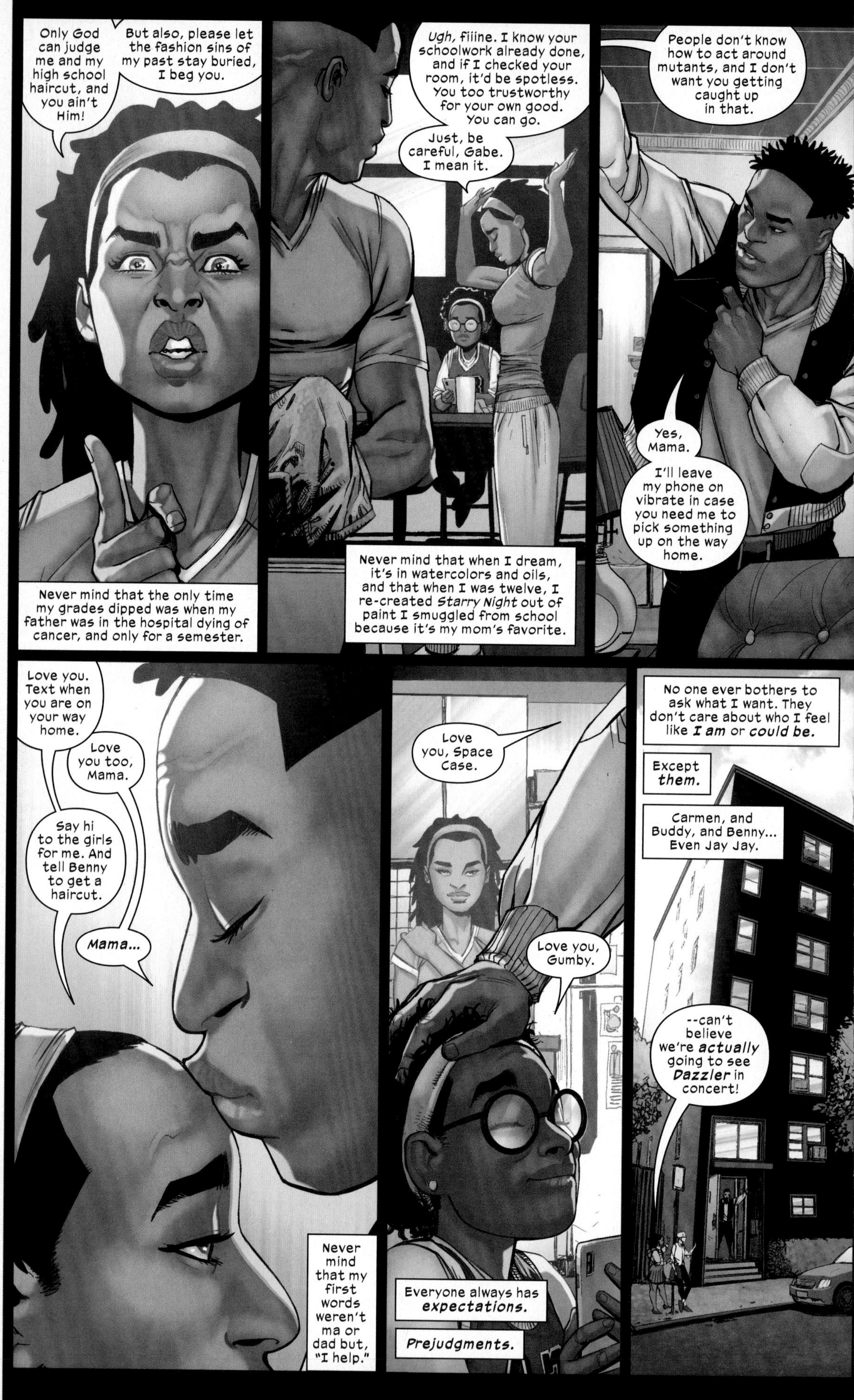

Only God can judge me and my high school haircut, and you ain't Him!
But also, please let the fashion sins of my past stay buried, I beg you.
Never mind that the only time my grades dipped was when my father was in the hospital dying of cancer, and only for a semester.
Ugh, fiiine. I know your schoolwork already done, and if I checked your room, it'd be spotless. You too trustworthy for your own good. You can go.
Just, be careful, Gabe. I mean it.
Never mind that when I dream, it's in watercolors and oils, and that when I was twelve, I re-created Starry Night out of paint I smuggled from school because it's my mom's favorite.
People don't know how to act around mutants, and I don't want you getting caught up in that.
Yes, Mama.
I'll leave my phone on vibrate in case you need me to pick something up on the way home.
Love you. Text when you are on your way home.
Love you too, Mama.
Say hi to the girls for me. And tell Benny to get a haircut.
Mama...
Never mind that my first words weren't ma or dad but, "I help."
Love you, Space Case.
Love you, Gumby.
Everyone always has expectations.
Prejudgments.
No one ever bothers to ask what I want. They don't care about who I feel like I am or could be.
Except them.
Carmen, and Buddy, and Benny... Even Jay Jay.
--can't believe we're actually going to see Dazzler in concert!

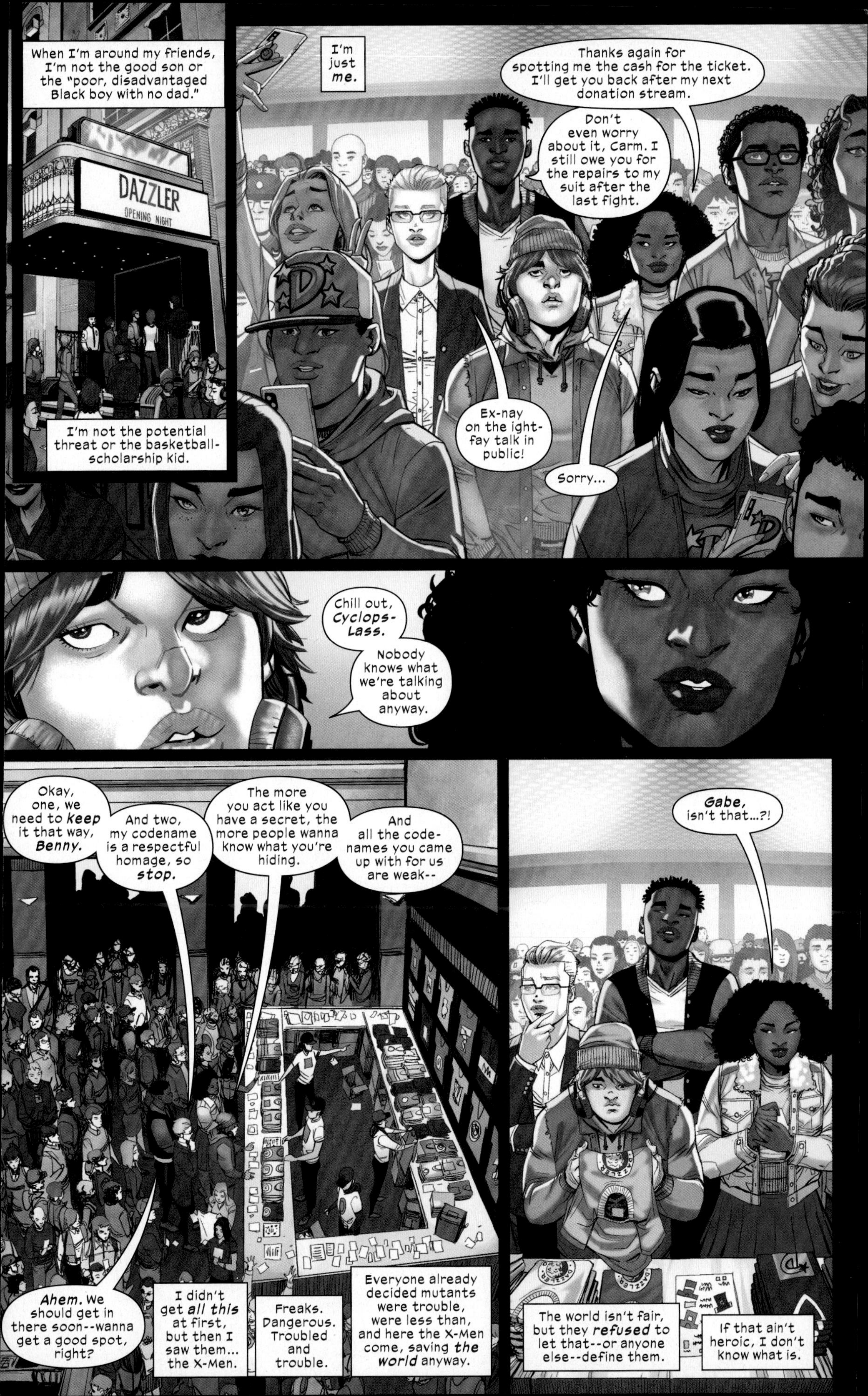
When I'm around my friends, I'm not the good son or the "poor, disadvantaged Black boy with no dad."
DAZZLER
OPENING NIGHT
I'm not the potential threat or the basketball-scholarship kid.
I'm just me.
Thanks again for spotting me the cash for the ticket. I'll get you back after my next donation stream.
Don't even worry about it, Carm. I still owe you for the repairs to my suit after the last fight.
Ex-nay on the ight-fay talk in public!
Sorry...
Chill out, Cyclops-Lass.
Nobody knows what we're talking about anyway.
Okay, one, we need to keep it that way, Benny.
And two, my codename is a respectful homage, so stop.
The more you act like you have a secret, the more people wanna know what you're hiding.
And all the code-names you came up with for us are weak--
Ahem. We should get in there soon--wanna get a good spot, right?
I didn't get all this at first, but then I saw them... the X-Men.
Freaks. Dangerous. Troubled and trouble.
Everyone already decided mutants were trouble, were less than, and here the X-Men come, saving the world anyway.
Gabe, isn't that...?!
The world isn't fair, but they refused to let that--or anyone else--define them.
If that ain't heroic, I don't know what is.

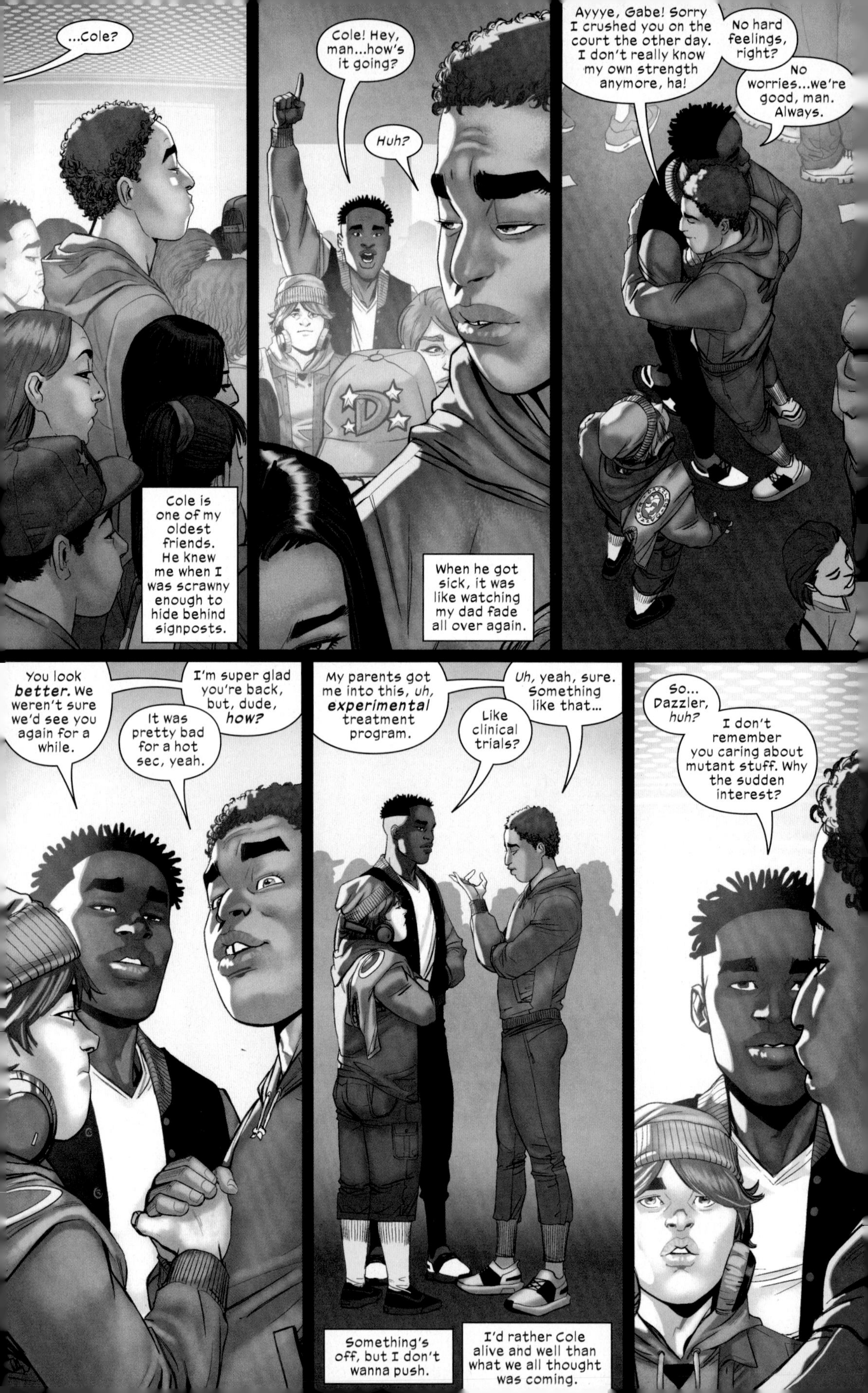
...Cole?
Cole is one of my oldest friends. He knew me when I was scrawny enough to hide behind signposts.
Cole! Hey, man...how's it going?
Huh?
When he got sick, it was like watching my dad fade all over again.
Ayyye, Gabe! Sorry I crushed you on the court the other day. I don't really know my own strength anymore, ha!
No hard feelings, right?
No worries...we're good, man. Always.
You look better. We weren't sure we'd see you again for a while.
I'm super glad you're back, but, dude, how?
It was pretty bad for a hot sec, yeah.
My parents got me into this, uh, experimental treatment program.
Uh, yeah, sure. Something like that...
Like clinical trials?
Something's off, but I don't wanna push.
I'd rather Cole alive and well than what we all thought was coming.
So... Dazzler, huh?
I don't remember you caring about mutant stuff. Why the sudden interest?

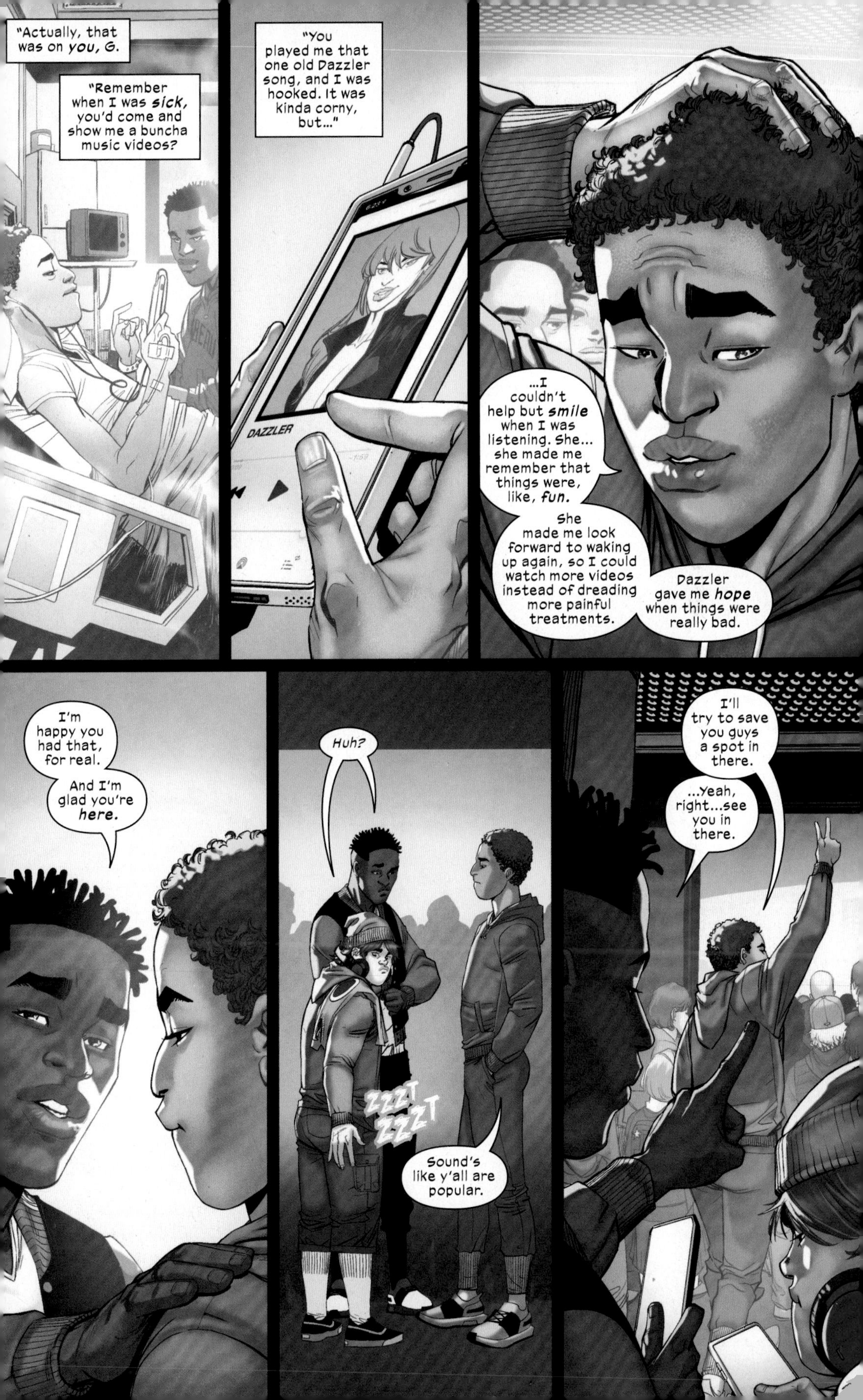
"Actually, that was on you, G.
"Remember when I was sick, you'd come and show me a buncha music videos?
"You played me that one old Dazzler song, and I was hooked. It was kinda corny, but..."
DAZZLER
...I couldn't help but smile when I was listening. She... she made me remember that things were, like, fun.
She made me look forward to waking up again, so I could watch more videos instead of dreading more painful treatments.
Dazzler gave me hope when things were really bad.
I'm happy you had that, for real.
And I'm glad you're here.
Huh?
ZZZT ZZZT
Sound's like y'all are popular.
I'll try to save you guys a spot in there.
...Yeah, right...see you in there.

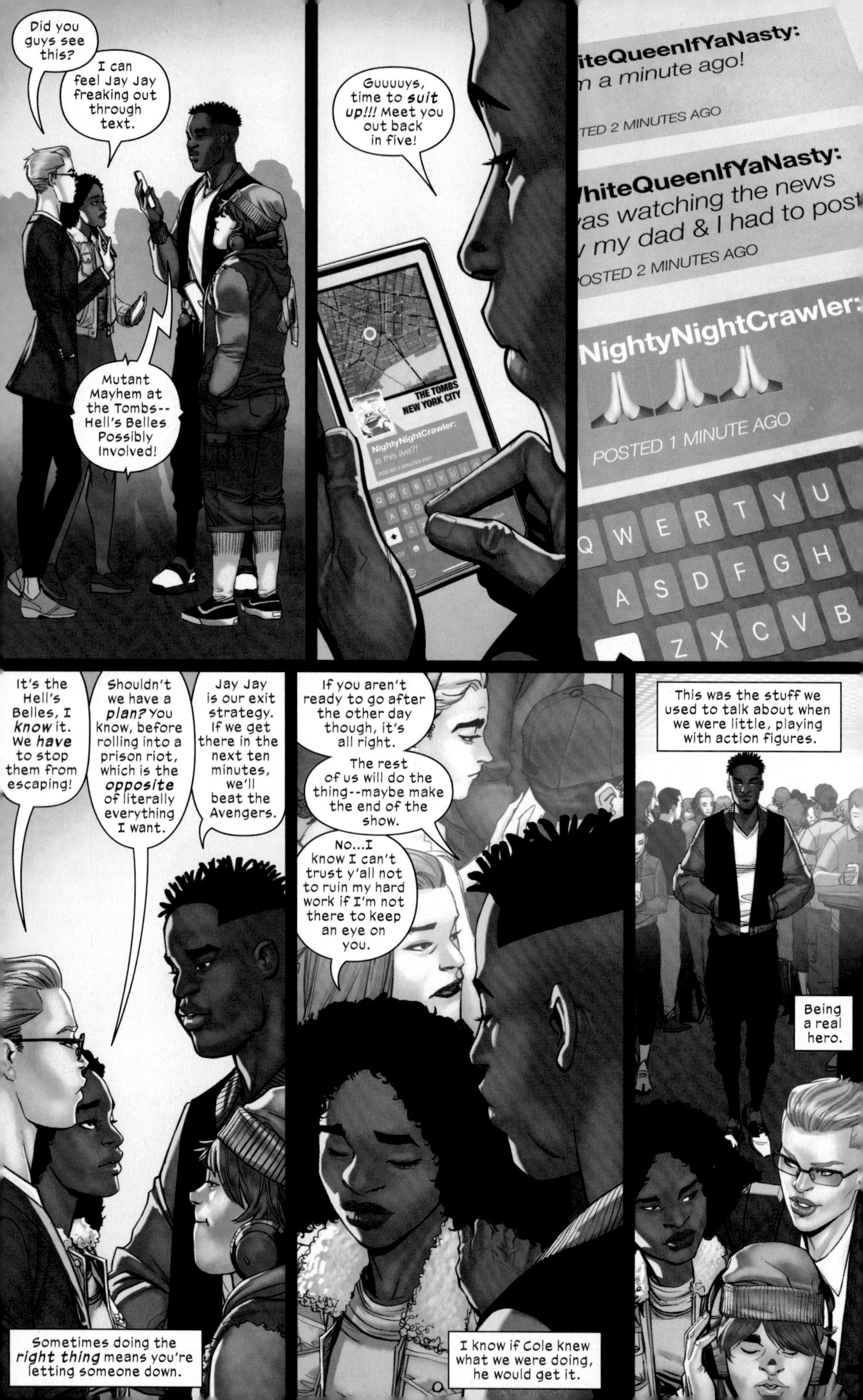
Did you guys see this?
I can feel Jay Jay freaking out through text.
Mutant Mayhem at the Tombs--Hell's Belles Possibly Involved!
Guuuuys, time to suit up!!! Meet you out back in five!
THE TOMBS NEW YORK CITY
NightyNightCrawler:
is this live?!
iteQueenIfYaNasty:
n a minute ago!
TED 2 MINUTES AGO
hiteQueenIfYaNasty:
as watching the news
y my dad & I had to post
OSTED 2 MINUTES AGO
NightyNightCrawler:
POSTED 1 MINUTE AGO
Q W E R T Y U
A S D F G H
Z X C V B
It's the Hell's Belles, I know it. We have to stop them from escaping!
Shouldn't we have a plan? You know, before rolling into a prison riot, which is the opposite of literally everything I want.
Jay Jay is our exit strategy. If we get there in the next ten minutes, we'll beat the Avengers.
Sometimes doing the right thing means you're letting someone down.
If you aren't ready to go after the other day though, it's all right.
The rest of us will do the thing--maybe make the end of the show.
No...I know I can't trust y'all not to ruin my hard work if I'm not there to keep an eye on you.
I know if Cole knew what we were doing, he would get it.
This was the stuff we used to talk about when we were little, playing with action figures.
Being a real hero.

[DAZZ....[04_14]
[LER!....[20:00]

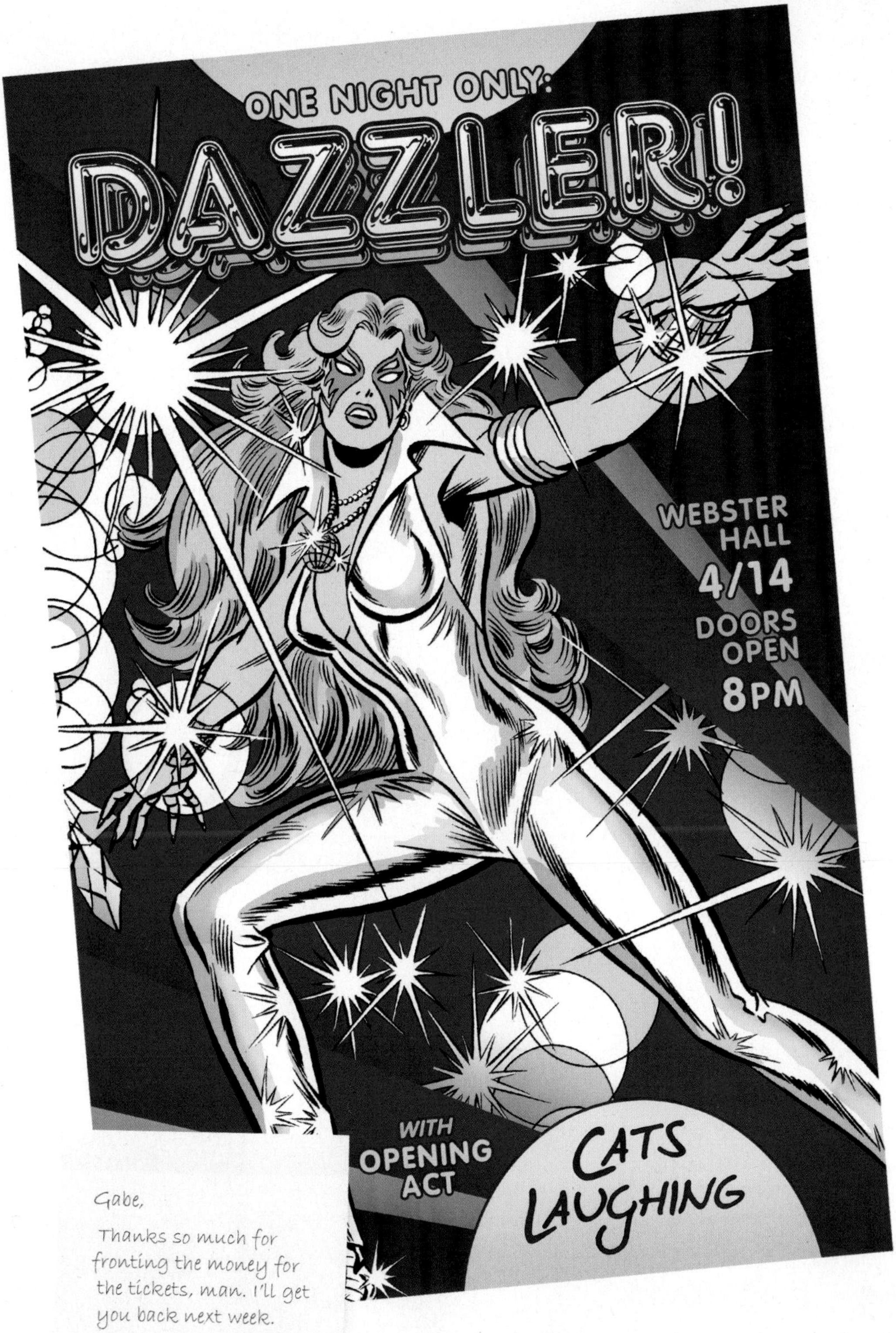

ONE NIGHT ONLY:
DAZZLER!
WEBSTER HALL
4/14
DOORS OPEN
8PM
WITH OPENING ACT
CATS LAUGHING

Gabe,

Thanks so much for fronting the money for the tickets, man. I'll get you back next week.

--Benny

[CA....[laug]
[TS....[hing]

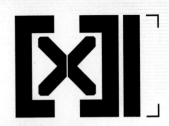

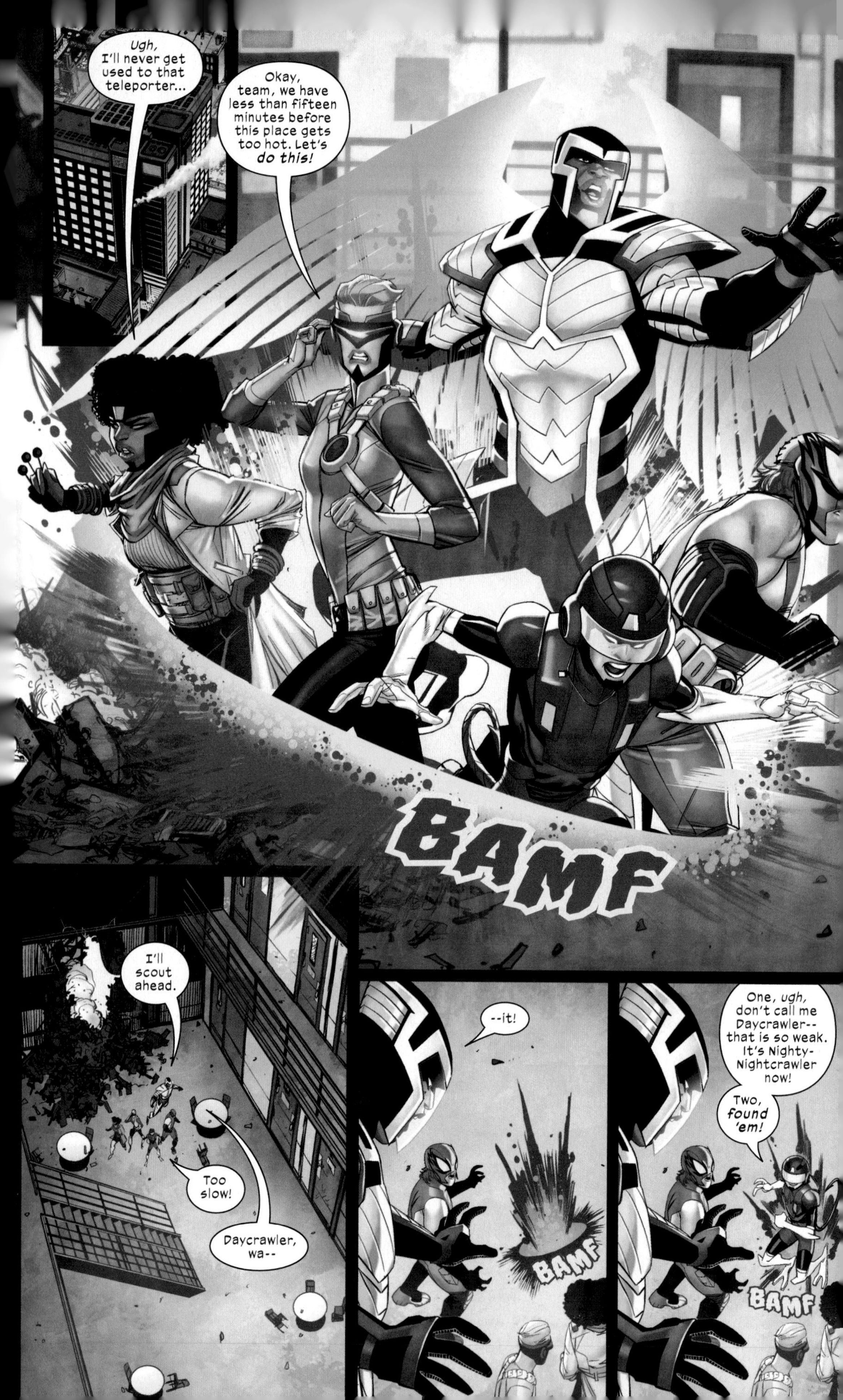

Ugh, I'll never get used to that teleporter...
Okay, team, we have less than fifteen minutes before this place gets too hot. Let's do this!
BAMF
I'll scout ahead.
Too slow!
Daycrawler, wa--
--it!
BAMF
One, ugh, don't call me Daycrawler-- that is so weak. It's Nighty-Nightcrawler now!
Two, found 'em!
BAMF

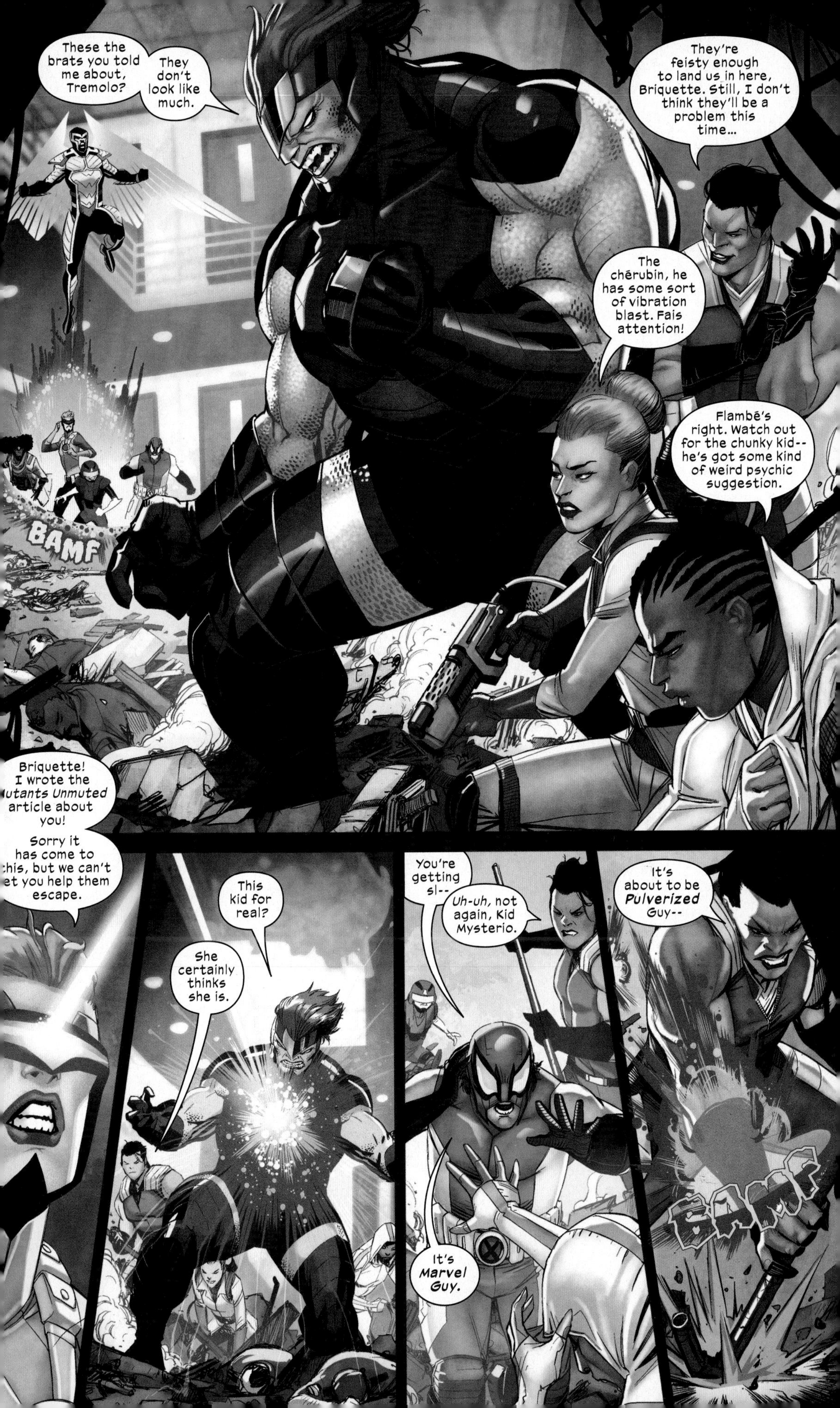
These the brats you told me about, Tremolo?
They don't look like much.
They're feisty enough to land us in here, Briquette. Still, I don't think they'll be a problem this time...
The chērubin, he has some sort of vibration blast. Fais attention!
Flambē's right. Watch out for the chunky kid-- he's got some kind of weird psychic suggestion.
BAMF
Briquette! I wrote the utants Unmuted article about you!
Sorry it has come to this, but we can't et you help them escape.
This kid for real?
She certainly thinks she is.
You're getting sl--
Uh-uh, not again, Kid Mysterio.
It's Marvel Guy.
It's about to be Pulverized Guy--

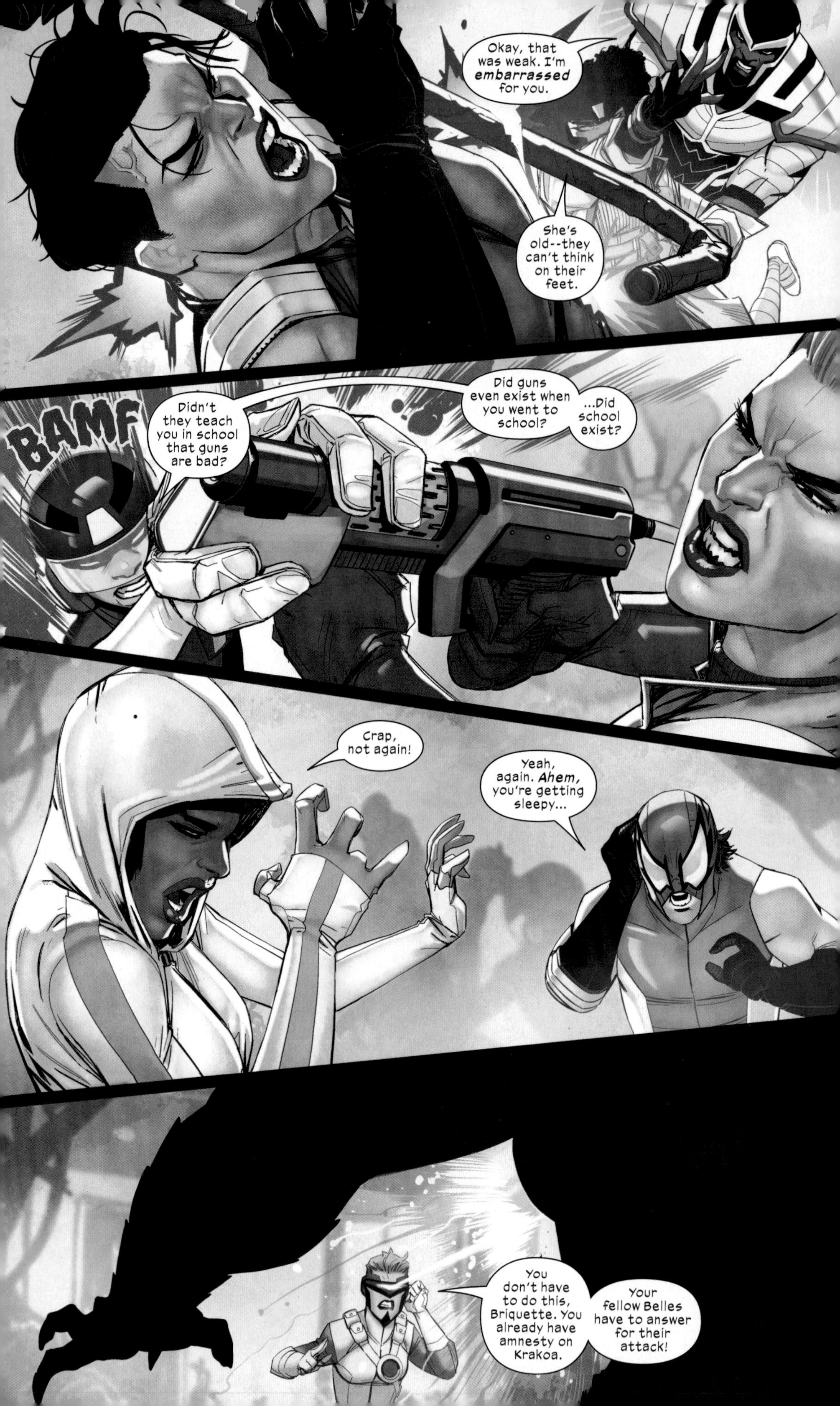
Okay, that was weak. I'm *embarrassed* for you.
She's old--they can't think on their feet.
BAMF
Didn't they teach you in school that guns are bad?
Did guns even exist when you went to school?
...Did school exist?
Crap, not again!
Yeah, again. *Ahem,* you're getting sleepy...
You don't have to do this, Briquette. You already have amnesty on Krakoa.
Your fellow Belles have to answer for their attack!

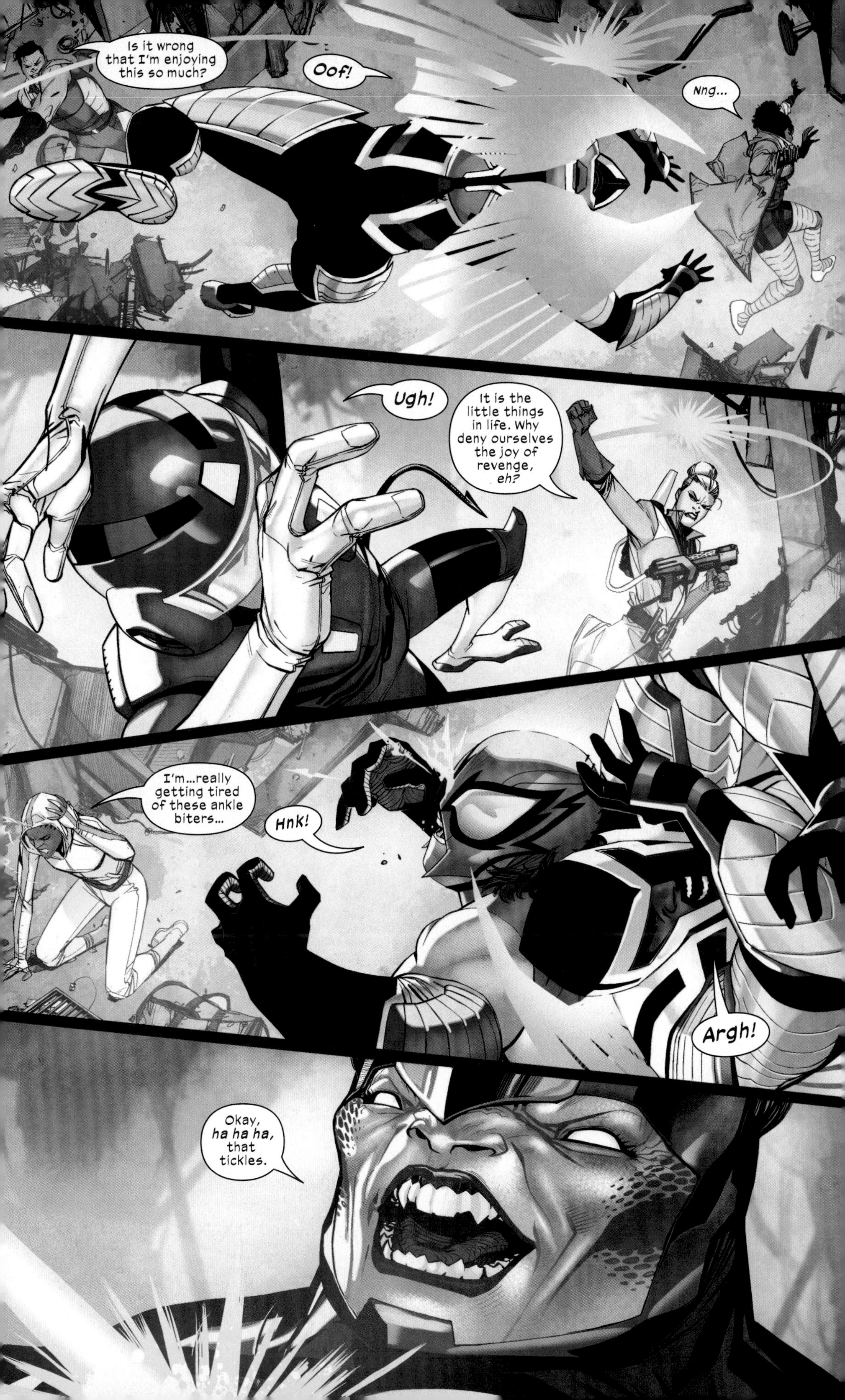
Is it wrong that I'm enjoying this so much?
Oof!
Nng...
Ugh!
It is the little things in life. Why deny ourselves the joy of revenge, eh?
I'm...really getting tired of these ankle biters...
Hnk!
Argh!
Okay, ha ha ha, that tickles.

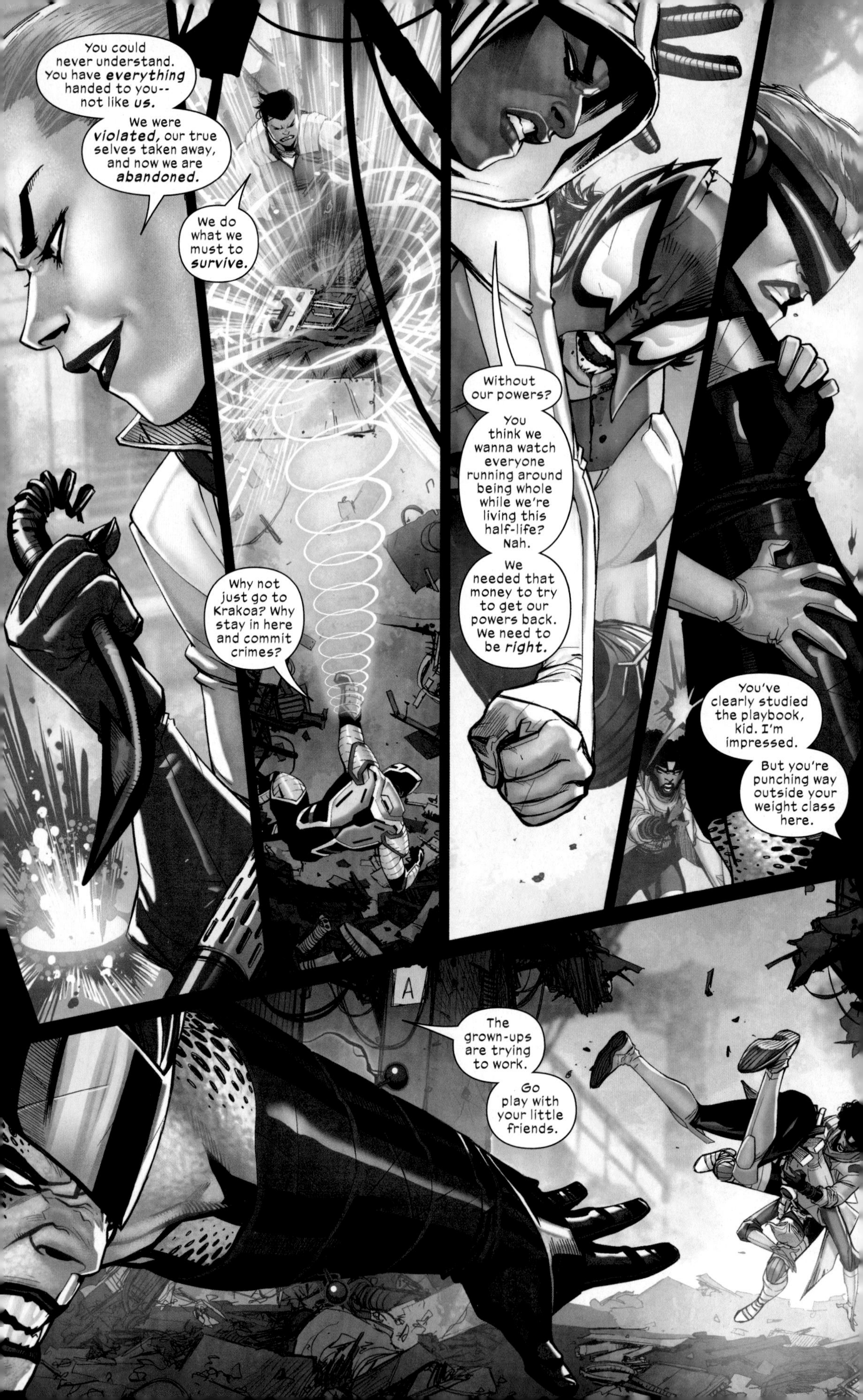
You could never understand. You have *everything* handed to you-- not like *us*.
We were *violated*, our true selves taken away, and now we are *abandoned*.
We do what we must to *survive*.
Why not just go to Krakoa? Why stay in here and commit crimes?
Without our powers?
You think we wanna watch everyone running around being whole while we're living this half-life? Nah.
We needed that money to try to get our powers back. We need to be *right*.
You've clearly studied the playbook, kid. I'm impressed.
But you're punching way outside your weight class here.
A
The grown-ups are trying to work.
Go play with your little friends.

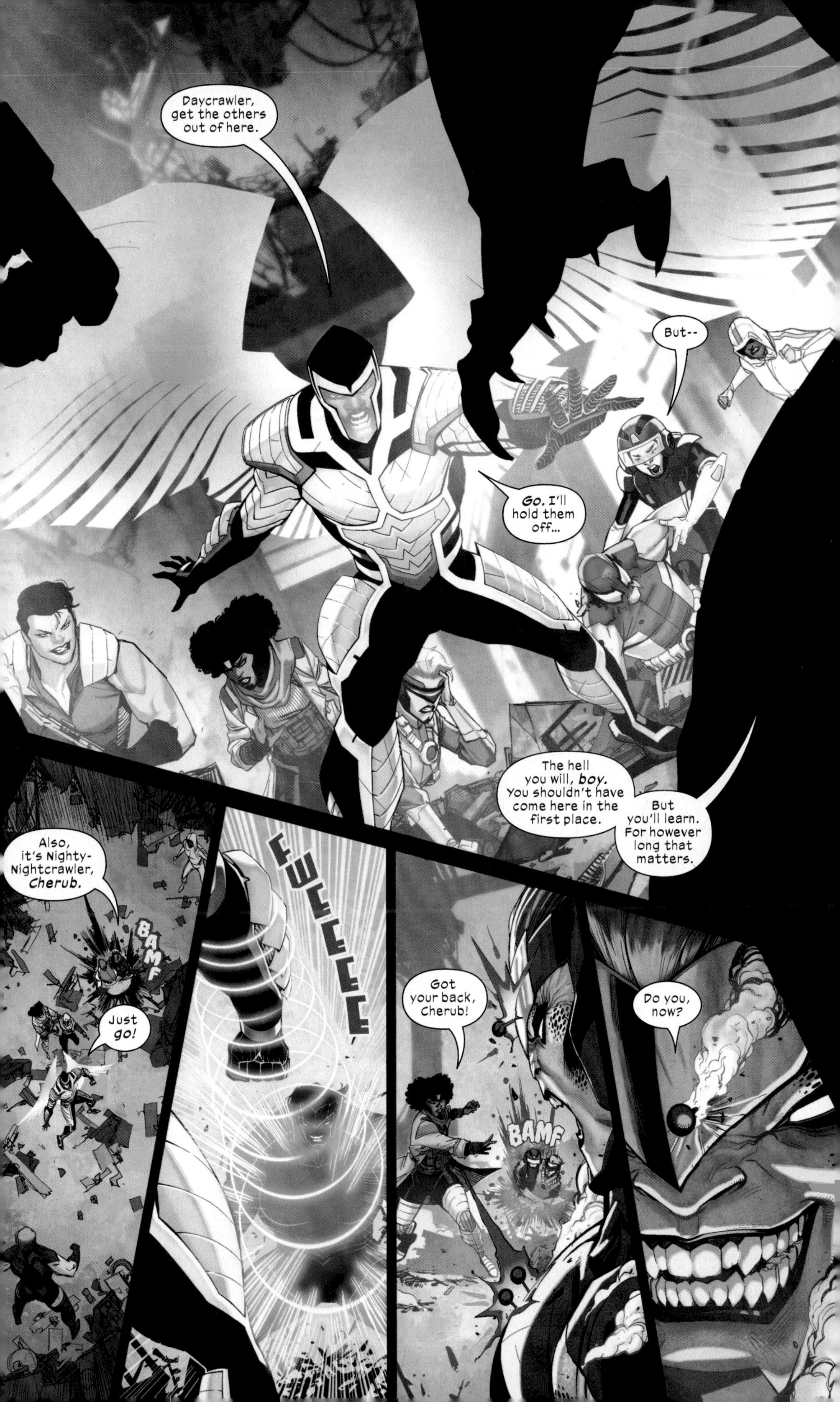
Daycrawler, get the others out of here.
But--
Go. I'll hold them off...
The hell you will, boy. You shouldn't have come here in the first place.
But you'll learn. For however long that matters.
Also, it's Nighty-Nightcrawler, Cherub.
BAMF
Just go!
FWEEEE
Got your back, Cherub!
BAMF
Do you, now?

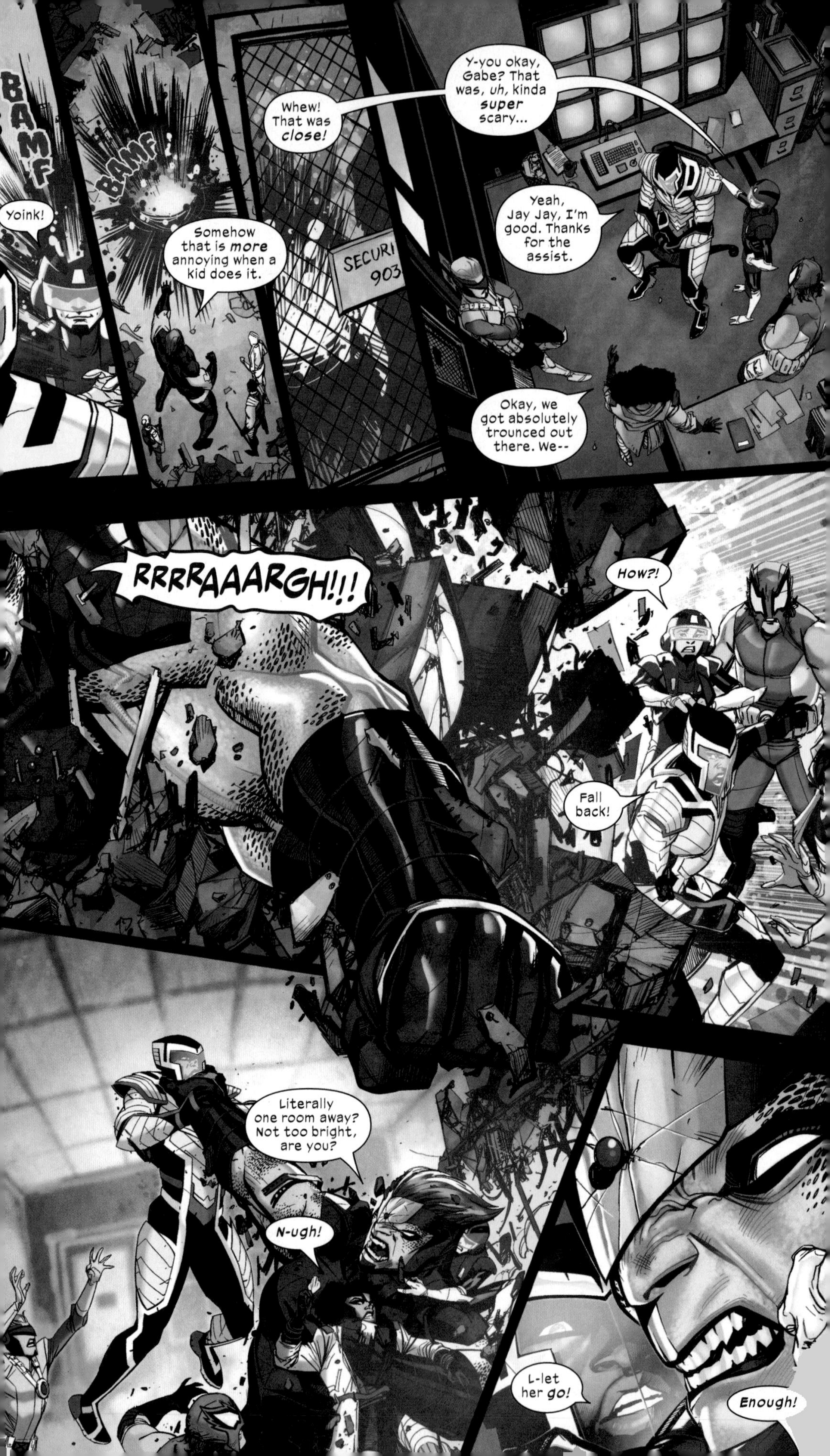
BAMF
Yoink!
BAMF
Somehow that is *more* annoying when a kid does it.
SECURI 903
Whew! That was *close!*
Y-you okay, Gabe? That was, *uh,* kinda ***super*** scary...
Yeah, Jay Jay, I'm good. Thanks for the assist.
Okay, we got absolutely trounced out there. We--
RRRRAAARGH!!!
How?!
Fall back!
Literally one room away? Not too bright, are you?
N-ugh!
L-let her *go!*
Enough!

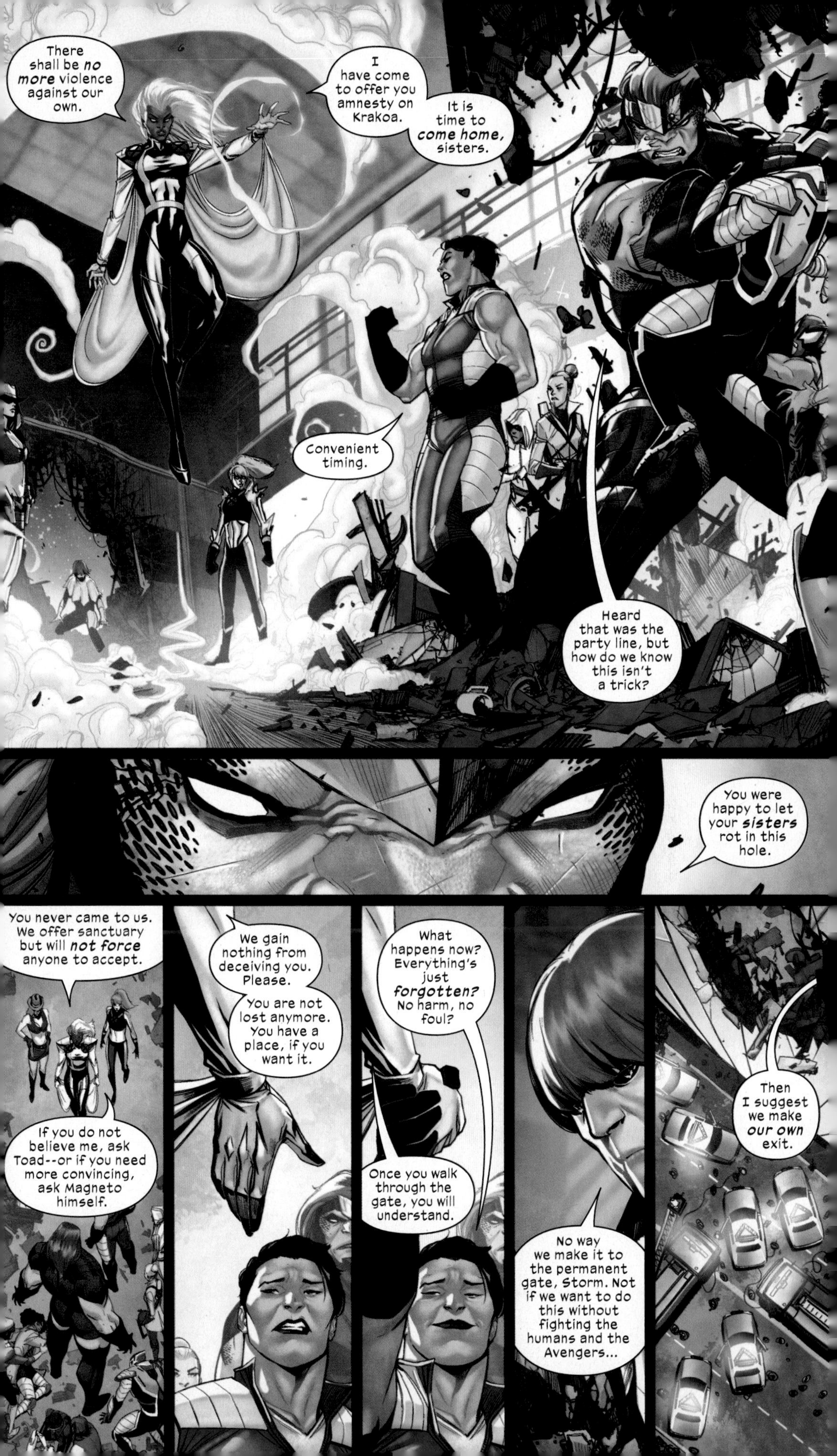

There shall be no more violence against our own.
I have come to offer you amnesty on Krakoa.
It is time to come home, sisters.
Convenient timing.
Heard that was the party line, but how do we know this isn't a trick?
You were happy to let your sisters rot in this hole.
You never came to us. We offer sanctuary but will not force anyone to accept.
If you do not believe me, ask Toad--or if you need more convincing, ask Magneto himself.
We gain nothing from deceiving you. Please.
You are not lost anymore. You have a place, if you want it.
What happens now? Everything's just forgotten? No harm, no foul?
Once you walk through the gate, you will understand.
No way we make it to the permanent gate, Storm. Not if we want to do this without fighting the humans and the Avengers...
Then I suggest we make our own exit.

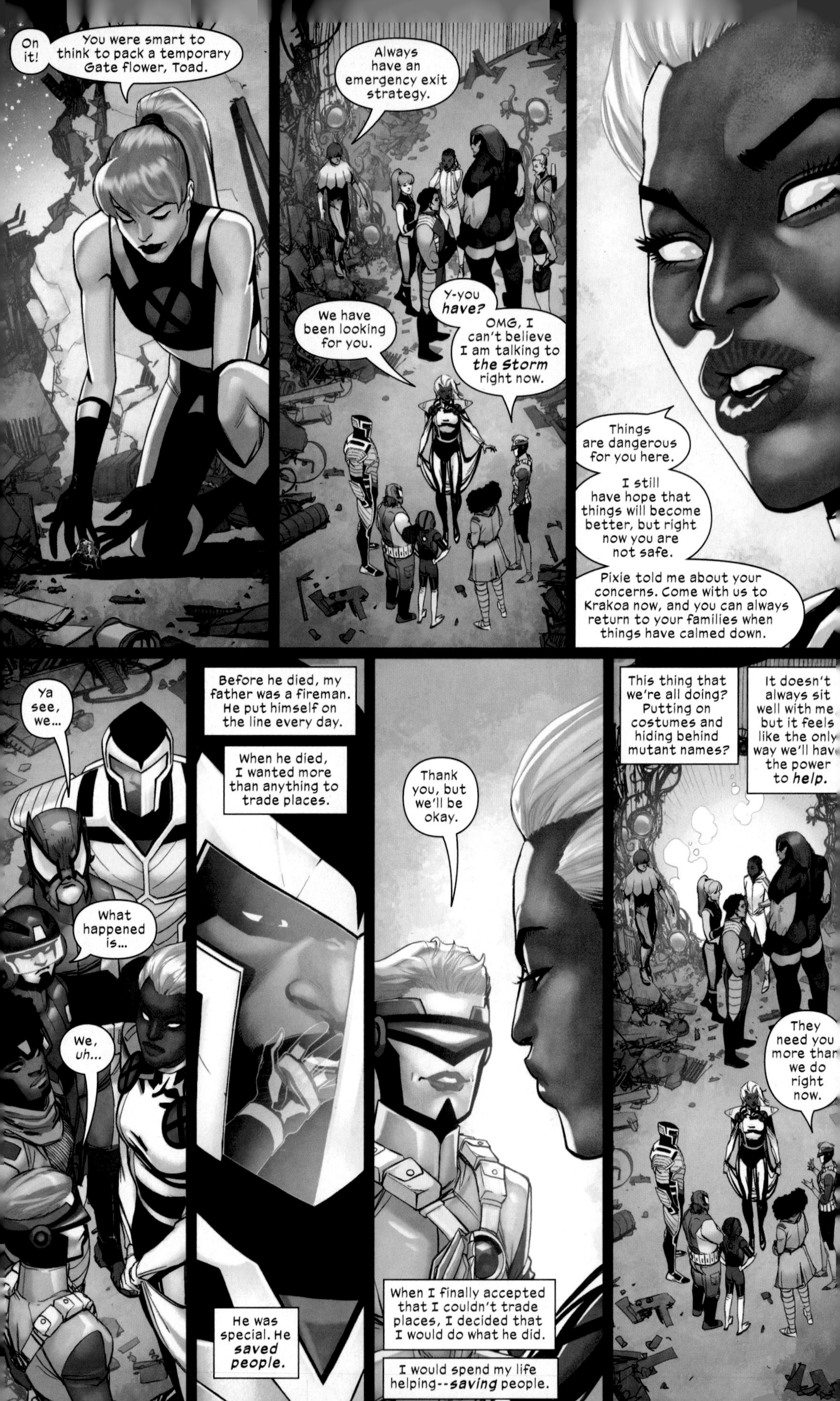

On it!
You were smart to think to pack a temporary Gate flower, Toad.
Always have an emergency exit strategy.
We have been looking for you.
Y-you *have?*
OMG, I can't believe I am talking to *the Storm* right now.
Things are dangerous for you here.
I still have hope that things will become better, but right now you are not safe.
Pixie told me about your concerns. Come with us to Krakoa now, and you can always return to your families when things have calmed down.
Ya see, we...
What happened is...
We, *uh...*
Before he died, my father was a fireman. He put himself on the line every day.
When he died, I wanted more than anything to trade places.
He was special. He ***saved people.***
Thank you, but we'll be okay.
When I finally accepted that I couldn't trade places, I decided that I would do what he did.
I would spend my life helping--*saving* people.
This thing that we're all doing? Putting on costumes and hiding behind mutant names?
It doesn't always sit well with me but it feels like the only way we'll hav the power to *help.*
They need you more thar we do right now.

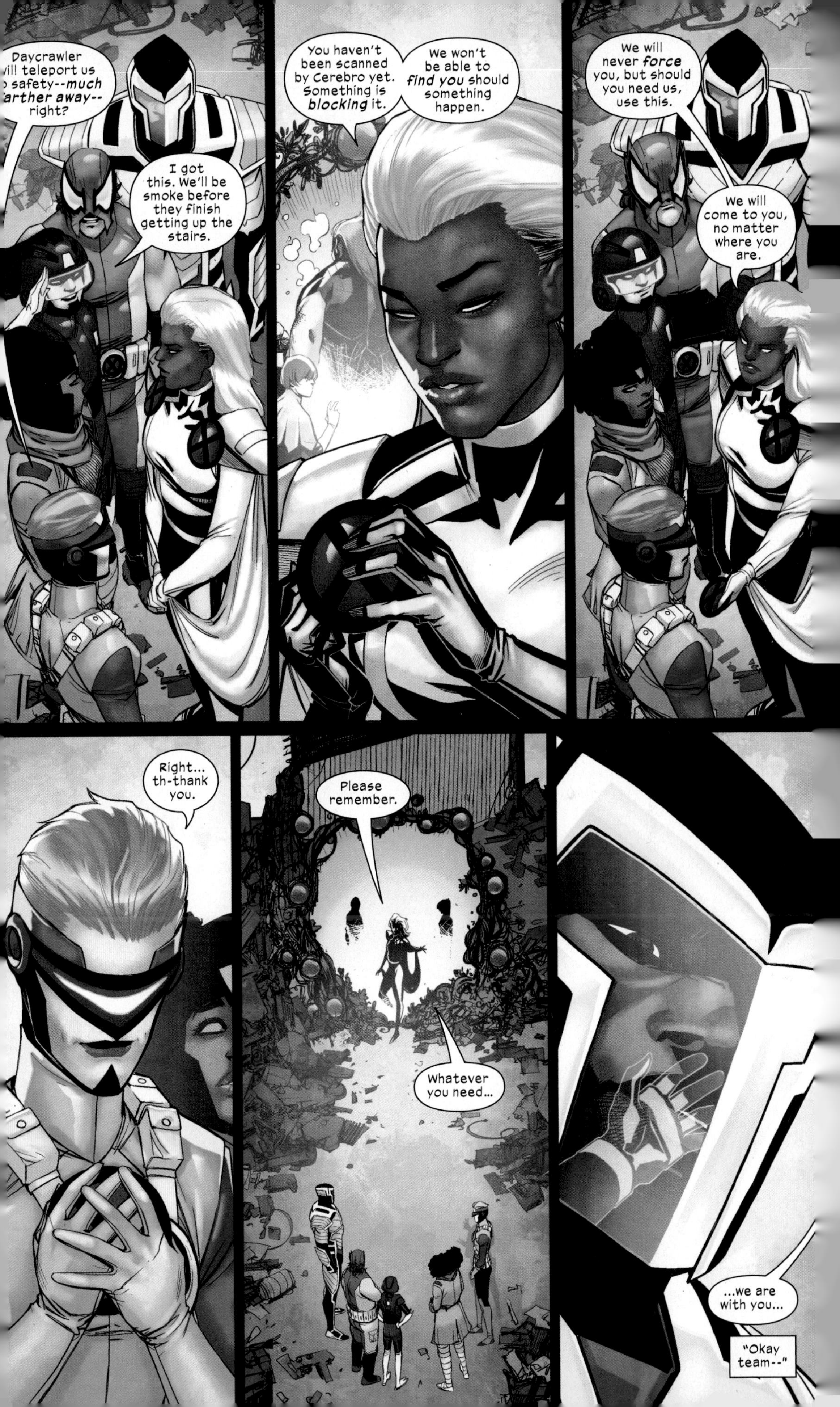

Daycrawler will teleport us to safety--*much farther away*--right?
I got this. We'll be smoke before they finish getting up the stairs.
You haven't been scanned by Cerebro yet. Something is *blocking* it.
We won't be able to *find you* should something happen.
We will never *force* you, but should you need us, use this.
We will come to you, no matter where you are.
Right... th-thank you.
Please remember.
Whatever you need...
...we are with you...
"Okay team--"

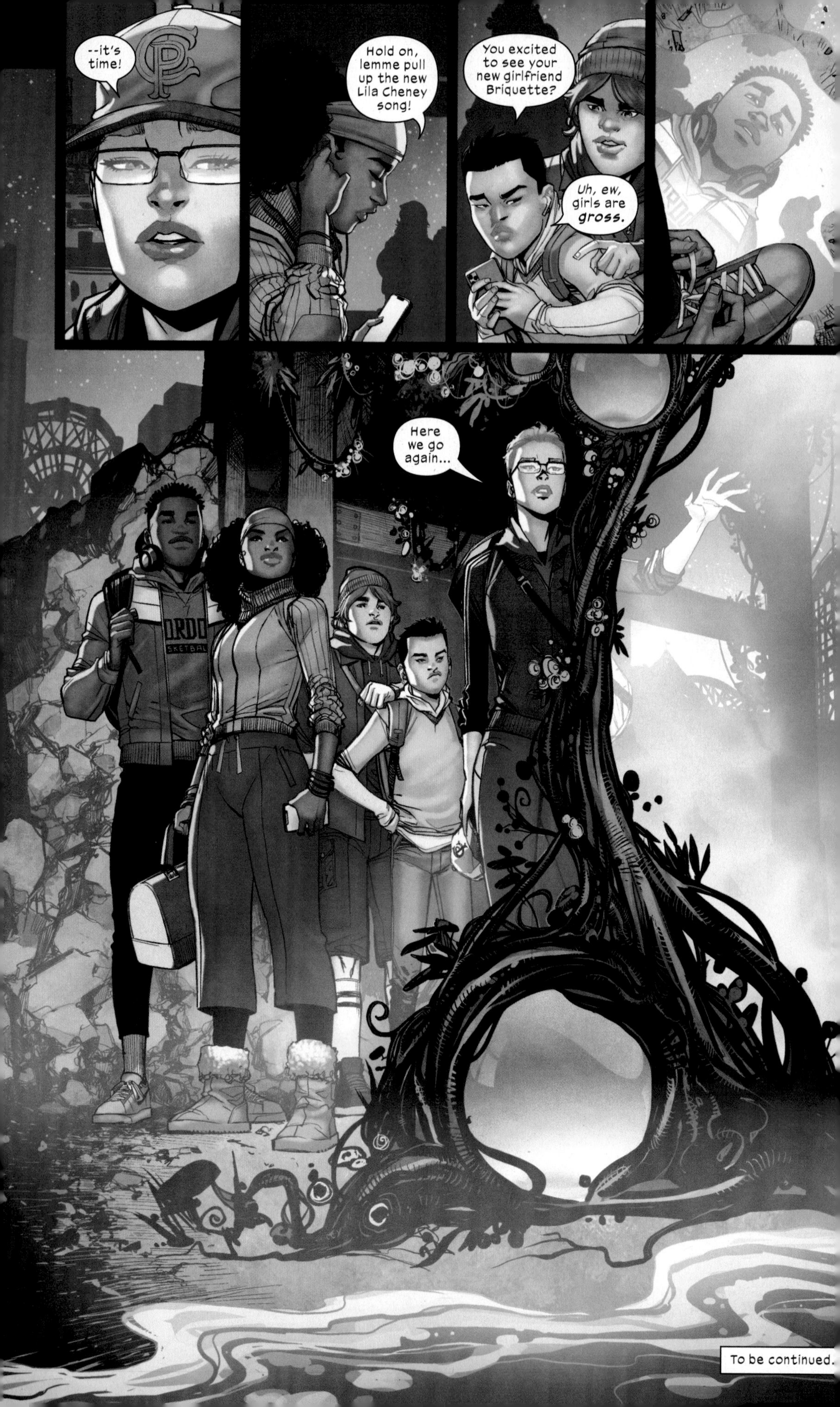

--it's time!
Hold on, lemme pull up the new Lila Cheney song!
You excited to see your new girlfriend Briquette?
Uh, ew, girls are gross.
Here we go again...
To be continued.

[reign_of_x]

[kra_]
[koa_]

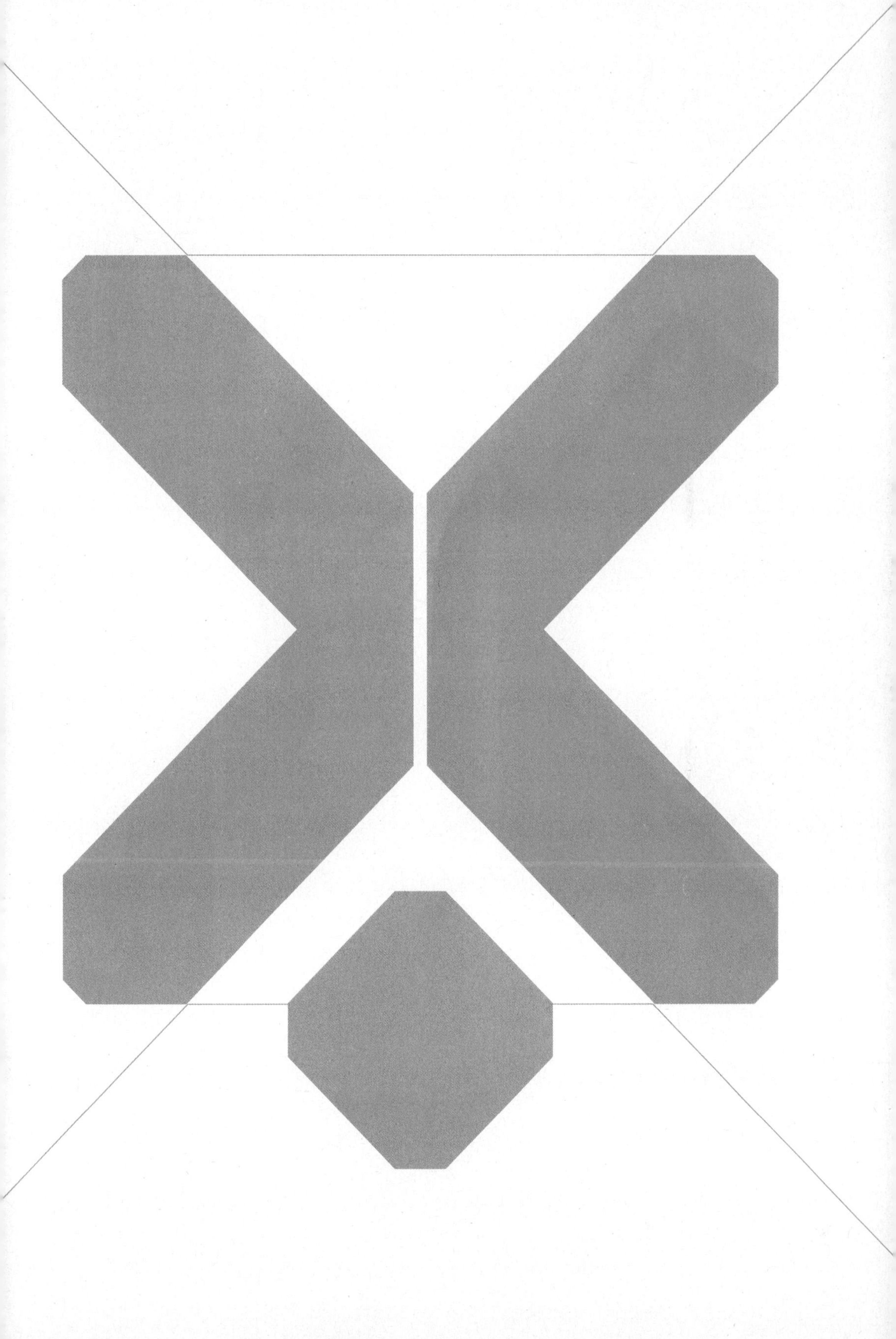

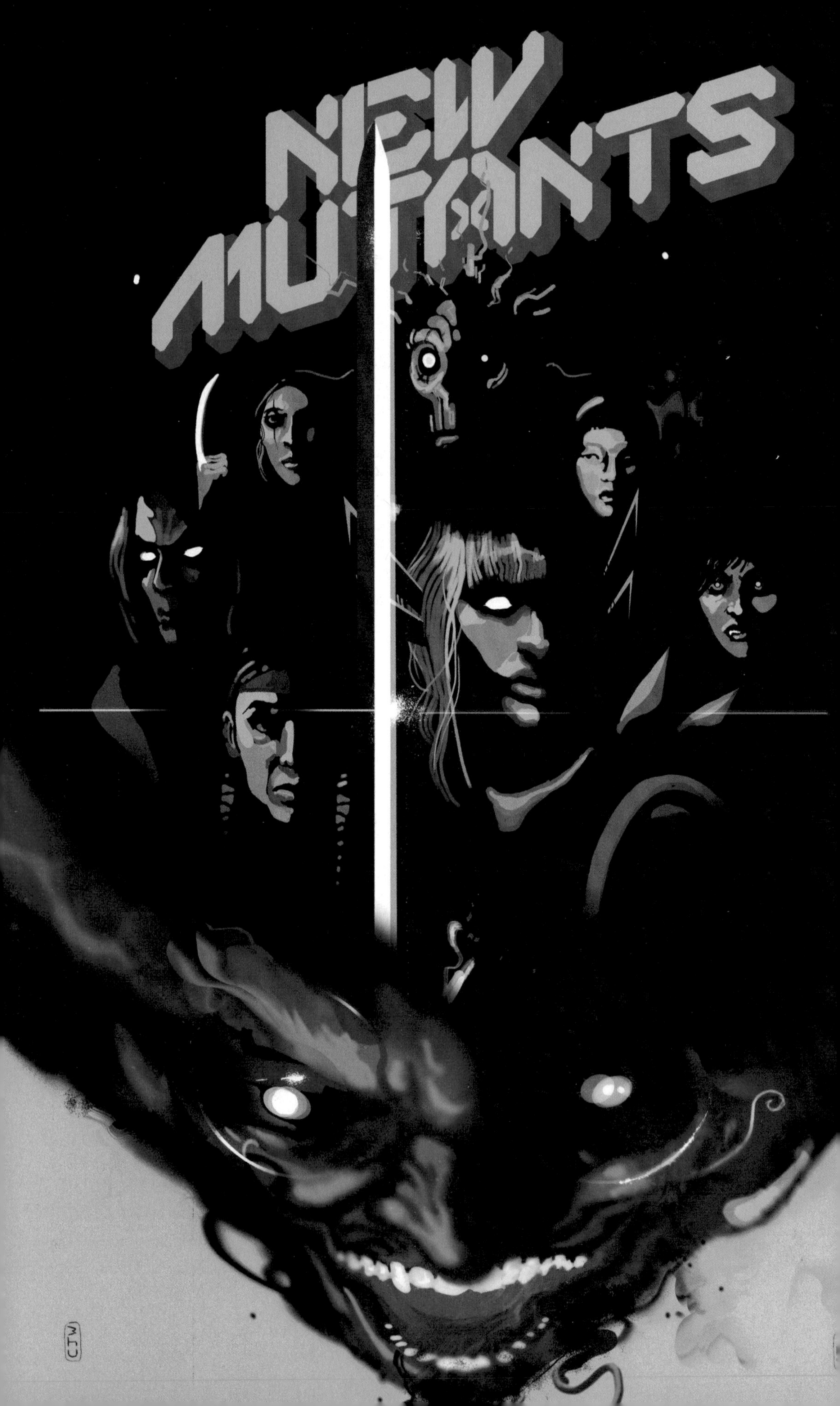
NEW MUTANTS

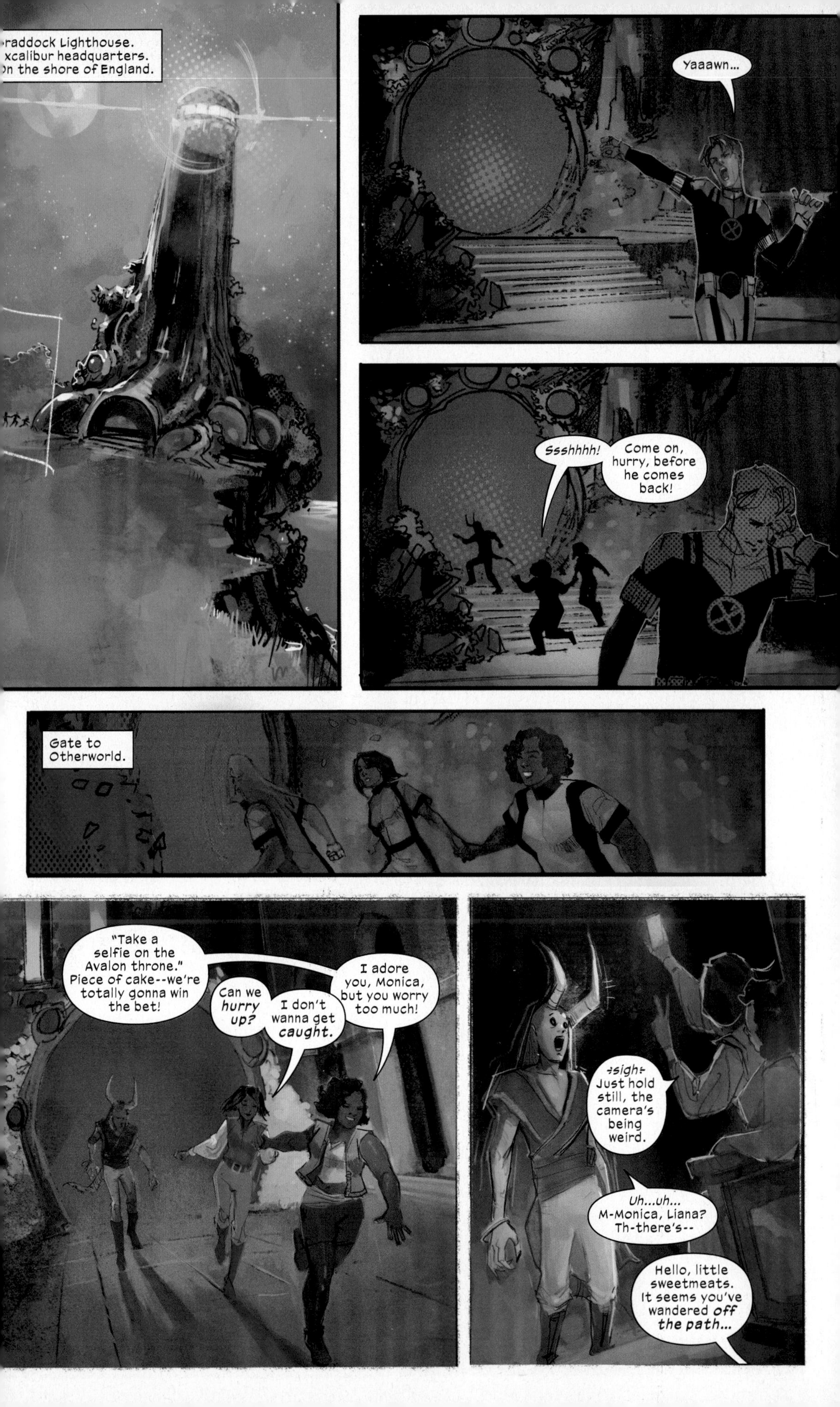

-raddock Lighthouse. xcalibur headquarters. On the shore of England.
Yaaawn...
Ssshhhh!
Come on, hurry, before he comes back!
Gate to Otherworld.
"Take a selfie on the Avalon throne." Piece of cake--we're totally gonna win the bet!
I adore you, Monica, but you worry too much!
Can we *hurry up?*
I don't wanna get *caught.*
sigh Just hold still, the camera's being weird.
Uh...uh... M-Monica, Liana? Th-there's--
Hello, little sweetmeats. It seems you've wandered *off the path...*

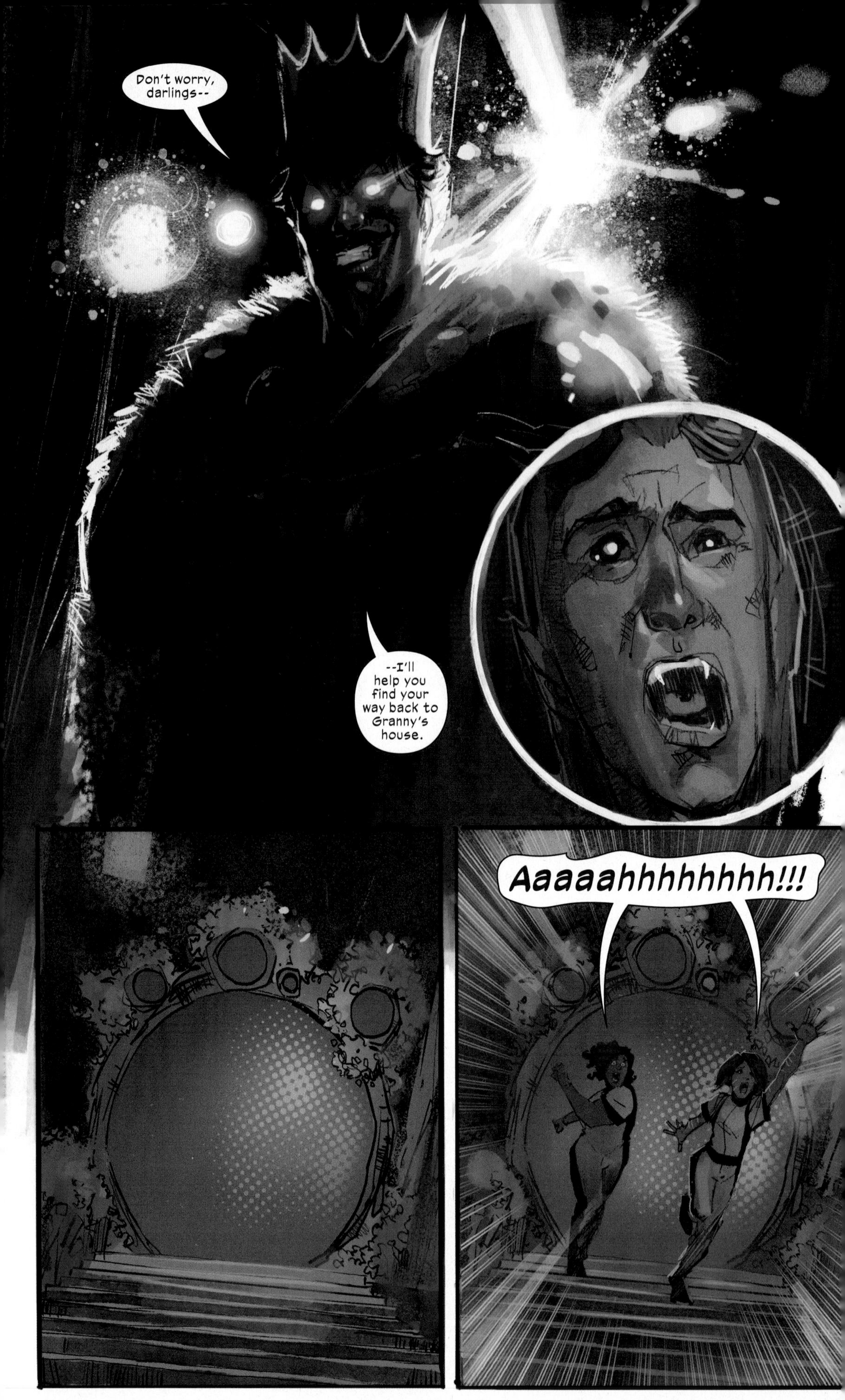
Don't worry, darlings--
--I'll help you find your way back to Granny's house.
Aaaaahhhhhhhh!!!

WARPATH JOURNAL, ENTRY 001

Pretty sure Moonstar got these questions out of a self-help book, but she's right: If we're going to guide, then we have to be willing to be led.

I doubt this will end up being useful, but I lose nothing by participating -- giving it a chance.

How do you view yourself?

With a mirror or other reflective surfaces. Sometimes in photos.

How do you view the world and others?

Generally with my eyes, but most of my other senses come into play. Sound and touch particularly help me get a sense of my environment.

Are you optimistic or pessimistic?

I think I misunderstood the last few questions, but since I used a pen, I'll press forward.

Being optimistic leaves you vulnerable to danger (internal and external). Being pessimistic cuts you off from possibilities. Neither is useful. Better to be a realist, to take things as they come and make any plans based on what you have observed.

Now let me circle back to the first two questions.

I view myself as a man who will do what needs to be done. I am a man who, even before Xavier's fancy machine, did not fear his own death, if it was what was needed. I am a man who hopes to help those that come after to do more than survive -- they deserve to thrive, more so because we didn't have the option.

The world supports and sustains life. It is an intricate, interconnected system of creation and destruction. Of balance. That is obvious.

Some people know how to be in harmony with the Earth's balance and some do not. It is unfortunate that the latter are able to exert their power so efficiently. That's where men like me come into the picture.

A FLUNG OPEN DOOR

The NEW MUTANTS have been tasked with training the youth of Krakoa -- teaching them to use and combine their mutant abilities! But that's hard to do when they're:

1. Sneaking into Otherworld, the one place that can kill them for good
2. Bullying each other
3. Getting suspiciously close to the Shadow King

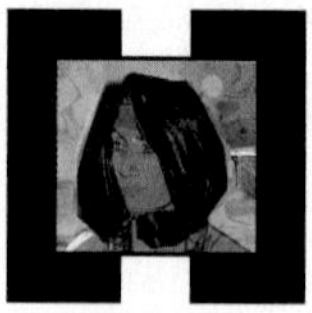

Dani Moonstar

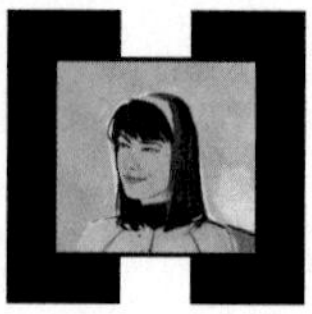

Karma

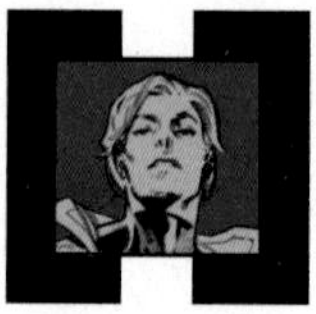

Cypher

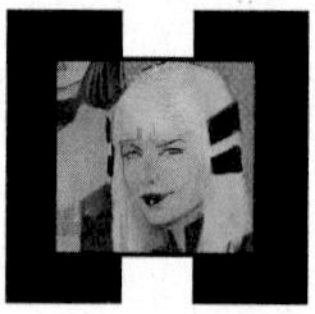

Magik

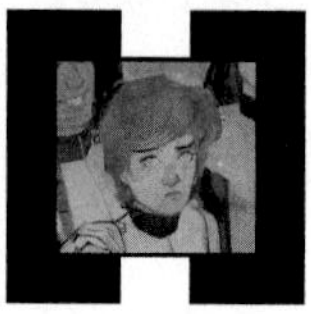

Wolfsbane

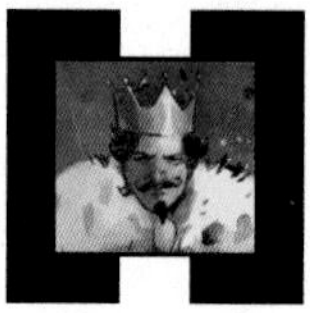

Jamie Braddock

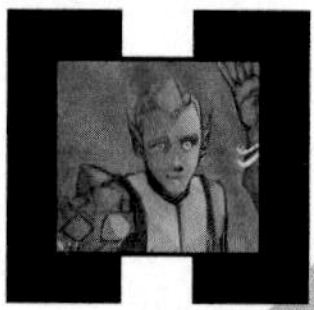

Anole

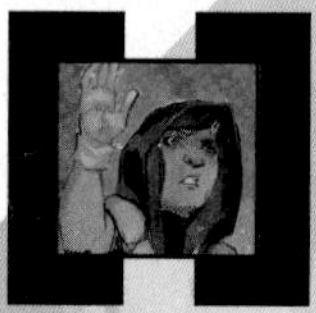

Scout

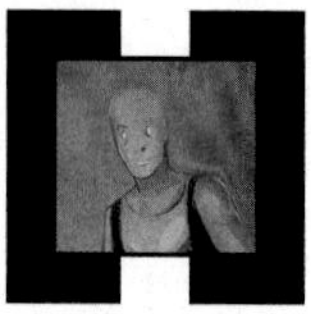

Rain Boy

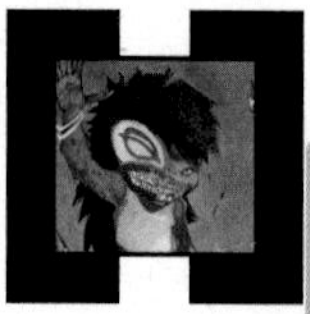

Cosmar

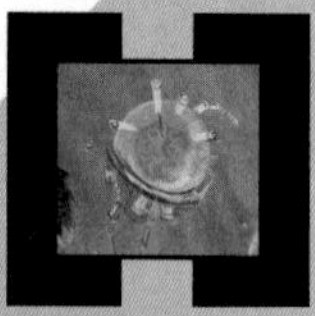

No-Girl

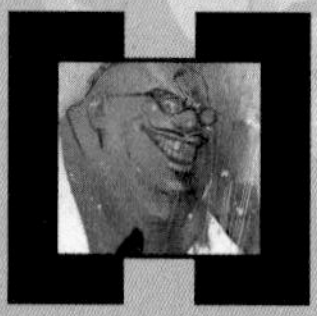

Shadow King

NEW MUTANTS
[X_16]

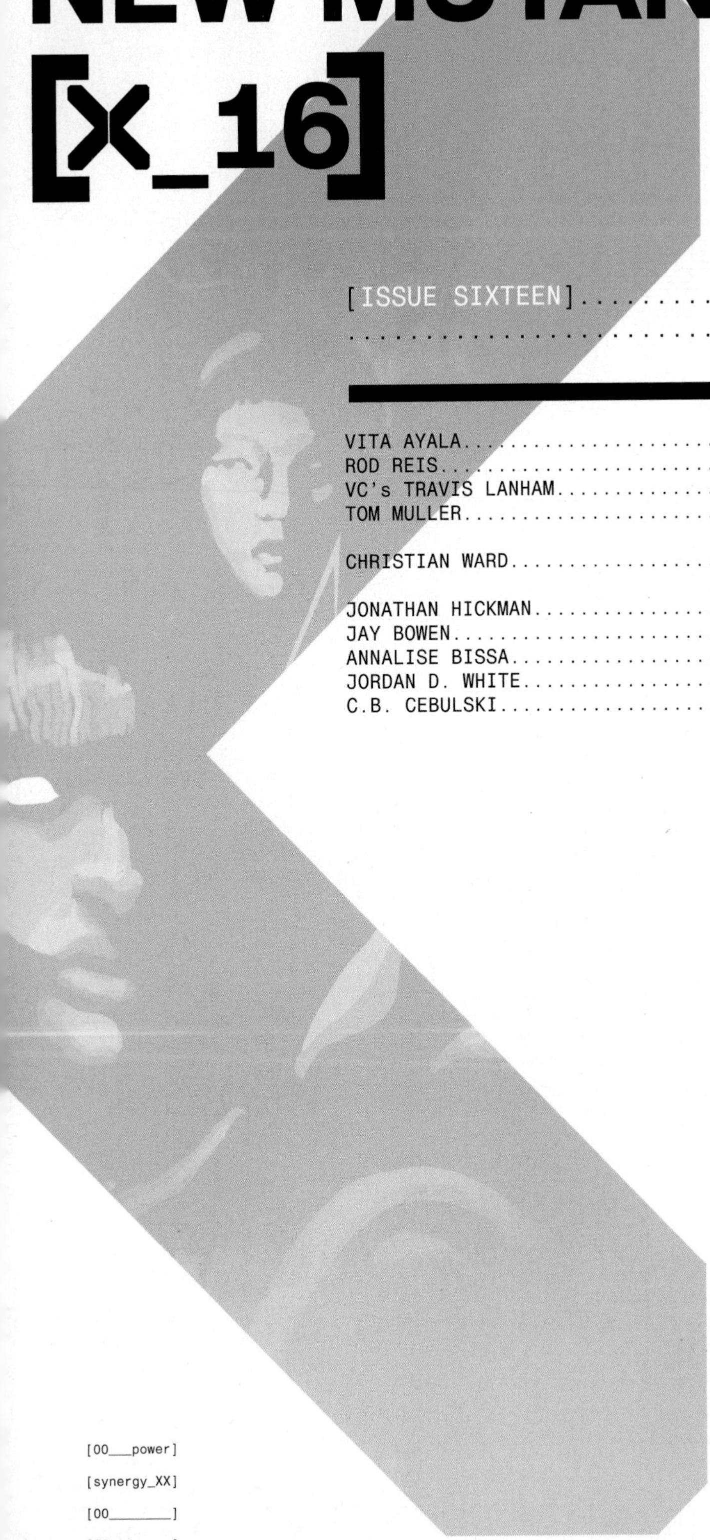

[ISSUE SIXTEEN]...............................
...........................ONE STEP BEHIND

VITA AYALA..[WRITER]
ROD REIS..[ARTIST]
VC's TRAVIS LANHAM...............................[LETTERER]
TOM MULLER..[DESIGN]

CHRISTIAN WARD...............................[COVER ARTIST]

JONATHAN HICKMAN...............................[HEAD OF X]
JAY BOWEN......................................[PRODUCTION]
ANNALISE BISSA....................................[EDITOR]
JORDAN D. WHITE............................[SENIOR EDITOR]
C.B. CEBULSKI............................[EDITOR IN CHIEF]

[00___power]

[synergy_XX]

[00_____]

[00_____]

[00_____in]

[00_____the]

[00___wild]

[00___hunt]

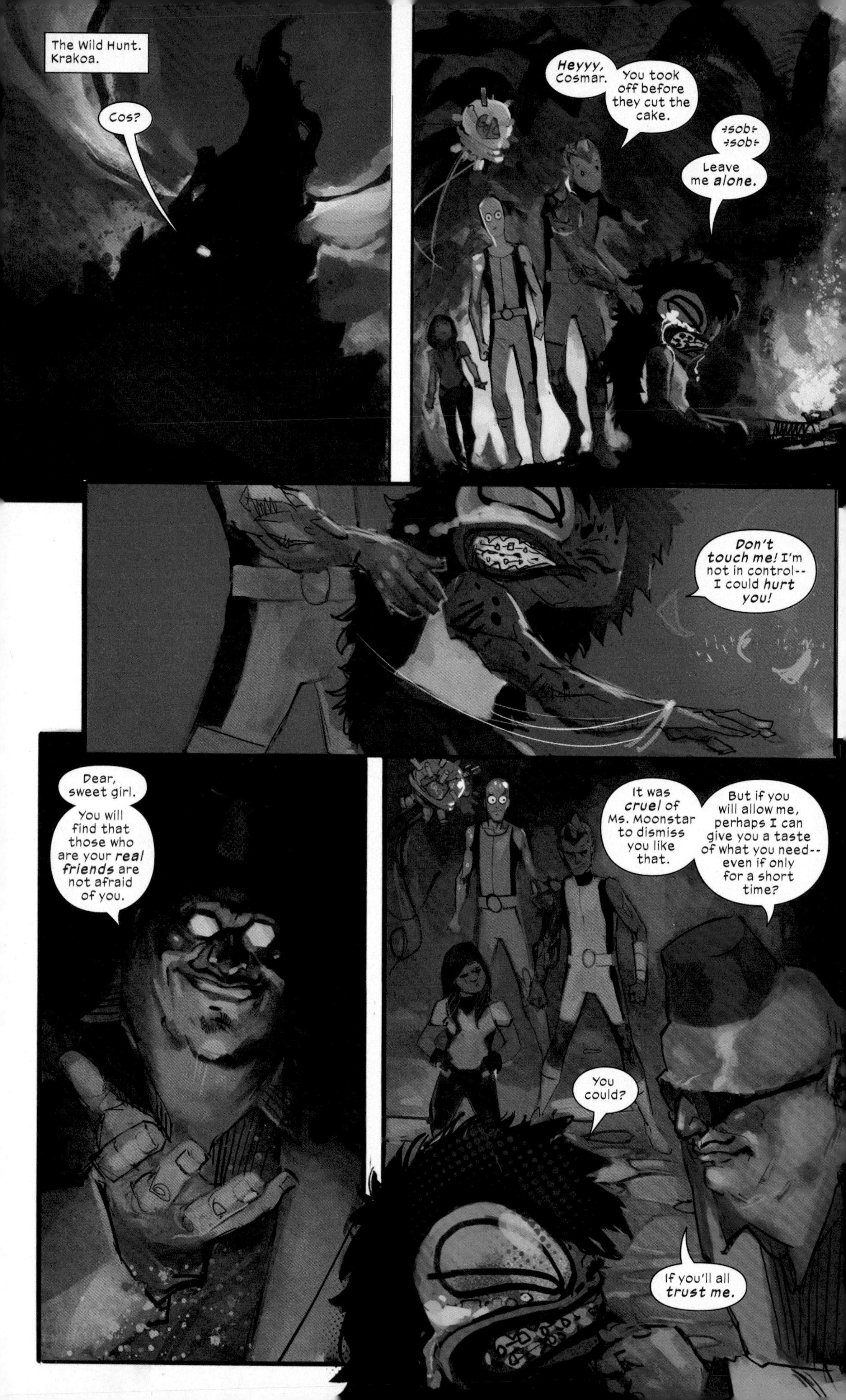
The Wild Hunt.
Krakoa.
Cos?
Heyyy, Cosmar.
You took off before they cut the cake.
sob *sob*
Leave me alone.
Don't touch me! I'm not in control-- I could hurt you!
Dear, sweet girl.
You will find that those who are your real friends are not afraid of you.
It was cruel of Ms. Moonstar to dismiss you like that.
But if you will allow me, perhaps I can give you a taste of what you need-- even if only for a short time?
You could?
If you'll all trust me.

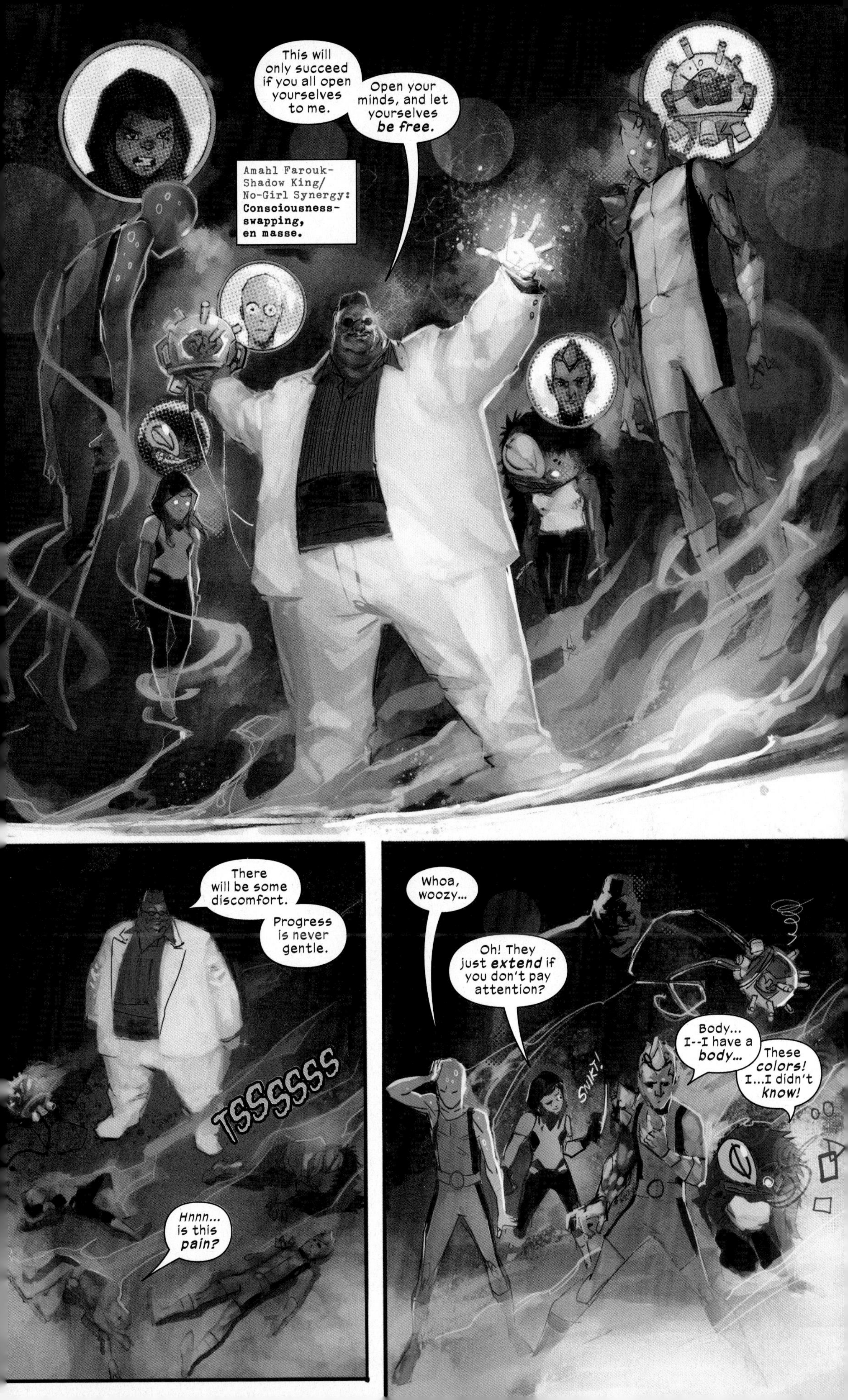

This will only succeed if you all open yourselves to me.
Open your minds, and let yourselves be free.
Amahl Farouk-Shadow King/ No-Girl Synergy: Consciousness-swapping, en masse.
There will be some discomfort.
Progress is never gentle.
TSSSSSS
Hnnn... is this pain?
Whoa, woozy...
Oh! They just extend if you don't pay attention?
SNIKT!
Body... I--I have a body...
These colors! I...I didn't know!

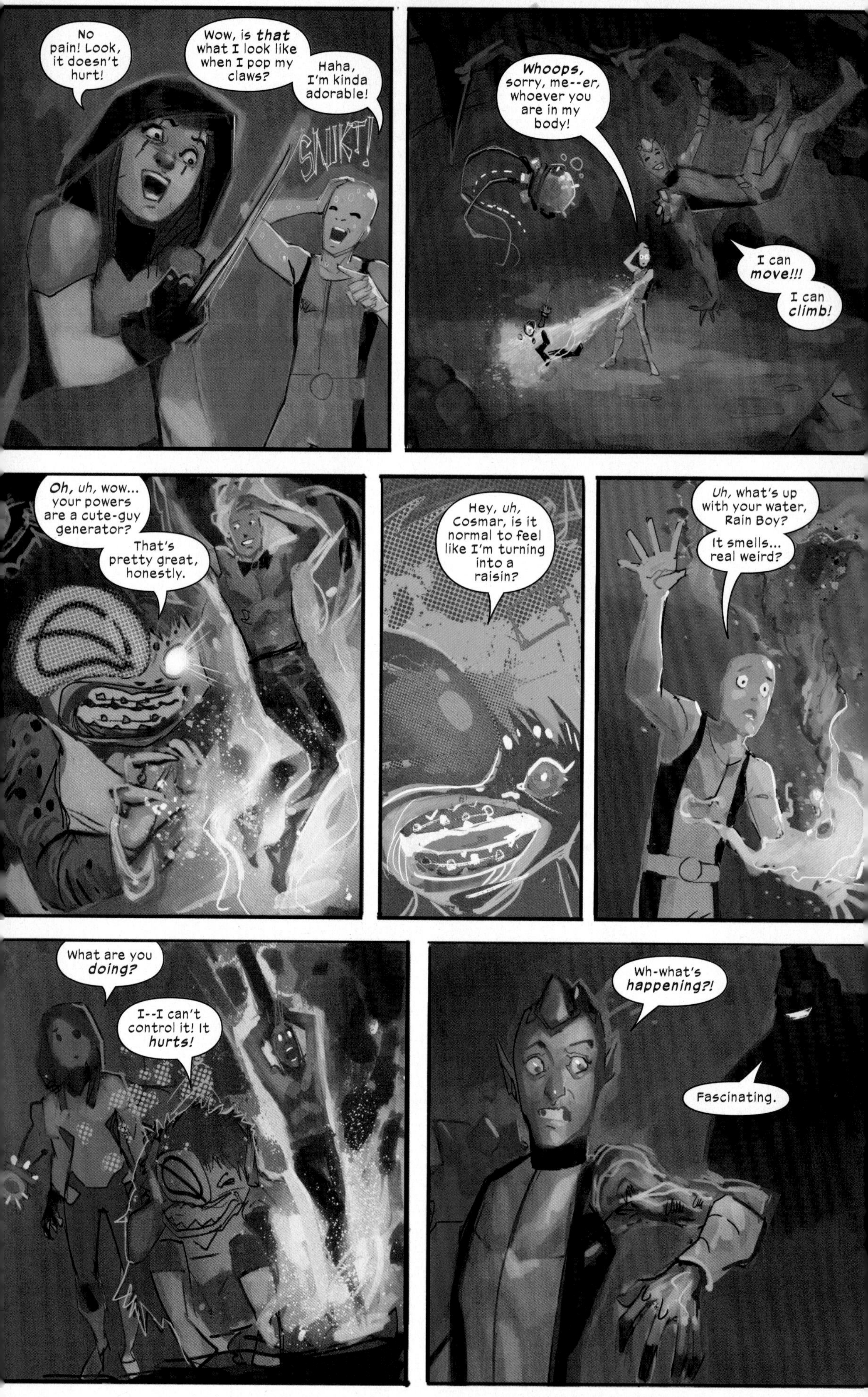
No pain! Look, it doesn't hurt!
Wow, is *that* what I look like when I pop my claws?
Haha, I'm kinda adorable!
SNIKT!
Whoops, sorry, me--*er,* whoever you are in my body!
I can *move!!!*
I can *climb!*
Oh, uh, wow... your powers are a cute-guy generator?
That's pretty great, honestly.
Hey, *uh,* Cosmar, is it normal to feel like I'm turning into a raisin?
Uh, what's up with your water, Rain Boy?
It smells... real weird?
What are you *doing?*
I--I can't control it! It *hurts!*
Wh-what's *happening?!*
Fascinating.

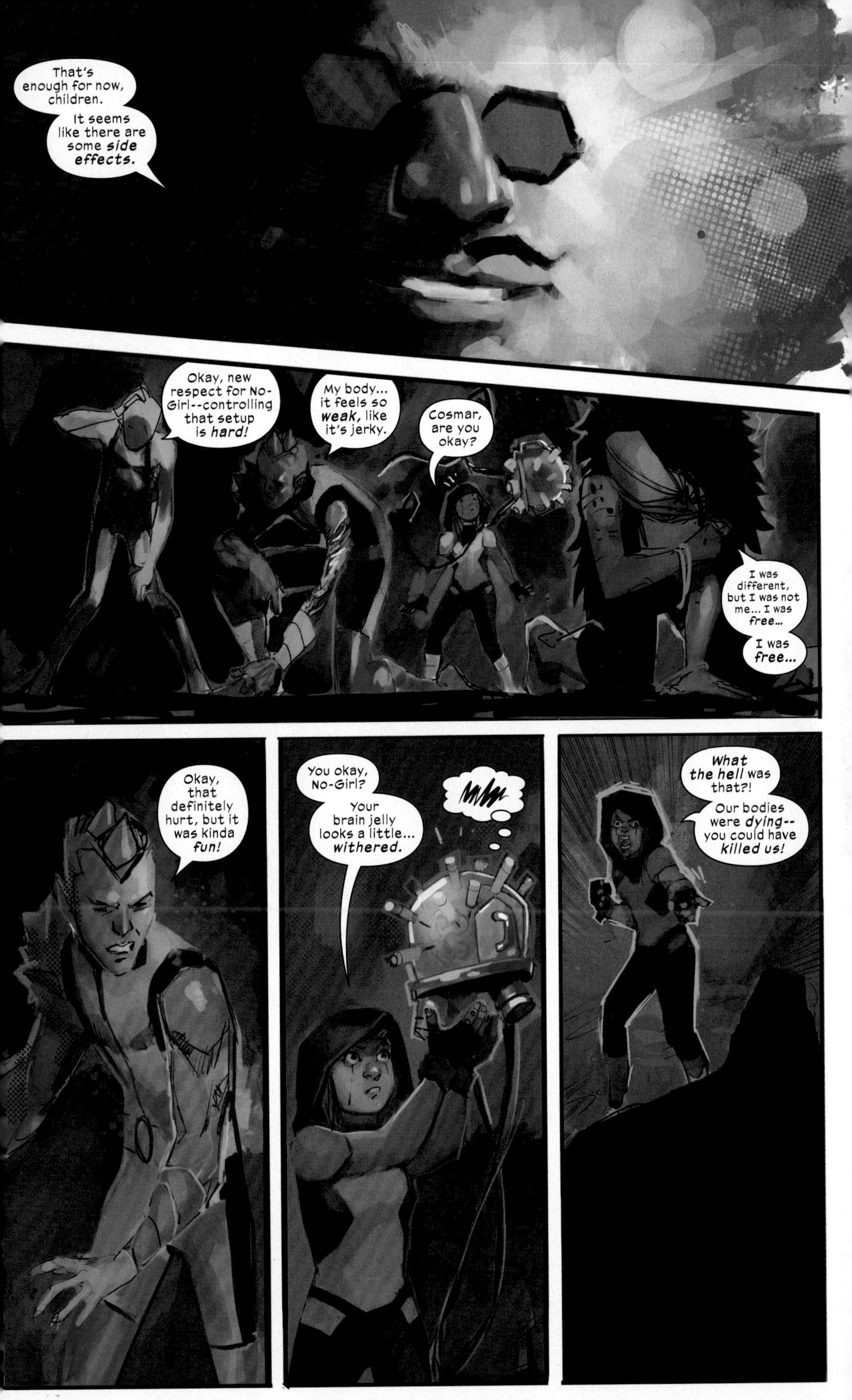
That's enough for now, children.
It seems like there are some side effects.
Okay, new respect for No-Girl--controlling that setup is hard!
My body... it feels so weak, like it's jerky.
Cosmar, are you okay?
I was different, but I was not me... I was free...
I was free...
Okay, that definitely hurt, but it was kinda fun!
You okay, No-Girl?
Your brain jelly looks a little... withered.
What the hell was that?!
Our bodies were dying-- you could have killed us!

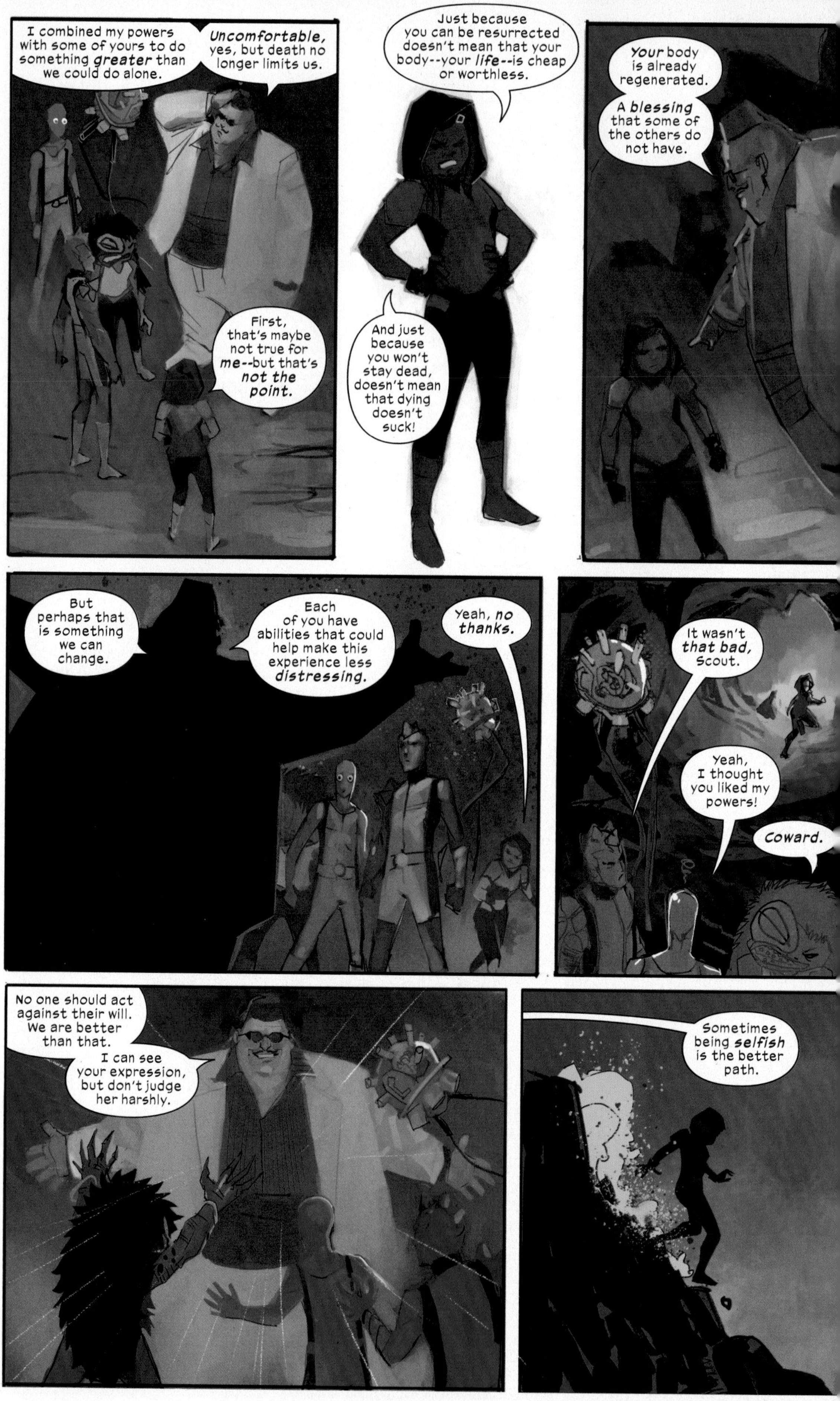
I combined my powers with some of yours to do something *greater* than we could do alone.
Uncomfortable, yes, but death no longer limits us.
First, that's maybe not true for *me*--but that's *not the point.*
Just because you can be resurrected doesn't mean that your body--your *life*--is cheap or worthless.
And just because you won't stay dead, doesn't mean that dying doesn't suck!
Your body is already regenerated.
A *blessing* that some of the others do not have.
But perhaps that is something we can change.
Each of you have abilities that could help make this experience less *distressing.*
Yeah, *no thanks.*
It wasn't *that bad,* Scout.
Yeah, I thought you liked my powers!
Coward.
No one should act against their will. We are better than that.
I can see your expression, but don't judge her harshly.
Sometimes being *selfish* is the better path.

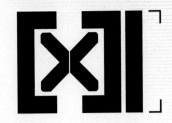

We here at the Crooked Caller pride ourselves on keeping you up to date on the happenings in all the kingdoms of Otherworld.

WHICH-BREED?

There've been reports of stragglers from Krakoa lingering about, sticking their noses in Otherworld business. And they're getting around.

The Caller's gotten word that a youngster has been seen in *Avalon*, *Sevalith*, the edges of *Blightspoke*, our own *Crooked Market* and all about the diplomatic ring.

As far as we can tell, there is no sinister agenda – mostly they've been reported to be interested in trade and asking nosy-but-benign questions--but seeing as they've had Actualization Essence and Candles of Revelation among their goods, we'll keep a close eye on them for future opportunities for our readers to get in on the action.

They also seem to have made a friend of the famously cantankerous Sheriff Whitechapel, which we wouldn't mention except that it could imply a new line to the riches of Blightspoke...

If any of you, discerning readers, have information on the movements of witchbreed* youth, let us know!

~ Quinn Crier, Staff Writer

*According to reports, the kid's anywhere between two and three meters tall, blue-skinned and horned. And, according to Ella the Gray from down near the border, the witchbreed also has quite the charming smile.

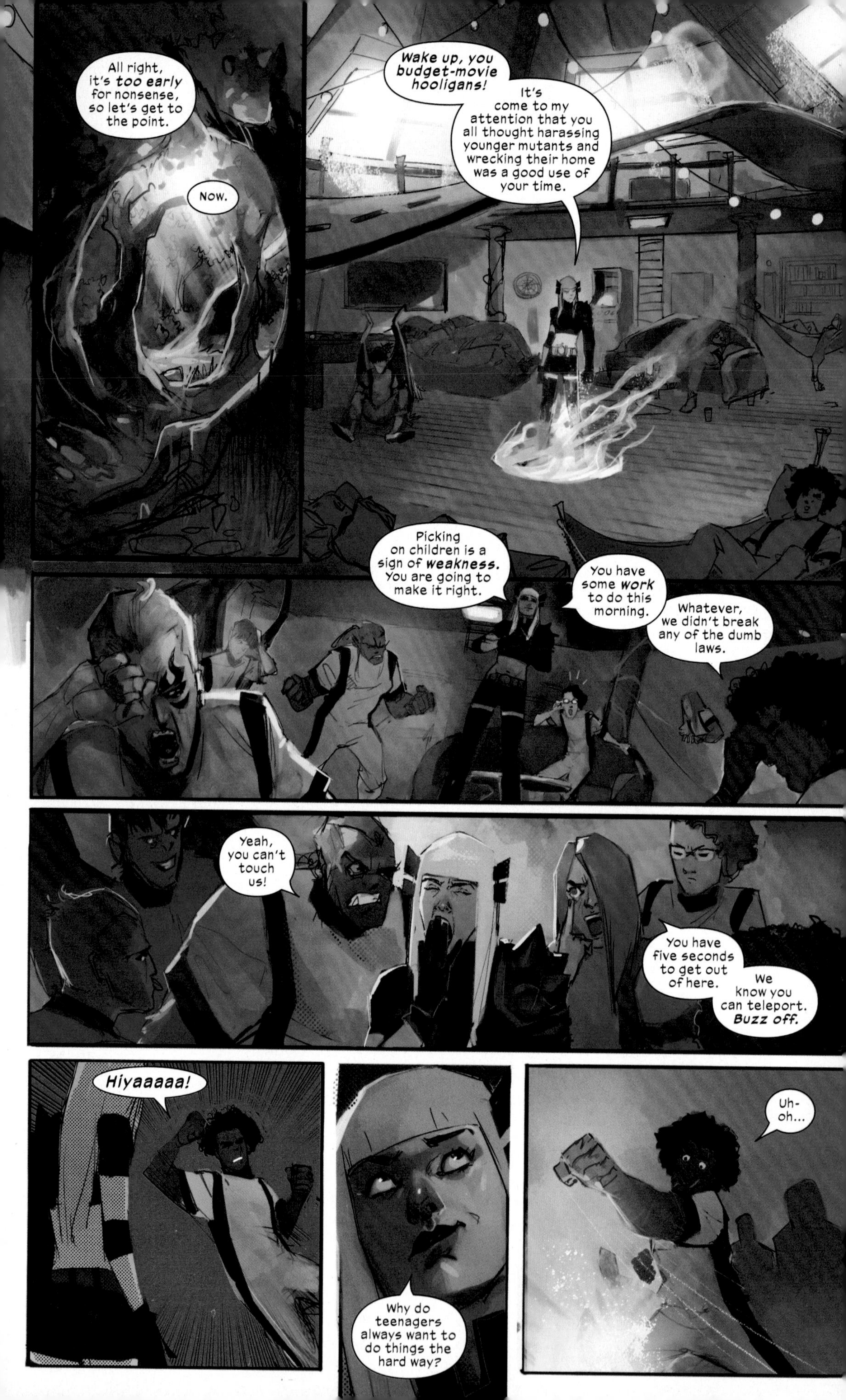
All right, it's *too early* for nonsense, so let's get to the point.
Now.
Wake up, you budget-movie hooligans!
It's come to my attention that you all thought harassing younger mutants and wrecking their home was a good use of your time.
Picking on children is a sign of ***weakness.*** You are going to make it right.
You have some ***work*** to do this morning.
Whatever, we didn't break any of the dumb laws.
Yeah, you can't touch us!
You have five seconds to get out of here.
We know you can teleport. ***Buzz off.***
Hiyaaaaa!
Why do teenagers always want to do things the hard way?
Uh-oh...

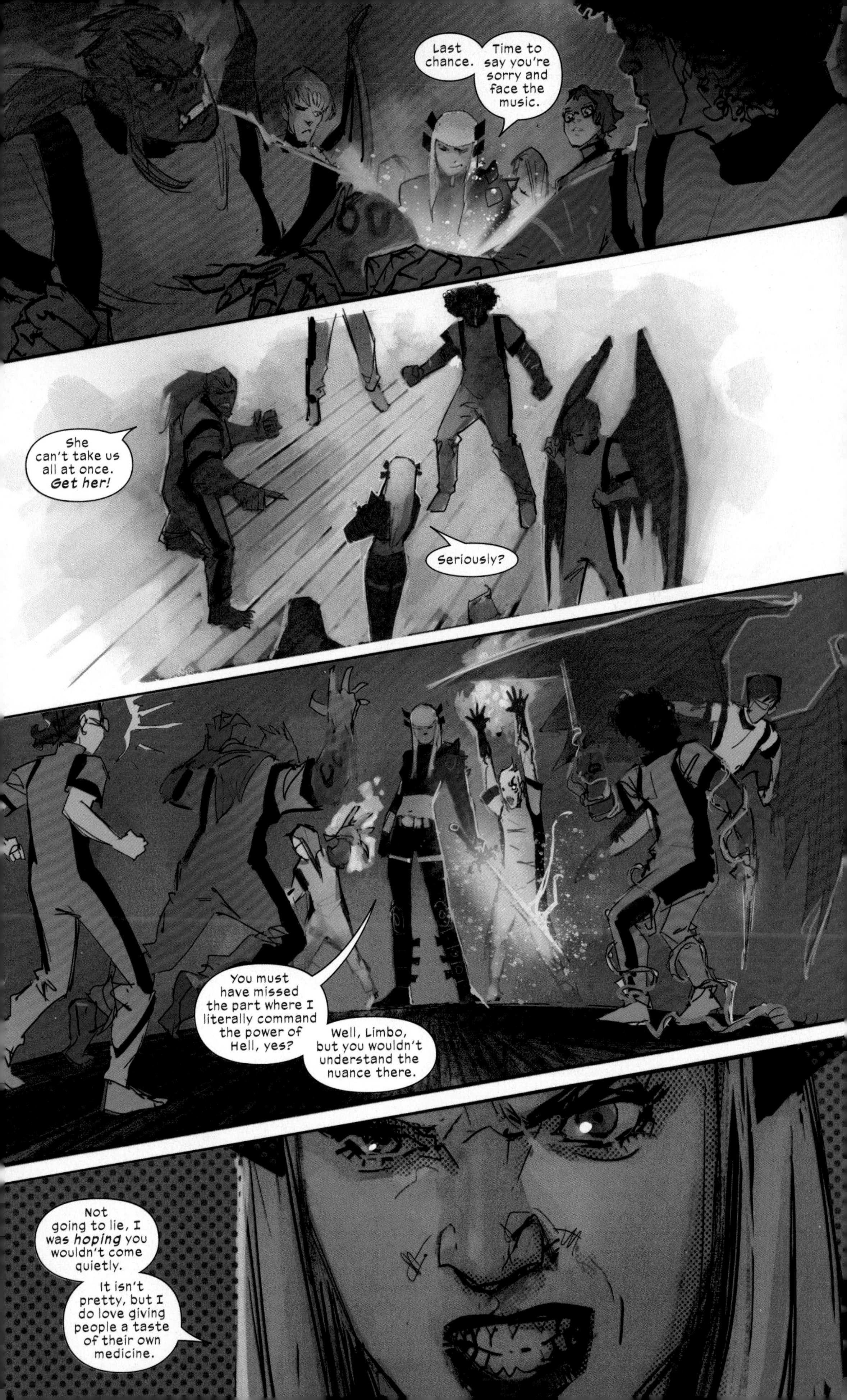
Last chance.
Time to say you're sorry and face the music.
She can't take us all at once. *Get her!*
Seriously?
You must have missed the part where I literally command the power of Hell, yes?
Well, Limbo, but you wouldn't understand the nuance there.
Not going to lie, I was *hoping* you wouldn't come quietly.
It isn't pretty, but I do love giving people a taste of their own medicine.

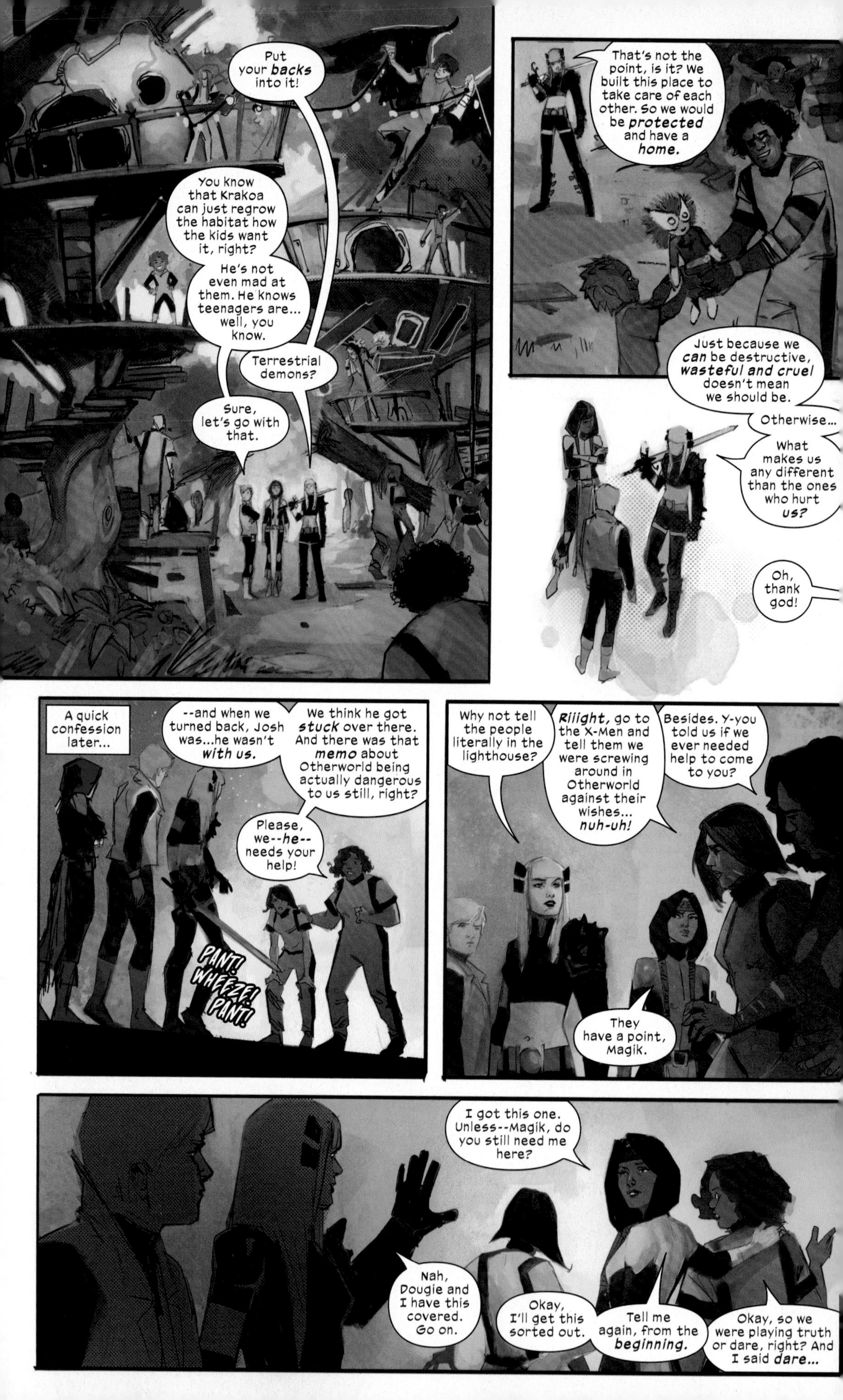

Put your backs into it!
You know that Krakoa can just regrow the habitat how the kids want it, right?
He's not even mad at them. He knows teenagers are... well, you know.
Terrestrial demons?
Sure, let's go with that.
That's not the point, is it? We built this place to take care of each other. So we would be protected and have a home.
Just because we can be destructive, wasteful and cruel doesn't mean we should be.
Otherwise...
What makes us any different than the ones who hurt us?
Oh, thank god!
A quick confession later...
--and when we turned back, Josh was...he wasn't with us.
We think he got stuck over there. And there was that memo about Otherworld being actually dangerous to us still, right?
Please, we--he--needs your help!
PANT! WHEEZE! PANT!
Why not tell the people literally in the lighthouse?
Riiight, go to the X-Men and tell them we were screwing around in Otherworld against their wishes... nuh-uh!
Besides. Y-you told us if we ever needed help to come to you?
They have a point, Magik.
I got this one. Unless--Magik, do you still need me here?
Nah, Dougie and I have this covered. Go on.
Okay, I'll get this sorted out.
Tell me again, from the beginning.
Okay, so we were playing truth or dare, right? And I said dare...

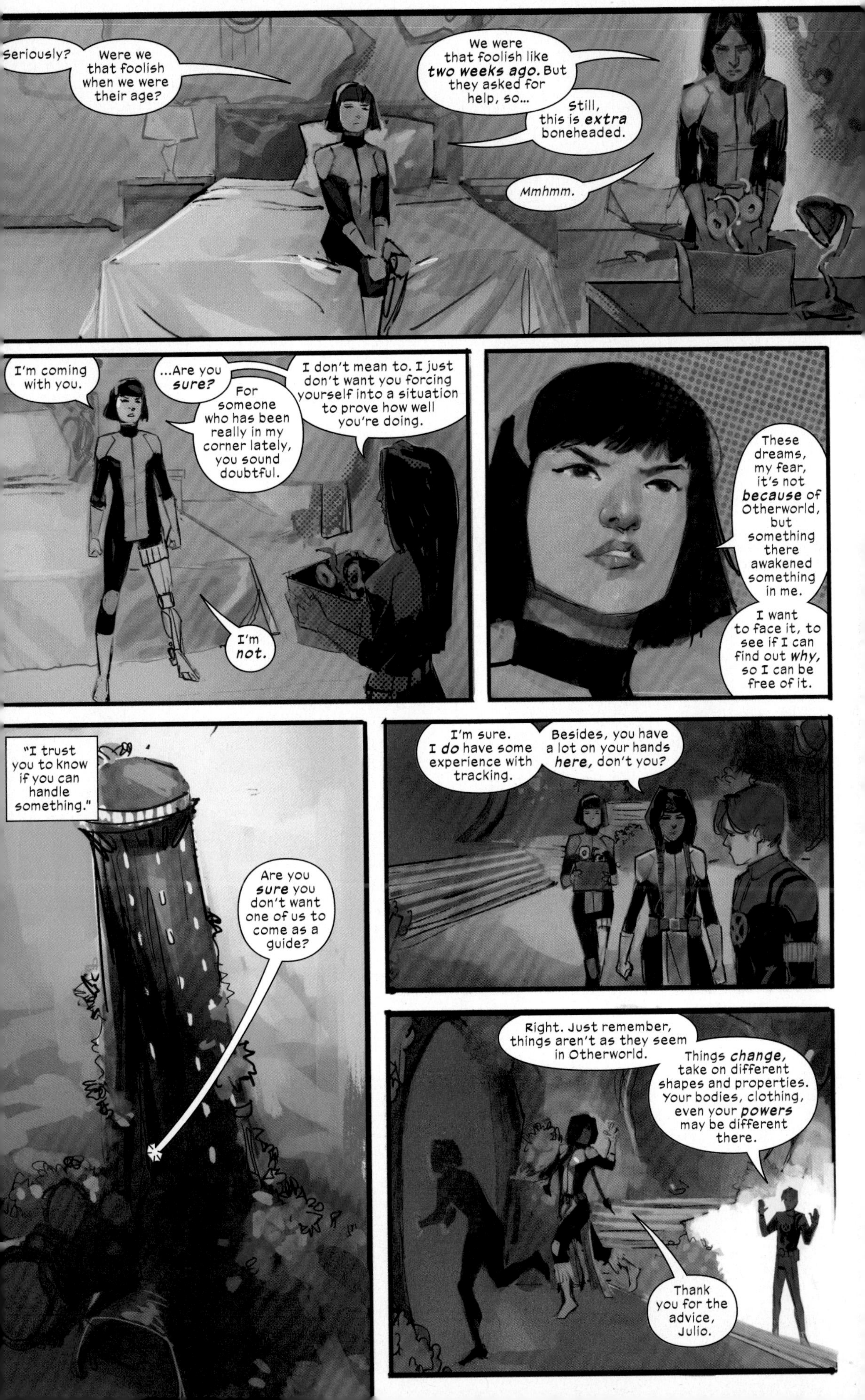
Seriously?
Were we that foolish when we were their age?
We were that foolish like two weeks ago. But they asked for help, so...
Still, this is extra boneheaded.
Mmhmm.
I'm coming with you.
...Are you sure?
For someone who has been really in my corner lately, you sound doubtful.
I don't mean to. I just don't want you forcing yourself into a situation to prove how well you're doing.
I'm not.
These dreams, my fear, it's not because of Otherworld, but something there awakened something in me.
I want to face it, to see if I can find out why, so I can be free of it.
"I trust you to know if you can handle something."
Are you sure you don't want one of us to come as a guide?
I'm sure. I do have some experience with tracking.
Besides, you have a lot on your hands here, don't you?
Right. Just remember, things aren't as they seem in Otherworld.
Things change, take on different shapes and properties. Your bodies, clothing, even your powers may be different there.
Thank you for the advice, Julio.

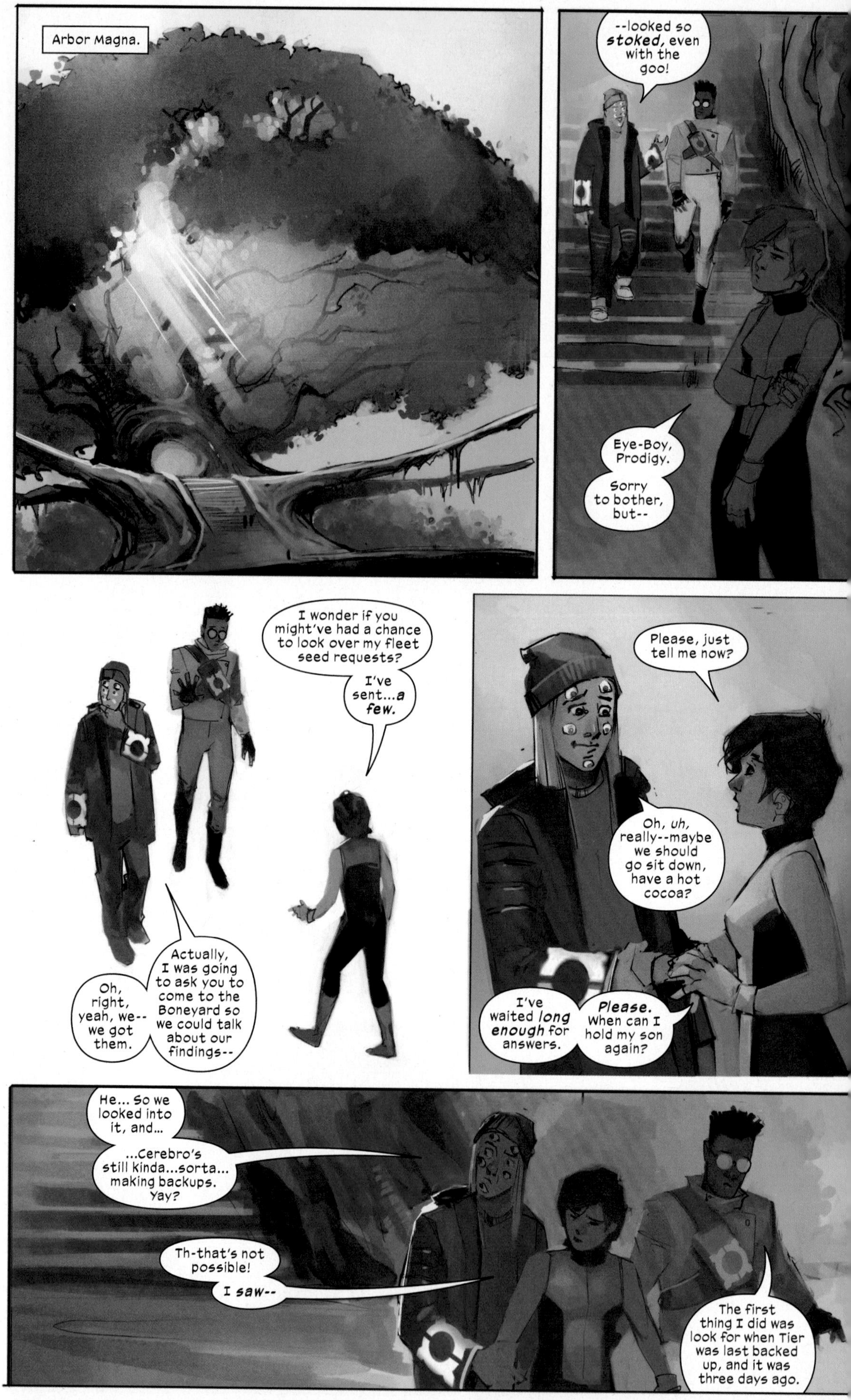
Arbor Magna.
--looked so *stoked,* even with the goo!
Eye-Boy, Prodigy.
Sorry to bother, but--
I wonder if you might've had a chance to look over my fleet seed requests?
I've sent...*a few.*
Actually, I was going to ask you to come to the Boneyard so we could talk about our findings--
Oh, right, yeah, we-- we got them.
Please, just tell me now?
Oh, *uh,* really--maybe we should go sit down, have a hot cocoa?
I've waited *long enough* for answers.
Please. When can I hold my son again?
He... So we looked into it, and...
...Cerebro's still kinda...sorta... making backups. Yay?
Th-that's not possible!
I *saw--*
The first thing I did was look for when Tier was last backed up, and it was three days ago.

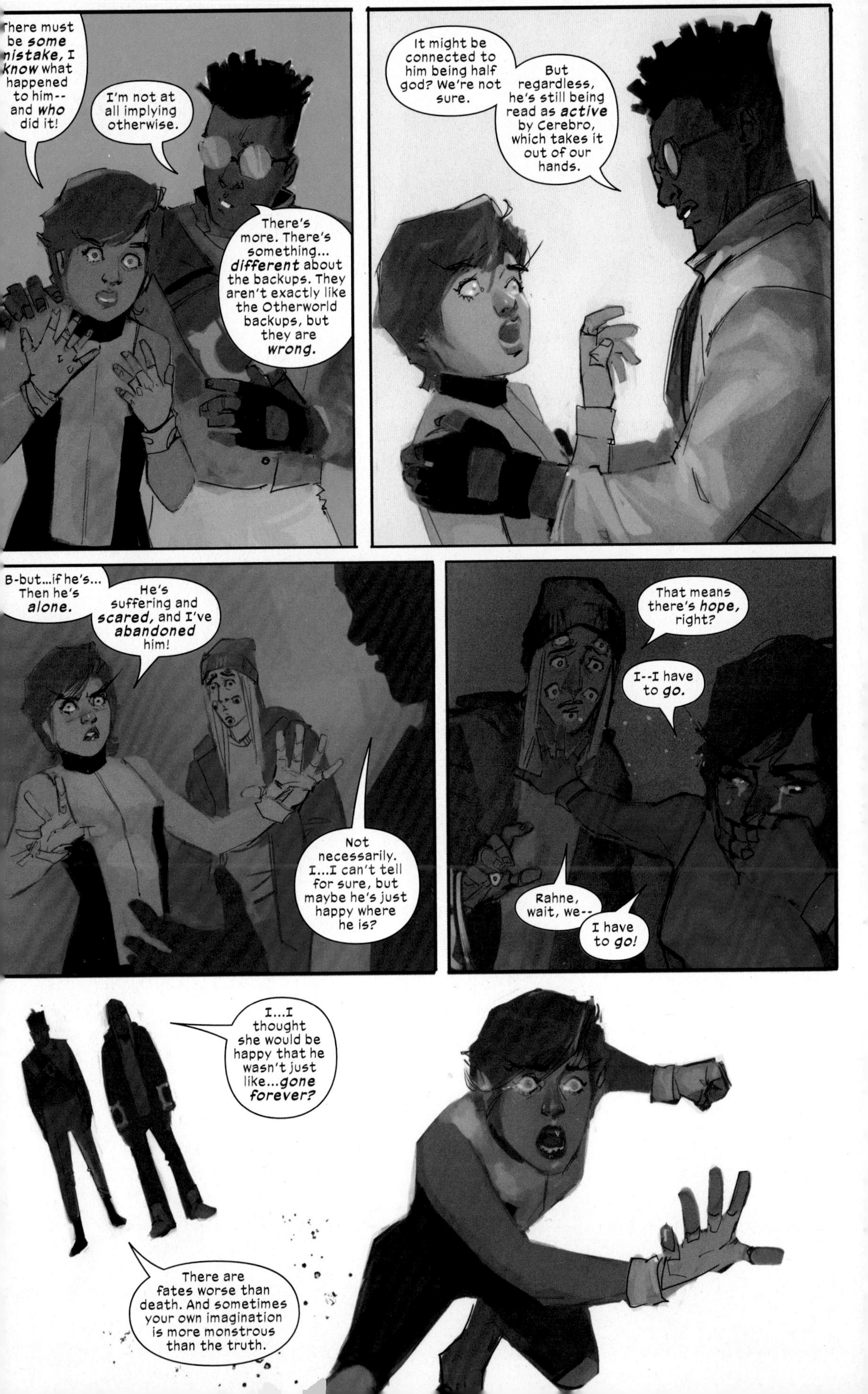
There must be some mistake, I know what happened to him-- and who did it!
I'm not at all implying otherwise.
There's more. There's something... different about the backups. They aren't exactly like the Otherworld backups, but they are wrong.
It might be connected to him being half god? We're not sure.
But regardless, he's still being read as active by Cerebro, which takes it out of our hands.
B-but...if he's... Then he's alone.
He's suffering and scared, and I've abandoned him!
Not necessarily. I...I can't tell for sure, but maybe he's just happy where he is?
That means there's hope, right?
I--I have to go.
Rahne, wait, we--
I have to go!
I...I thought she would be happy that he wasn't just like...gone forever?
There are fates worse than death. And sometimes your own imagination is more monstrous than the truth.

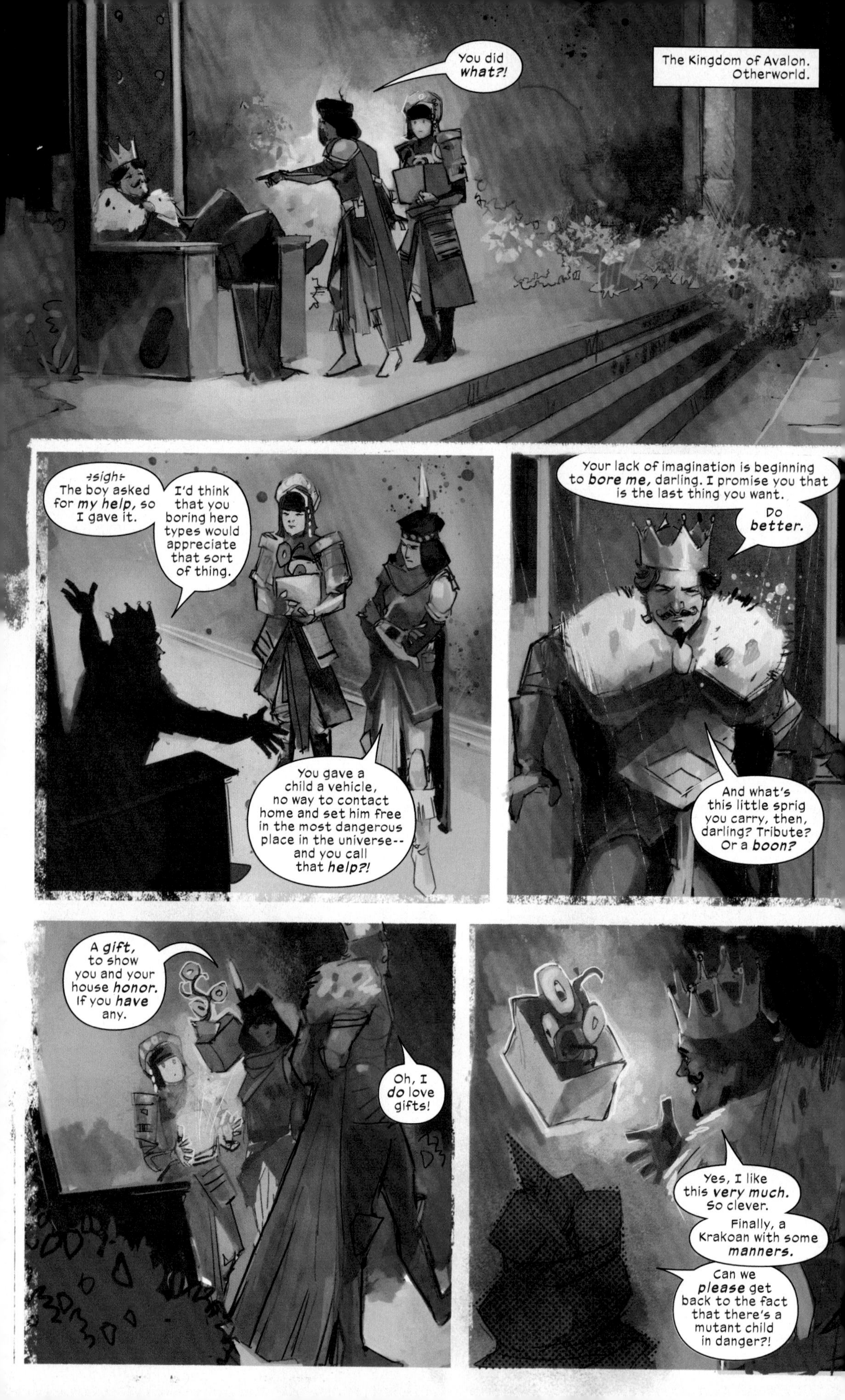

The Kingdom of Avalon. Otherworld.
You did what?!
-sigh- The boy asked for my help, so I gave it.
I'd think that you boring hero types would appreciate that sort of thing.
You gave a child a vehicle, no way to contact home and set him free in the most dangerous place in the universe--and you call that help?!
Your lack of imagination is beginning to bore me, darling. I promise you that is the last thing you want.
Do better.
And what's this little sprig you carry, then, darling? Tribute? Or a boon?
A gift, to show you and your house honor. If you have any.
Oh, I do love gifts!
Yes, I like this very much. So clever.
Finally, a Krakoan with some manners.
Can we please get back to the fact that there's a mutant child in danger?!

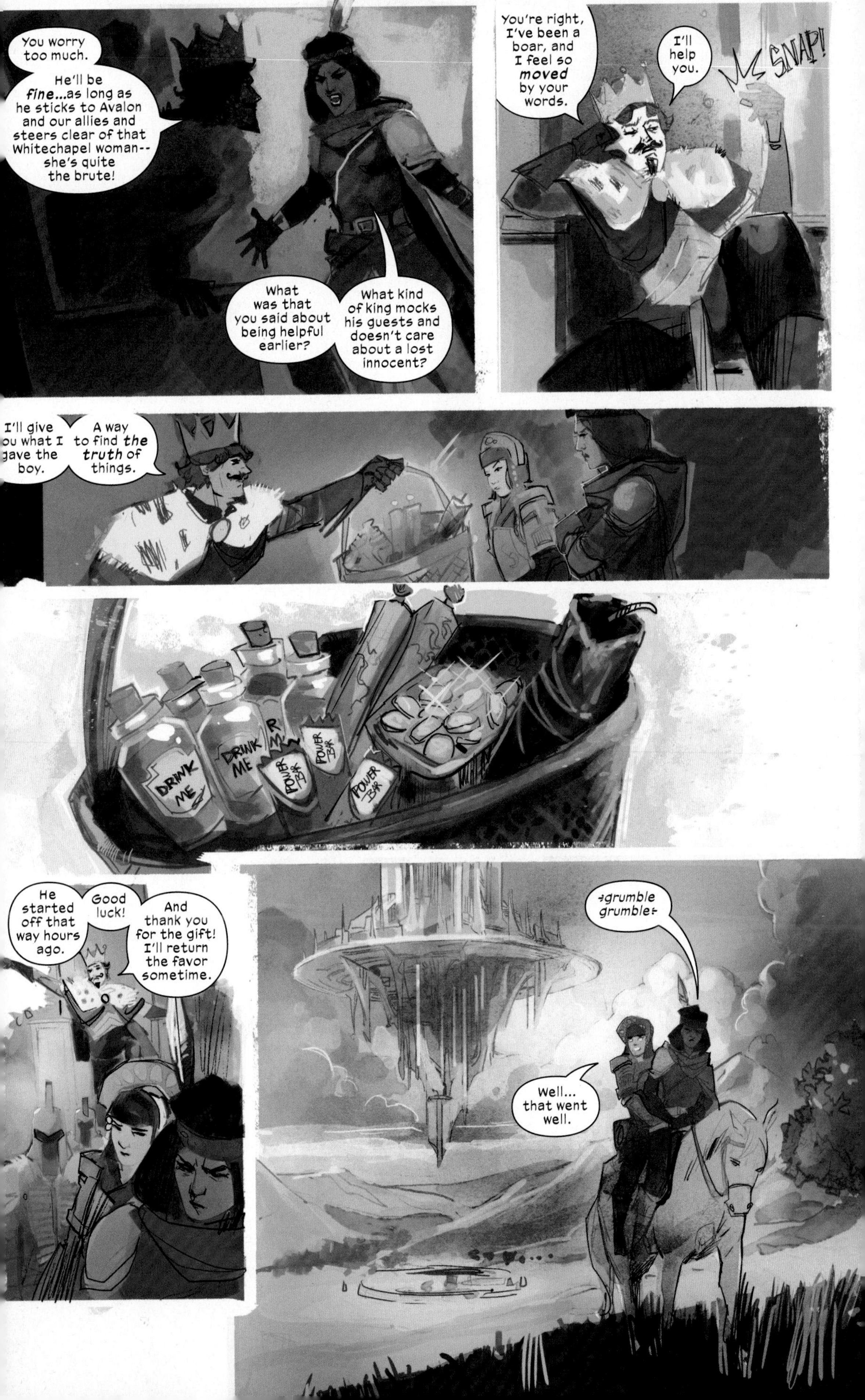

You worry too much.
He'll be *fine*...as long as he sticks to Avalon and our allies and steers clear of that Whitechapel woman--she's quite the brute!
What was that you said about being helpful earlier?
What kind of king mocks his guests and doesn't care about a lost innocent?
You're right, I've been a boar, and I feel so *moved* by your words.
I'll help you.
SNAP!
I'll give ou what I gave the boy.
A way to find *the truth* of things.
DRINK ME
DRINK ME
POWER BAR
POWER BAR
POWER BAR
He started off that way hours ago.
Good luck!
And thank you for the gift! I'll return the favor sometime.
grumble grumble
Well... that went well.

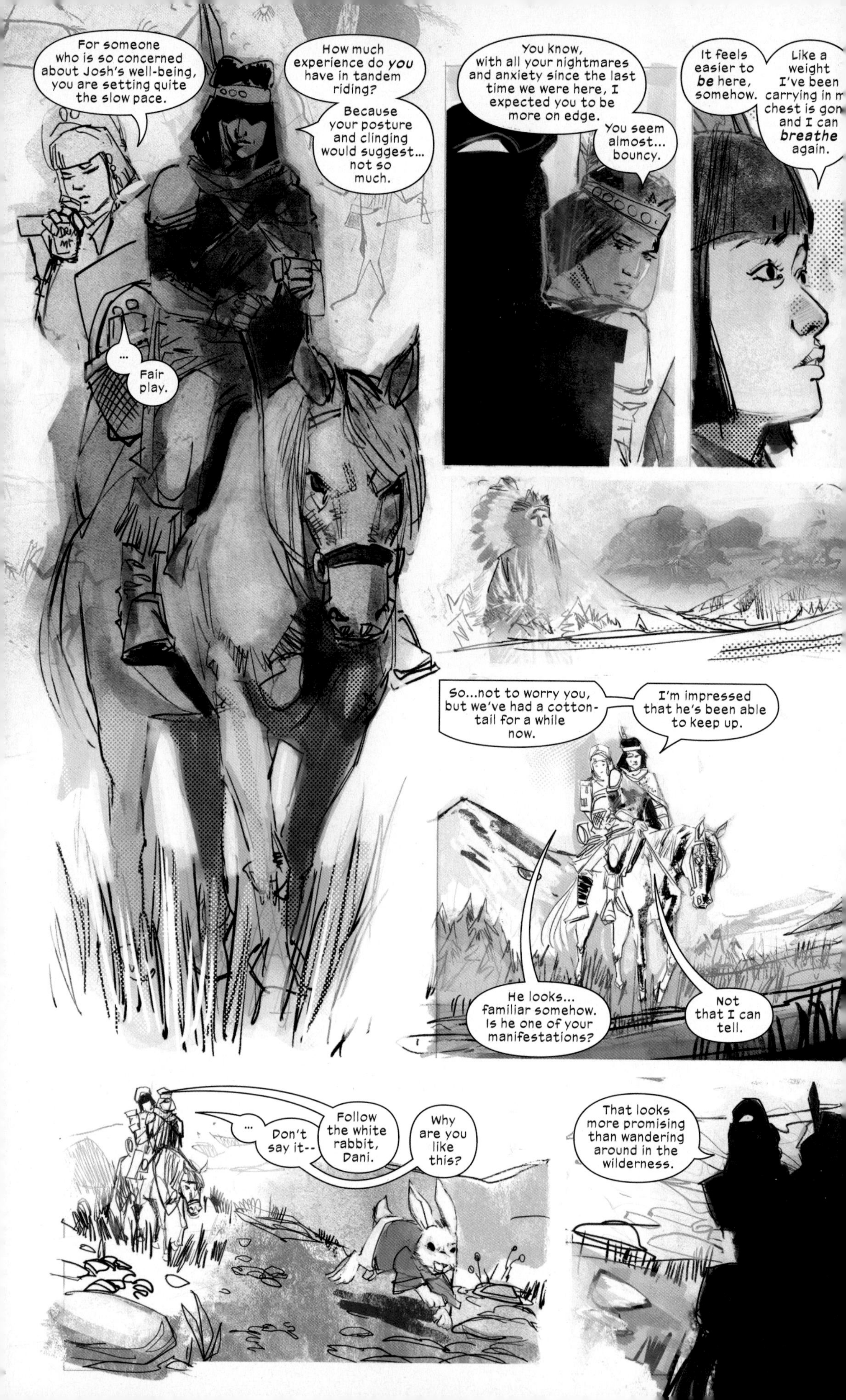
For someone who is so concerned about Josh's well-being, you are setting quite the slow pace.
How much experience do *you* have in tandem riding?
Because your posture and clinging would suggest... not so much.
... Fair play.
You know, with all your nightmares and anxiety since the last time we were here, I expected you to be more on edge.
You seem almost... bouncy.
It feels easier to *be* here, somehow.
Like a weight I've been carrying in m chest is gon and I can *breathe* again.
So...not to worry you, but we've had a cotton-tail for a while now.
I'm impressed that he's been able to keep up.
He looks... familiar somehow. Is he one of your manifestations?
Not that I can tell.
... Don't say it--
Follow the white rabbit, Dani.
Why are you like this?
That looks more promising than wandering around in the wilderness.

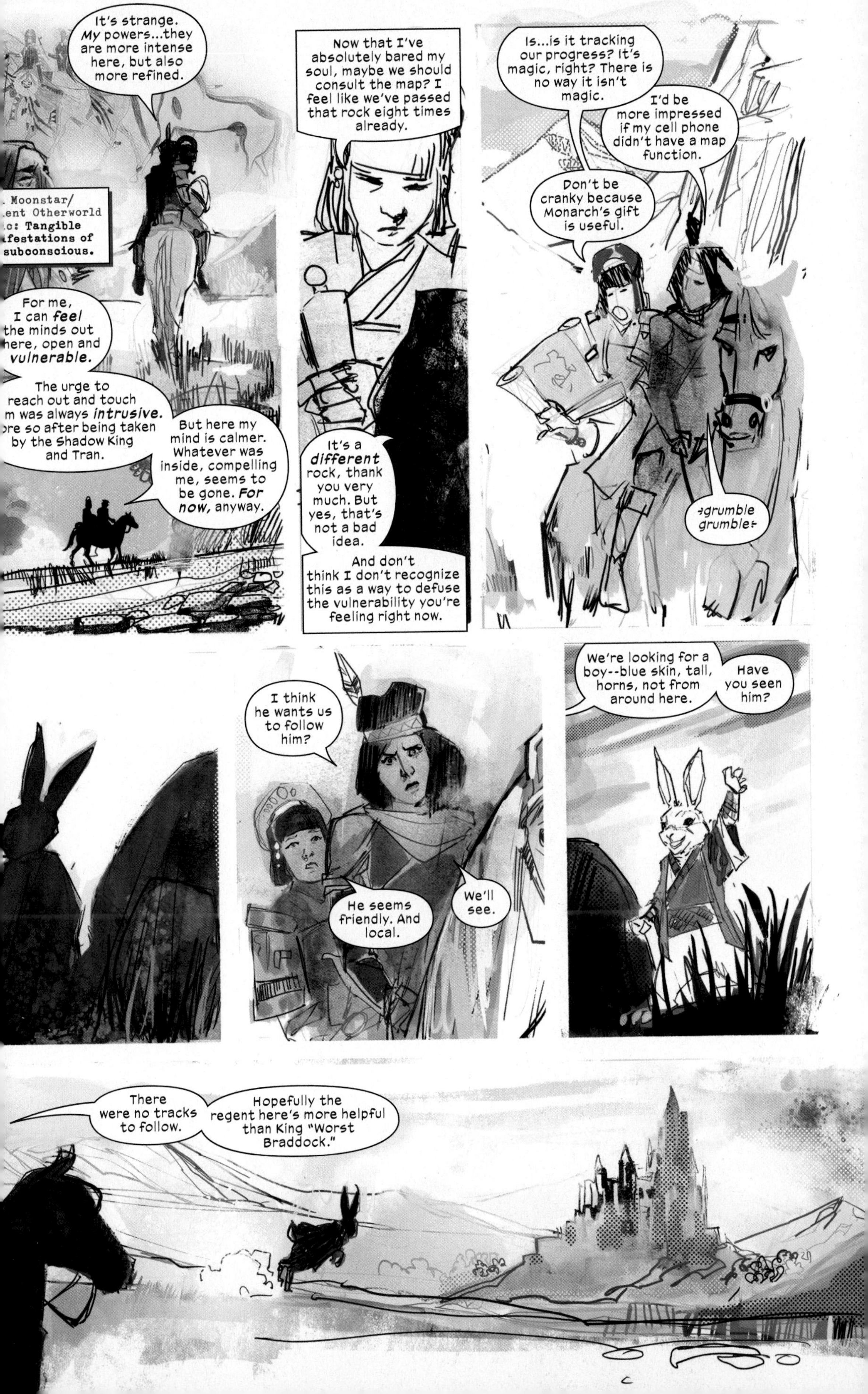
It's strange. My powers...they are more intense here, but also more refined.
Moonstar/ ent Otherworld c: Tangible festations of subconscious.
For me, I can feel the minds out here, open and vulnerable.
The urge to reach out and touch m was always intrusive. ore so after being taken by the Shadow King and Tran.
But here my mind is calmer. Whatever was inside, compelling me, seems to be gone. For now, anyway.
Now that I've absolutely bared my soul, maybe we should consult the map? I feel like we've passed that rock eight times already.
It's a different rock, thank you very much. But yes, that's not a bad idea.
And don't think I don't recognize this as a way to defuse the vulnerability you're feeling right now.
Is...is it tracking our progress? It's magic, right? There is no way it isn't magic.
I'd be more impressed if my cell phone didn't have a map function.
Don't be cranky because Monarch's gift is useful.
grumble grumble
I think he wants us to follow him?
He seems friendly. And local.
We'll see.
We're looking for a boy--blue skin, tall, horns, not from around here.
Have you seen him?
There were no tracks to follow.
Hopefully the regent here's more helpful than King "Worst Braddock."

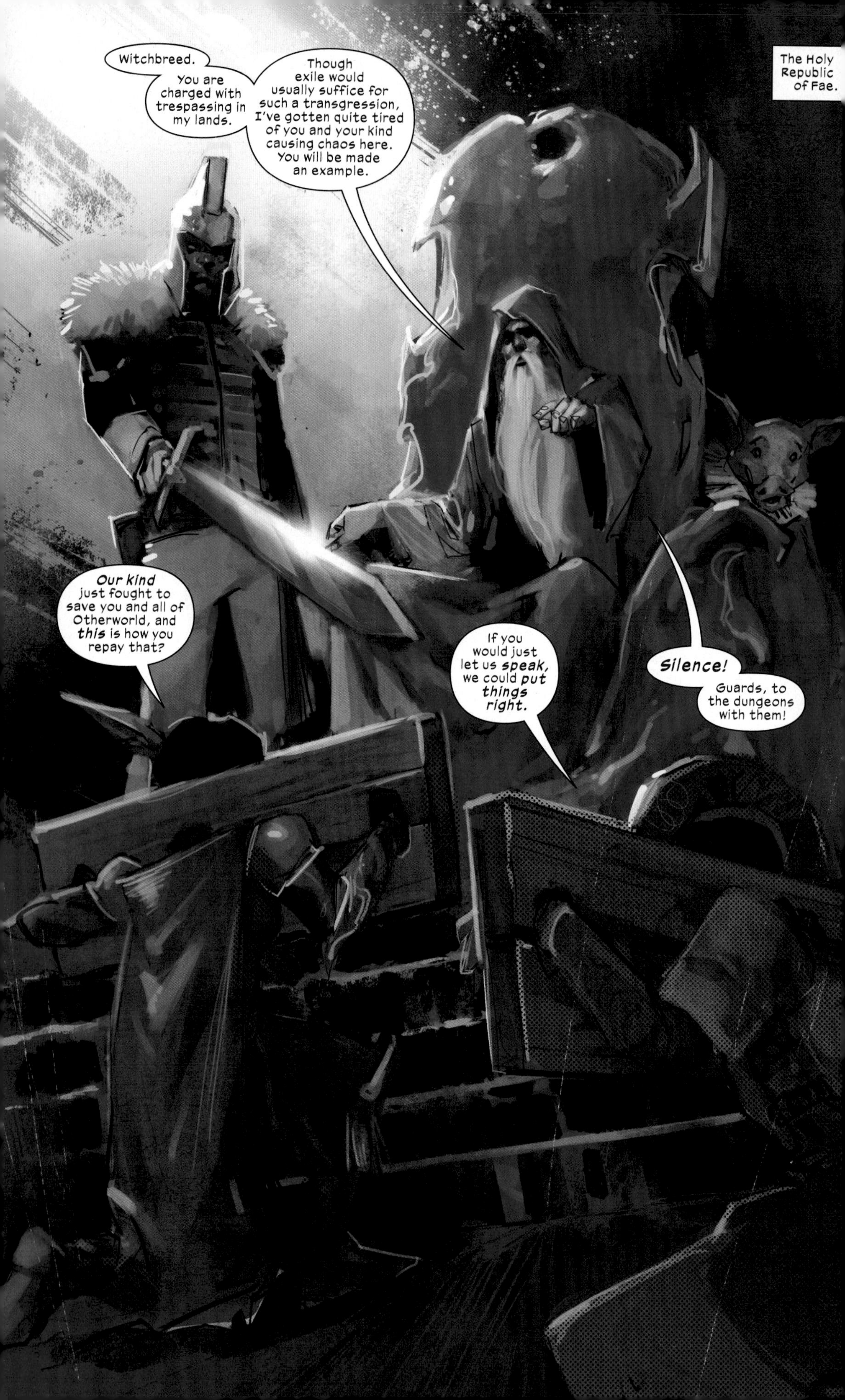

The Holy Republic of Fae.
Witchbreed.
You are charged with trespassing in my lands.
Though exile would usually suffice for such a transgression, I've gotten quite tired of you and your kind causing chaos here. You will be made an example.
Our kind just fought to save you and all of Otherworld, and *this* is how you repay that?
If you would just let us *speak*, we could *put things right*.
Silence!
Guards, to the dungeons with them!

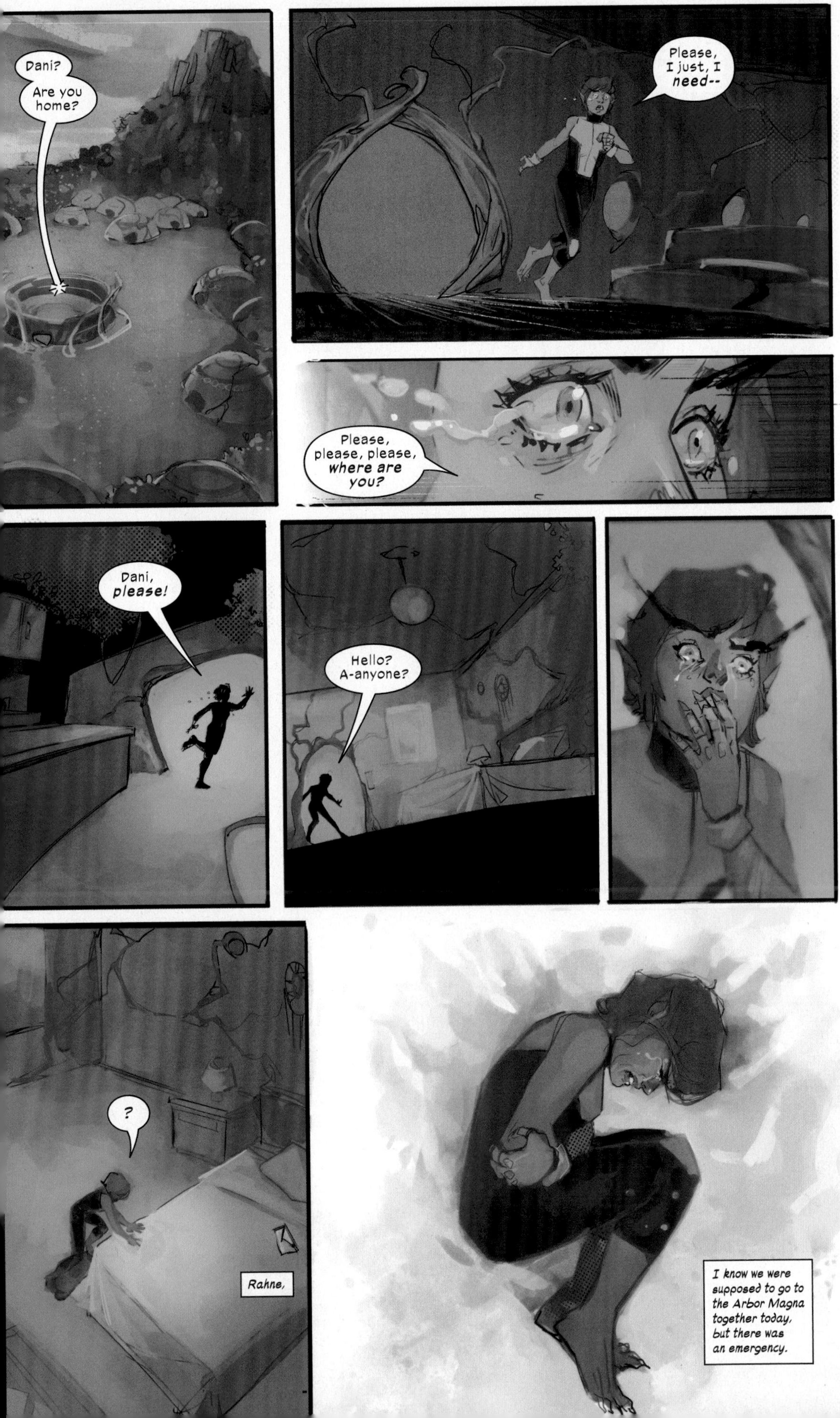
Dani?
Are you home?
Please, I just, I *need--*
Please, please, please, *where are you?*
Dani, *please!*
Hello? A-anyone?
?
Rahne,
I know we were supposed to go to the Arbor Magna together today, but there was an emergency.

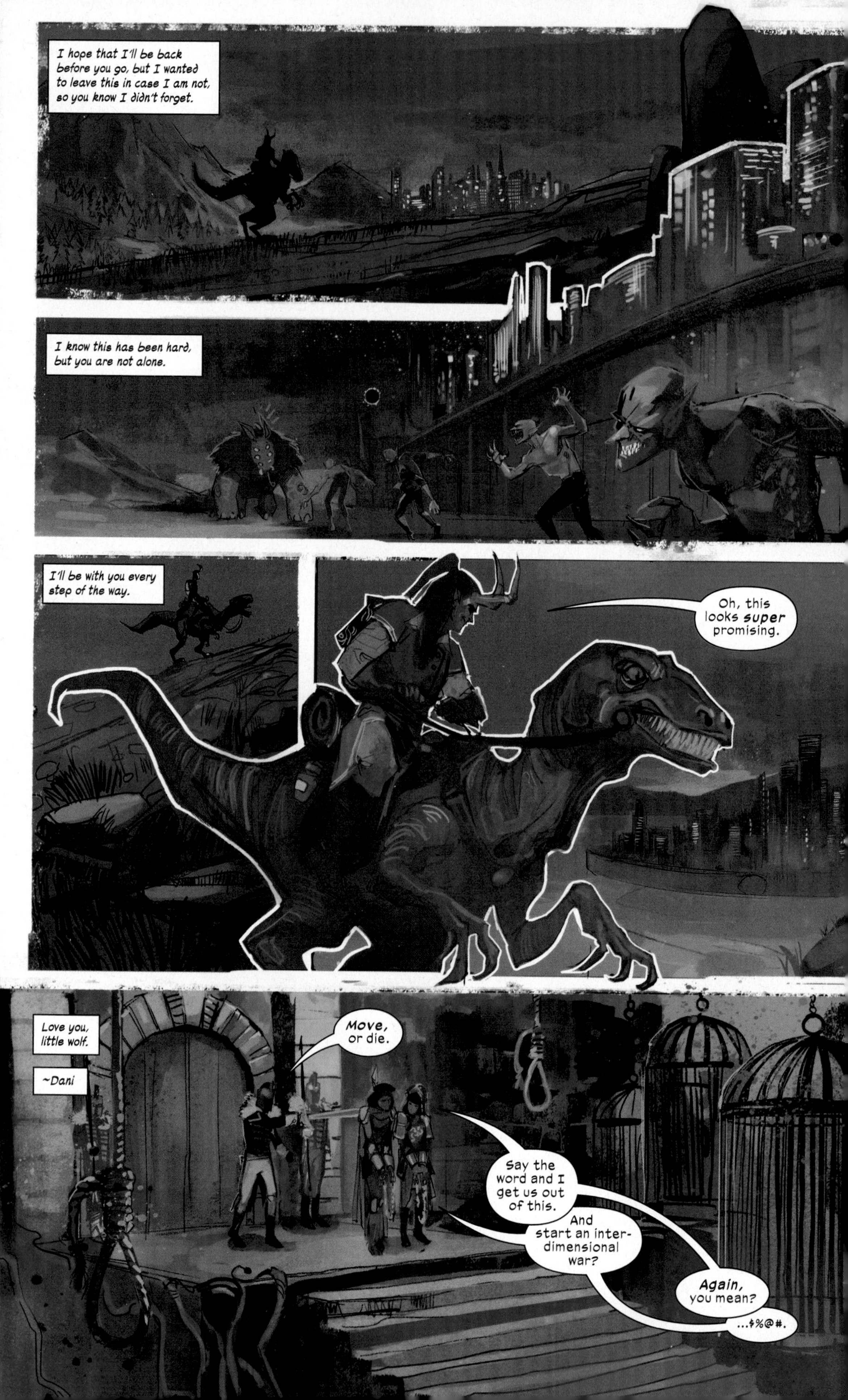
I hope that I'll be back before you go, but I wanted to leave this in case I am not, so you know I didn't forget.
I know this has been hard, but you are not alone.
I'll be with you every step of the way.
Oh, this looks *super* promising.
Love you, little wolf.
~Dani
Move, or die.
Say the word and I get us out of this.
And start an inter-dimensional war?
Again, you mean?
...$%@#.

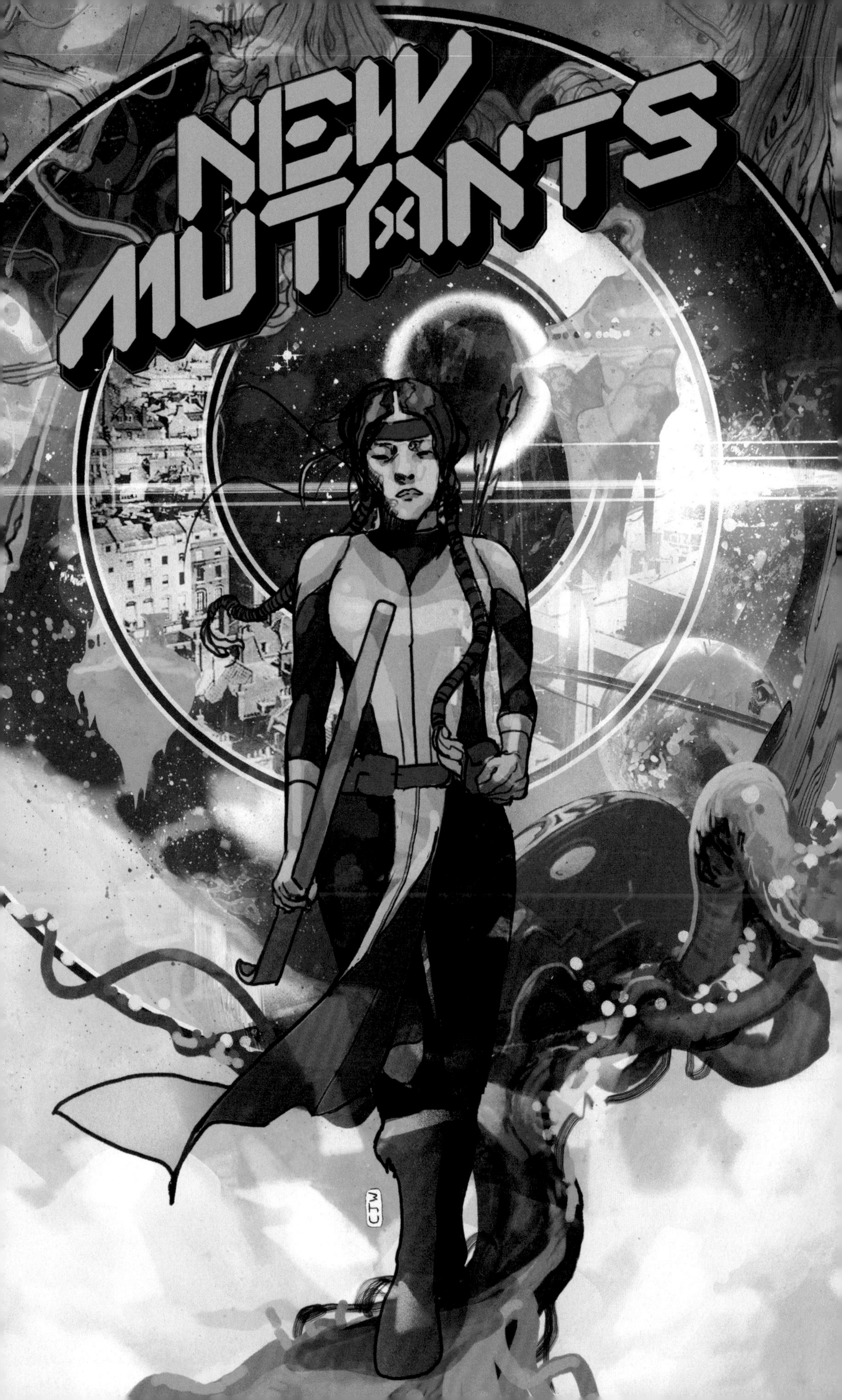
NEW MUTANTS
CJW

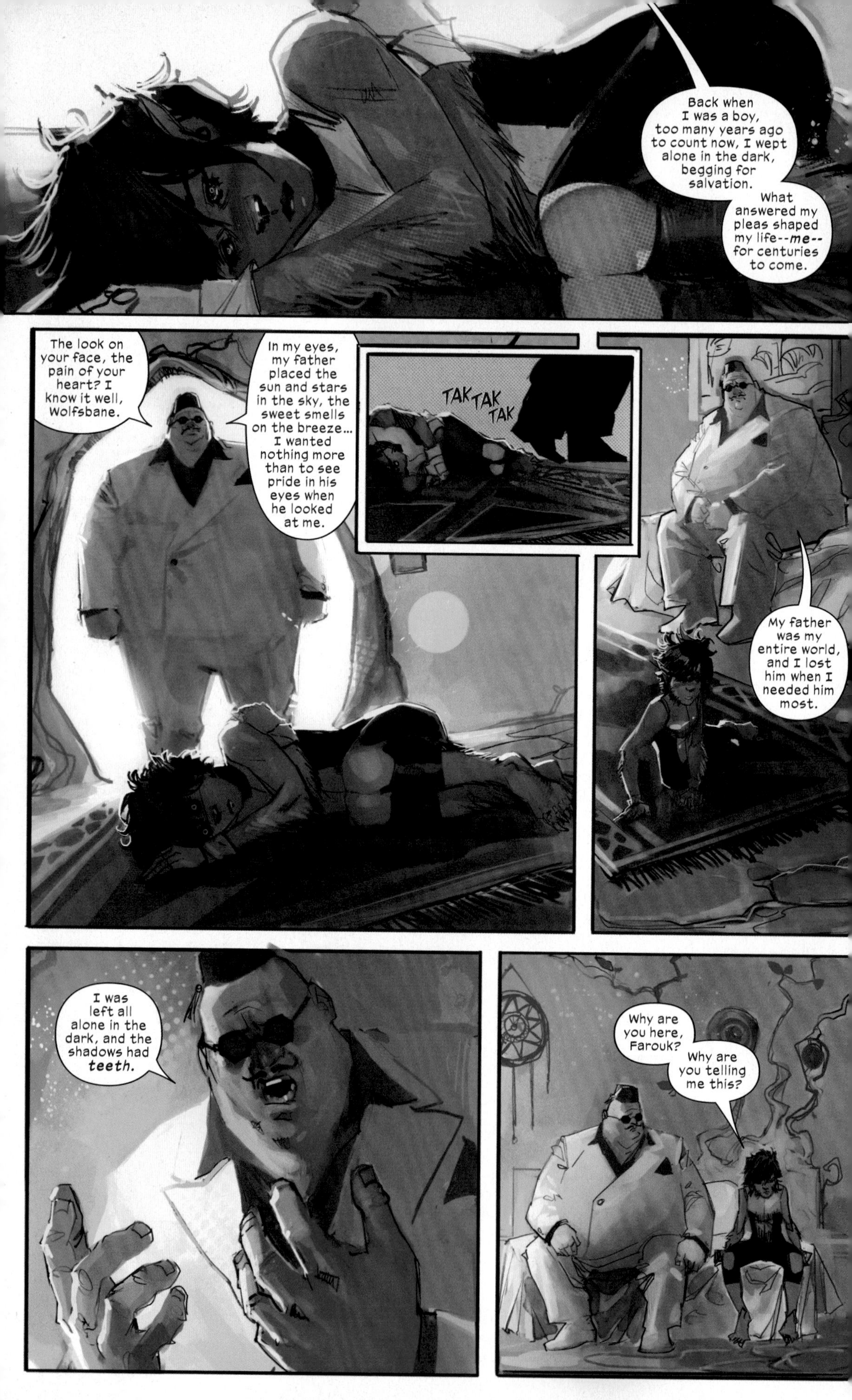

Back when I was a boy, too many years ago to count now, I wept alone in the dark, begging for salvation.
What answered my pleas shaped my life--*me*--for centuries to come.
The look on your face, the pain of your heart? I know it well, Wolfsbane.
In my eyes, my father placed the sun and stars in the sky, the sweet smells on the breeze... I wanted nothing more than to see pride in his eyes when he looked at me.
TAK TAK TAK
My father was my entire world, and I lost him when I needed him most.
I was left all alone in the dark, and the shadows had *teeth.*
Why are you here, Farouk?
Why are you telling me this?

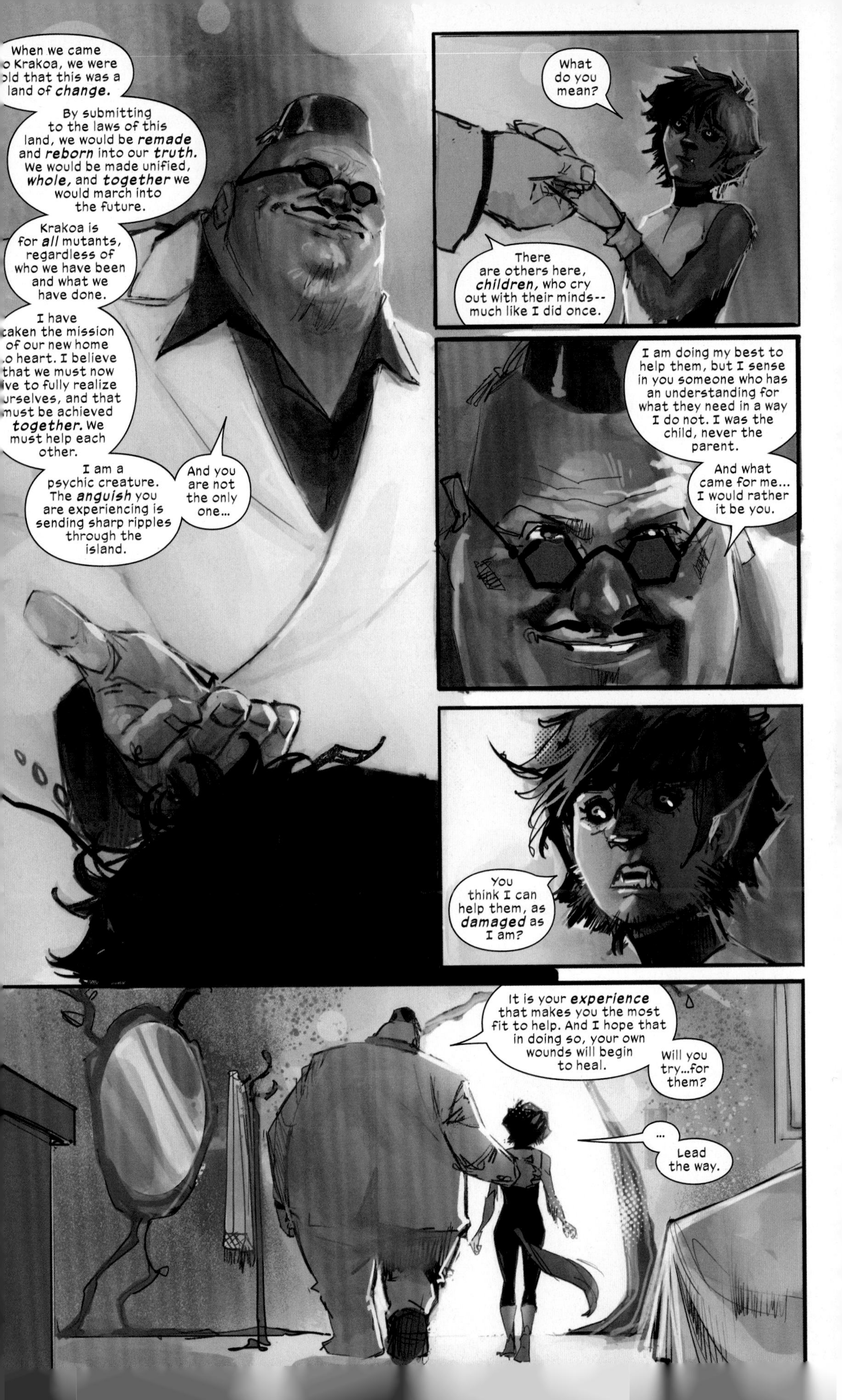
When we came o Krakoa, we were old that this was a land of *change.*
By submitting to the laws of this land, we would be *remade* and *reborn* into our *truth.* We would be made unified, *whole,* and *together* we would march into the future.
Krakoa is for *all* mutants, regardless of who we have been and what we have done.
I have taken the mission of our new home o heart. I believe that we must now ive to fully realize urselves, and that must be achieved *together.* We must help each other.
I am a psychic creature. The *anguish* you are experiencing is sending sharp ripples through the island.
And you are not the only one...
What do you mean?
There are others here, *children,* who cry out with their minds--much like I did once.
I am doing my best to help them, but I sense in you someone who has an understanding for what they need in a way I do not. I was the child, never the parent.
And what came for me... I would rather it be you.
You think I can help them, as *damaged* as I am?
It is your *experience* that makes you the most fit to help. And I hope that in doing so, your own wounds will begin to heal.
Will you try...for them?
...
Lead the way.

[00_synergy_X]
[X__power__00]

WHAT THE LIGHT ILLUMINATES

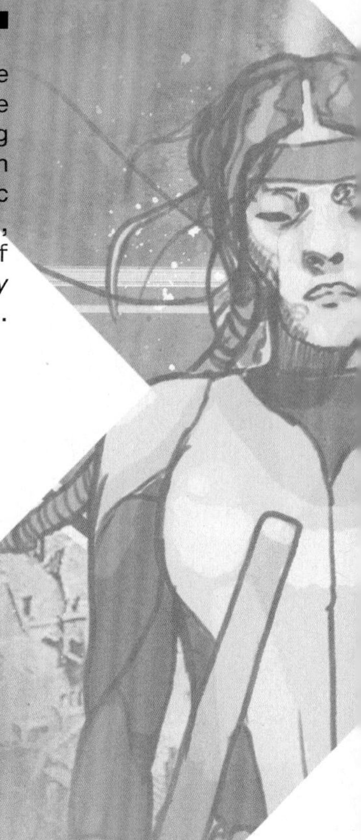

The NEW MUTANTS have been tasked with training the youth of Krakoa -- teaching them to use and combine their mutant abilities! But basic training isn't working for everyone -- a group of young mutants have fallen in with the Shadow King, who's been using his psychic powers to experiment with body-swapping. Meanwhile, Dani and Xi'an's rescue mission to track down one of their missing charges in Otherworld has gone *incredibly* wrong, landing them under the iron fist of the cruel Merlyn.

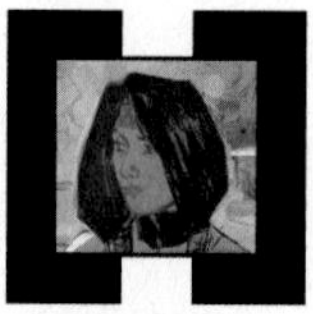
Dani Moonstar

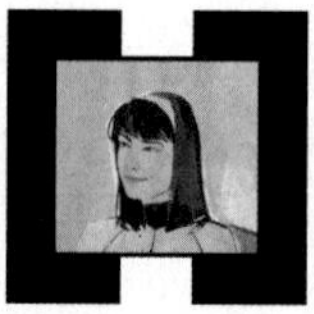
Karma

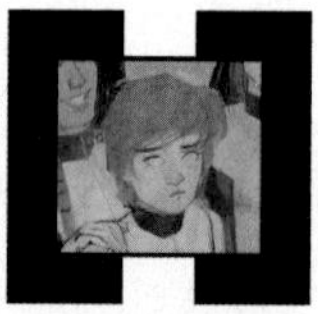
Wolfsbane

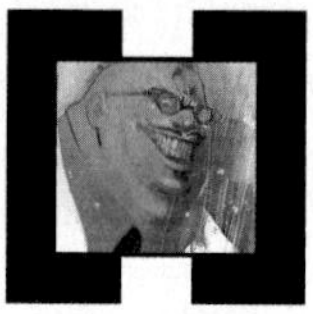
Shadow King

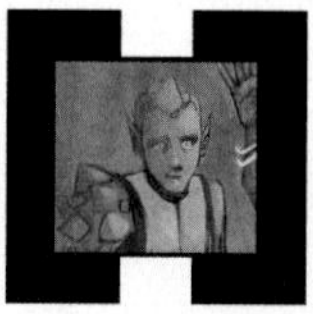
Anole

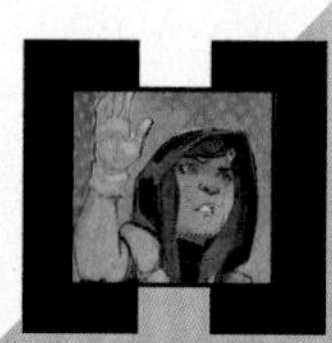
Scout

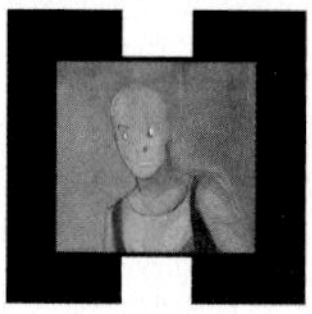
Rain Boy

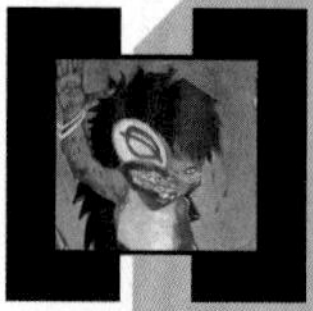
Cosmar

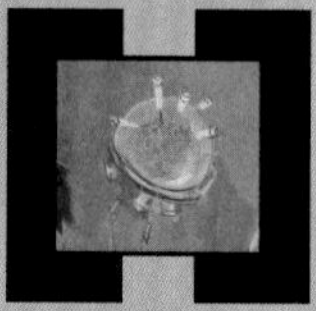
No-Girl

NEW MUTANTS
[X_17]

[ISSUE SEVENTEEN]............................
....................FOLLOW THE WHITE RABBIT

VITA AYALA...[WRITER]
ROD REIS...[ARTIST]
VC's TRAVIS LANHAM...............................[LETTERER]
TOM MULLER..[DESIGN]

CHRISTIAN WARD..............................[COVER ARTIST]

BOB McLEOD..........................[VARIANT COVER ARTIST]

JONATHAN HICKMAN..............................[HEAD OF X]
JAY BOWEN.....................................[PRODUCTION]
ANNALISE BISSA....................................[EDITOR]
JORDAN D. WHITE............................[SENIOR EDITOR]
C.B. CEBULSKI...........................[EDITOR IN CHIEF]

[00___power]

[synergy_XX]

[00_____]

[00_____]

[00_____in]

[00_____the]

[00____wild]

[00____hunt]

A PACT WITH HIS EXCELLENCY MERLYN, RULER OF THE HOLY REPUBLIC OF FAE

The witchbreed blasphemers, Danielle Moonstar and Xi'an Coy Manh, stand accused of crimes against The Holy Republic of Fae. Their crimes include trespassing, threatening the royal guard and speaking out of turn.

The punishment for these crimes: death.

His Excellency Merlyn has chosen mercy, and offered the witchbreed the following alternative:

Danielle Moonstar and Xi'an Coy Manh swear by blood and word, under penalty of instantaneous death, to infiltrate the blasphemous Kingdom of Roma Regina and reclaim a vessel stolen by the Lady Roma.

Success will result in a full pardon of all crimes.

Failure, desertion or any other breach of this pact will result in death by boiling blood.

Should they die during their mission, a posthumous pardon will be granted, as his Excellency is merciful.

This pact is sealed in blood and bound by his Excellency's power.

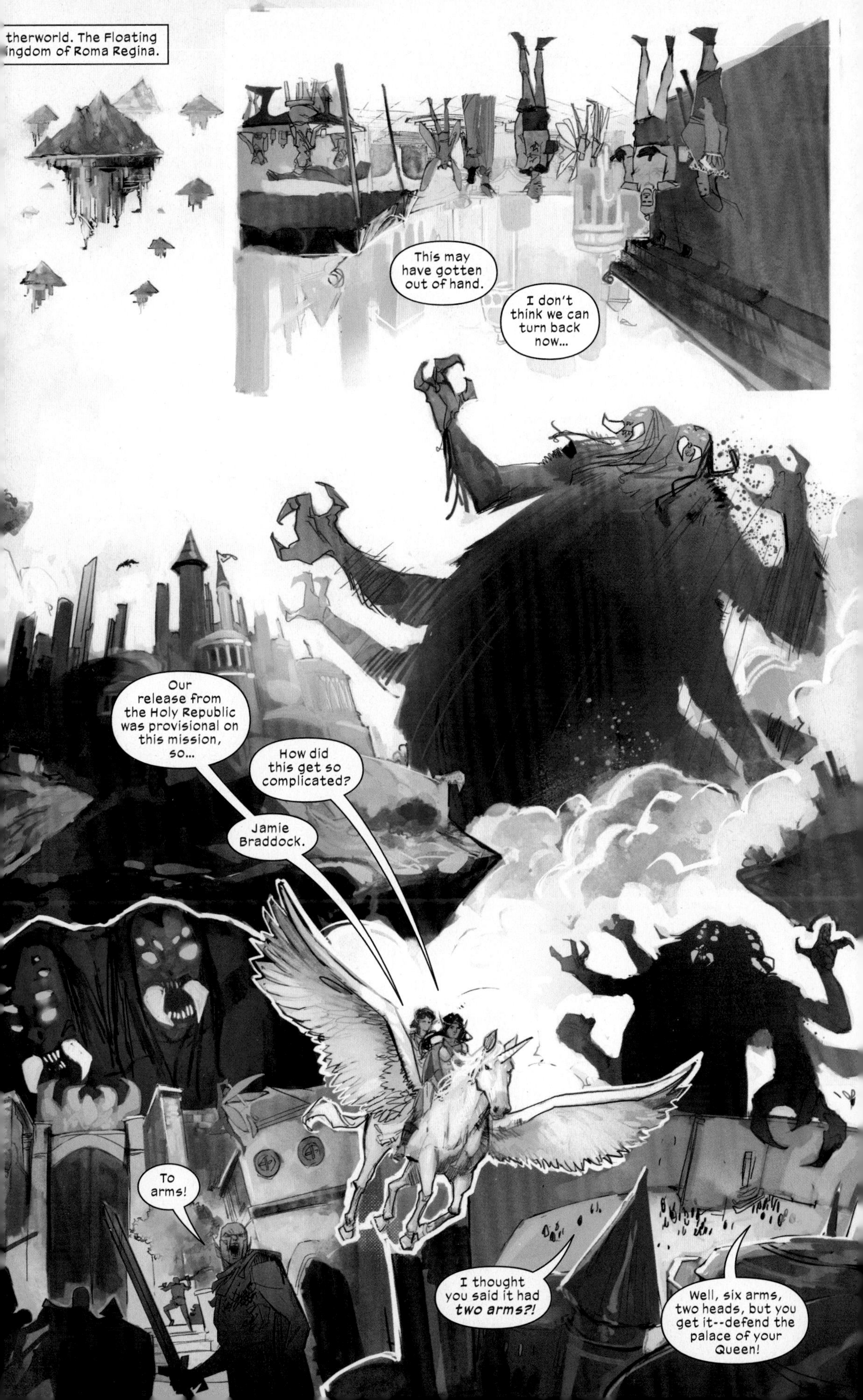
therworld. The Floating
ingdom of Roma Regina.
This may have gotten out of hand.
I don't think we can turn back now...
Our release from the Holy Republic was provisional on this mission, so...
How did this get so complicated?
Jamie Braddock.
To arms!
I thought you said it had *two arms?!*
Well, six arms, two heads, but you get it--defend the palace of your Queen!

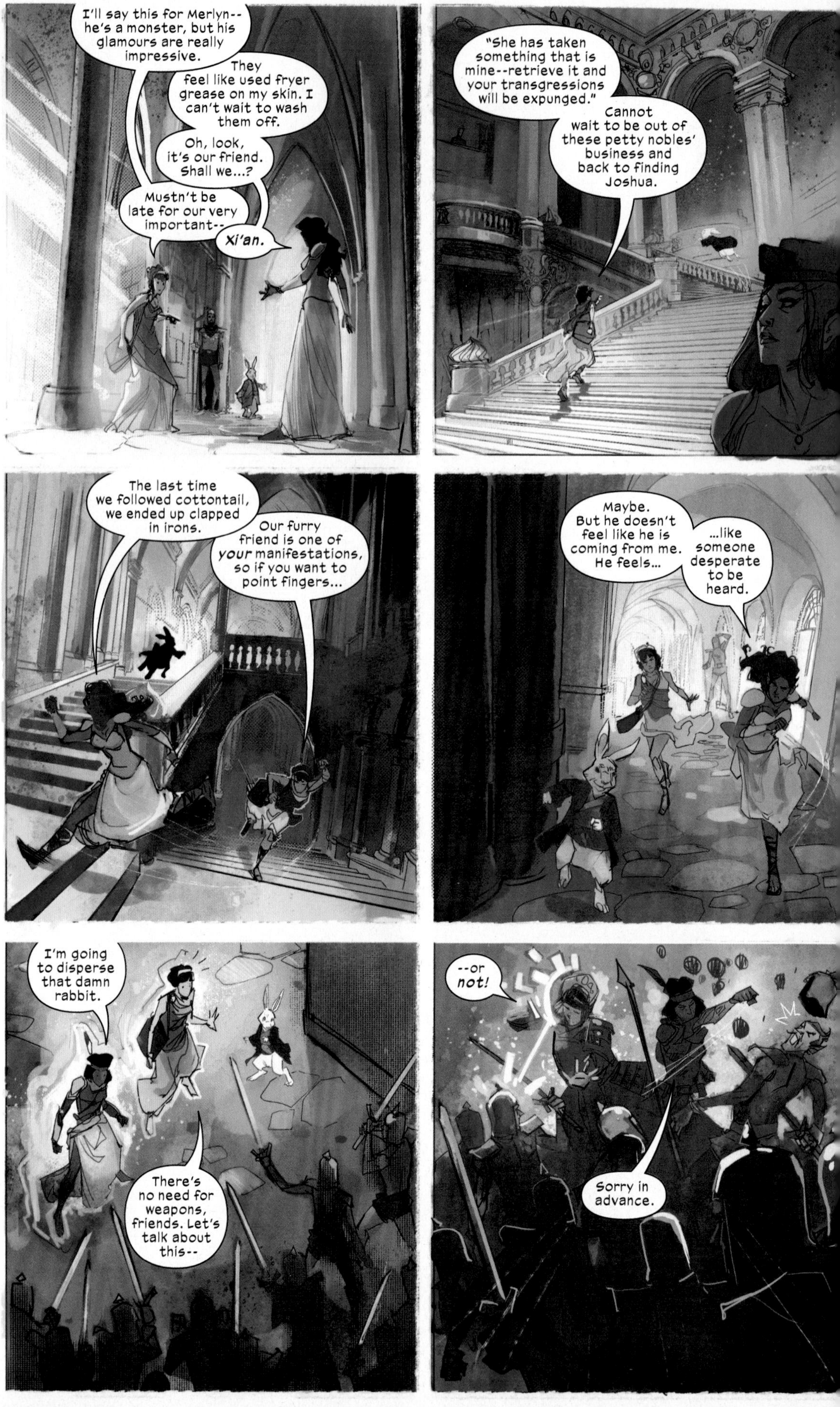
I'll say this for Merlyn--he's a monster, but his glamours are really impressive.
They feel like used fryer grease on my skin. I can't wait to wash them off.
Oh, look, it's our friend. Shall we...?
Mustn't be late for our very important--
Xi'an.
"She has taken something that is mine--retrieve it and your transgressions will be expunged."
Cannot wait to be out of these petty nobles' business and back to finding Joshua.
The last time we followed cottontail, we ended up clapped in irons.
Our furry friend is one of your manifestations, so if you want to point fingers...
Maybe. But he doesn't feel like he is coming from me. He feels...
...like someone desperate to be heard.
I'm going to disperse that damn rabbit.
There's no need for weapons, friends. Let's talk about this--
--or not!
Sorry in advance.

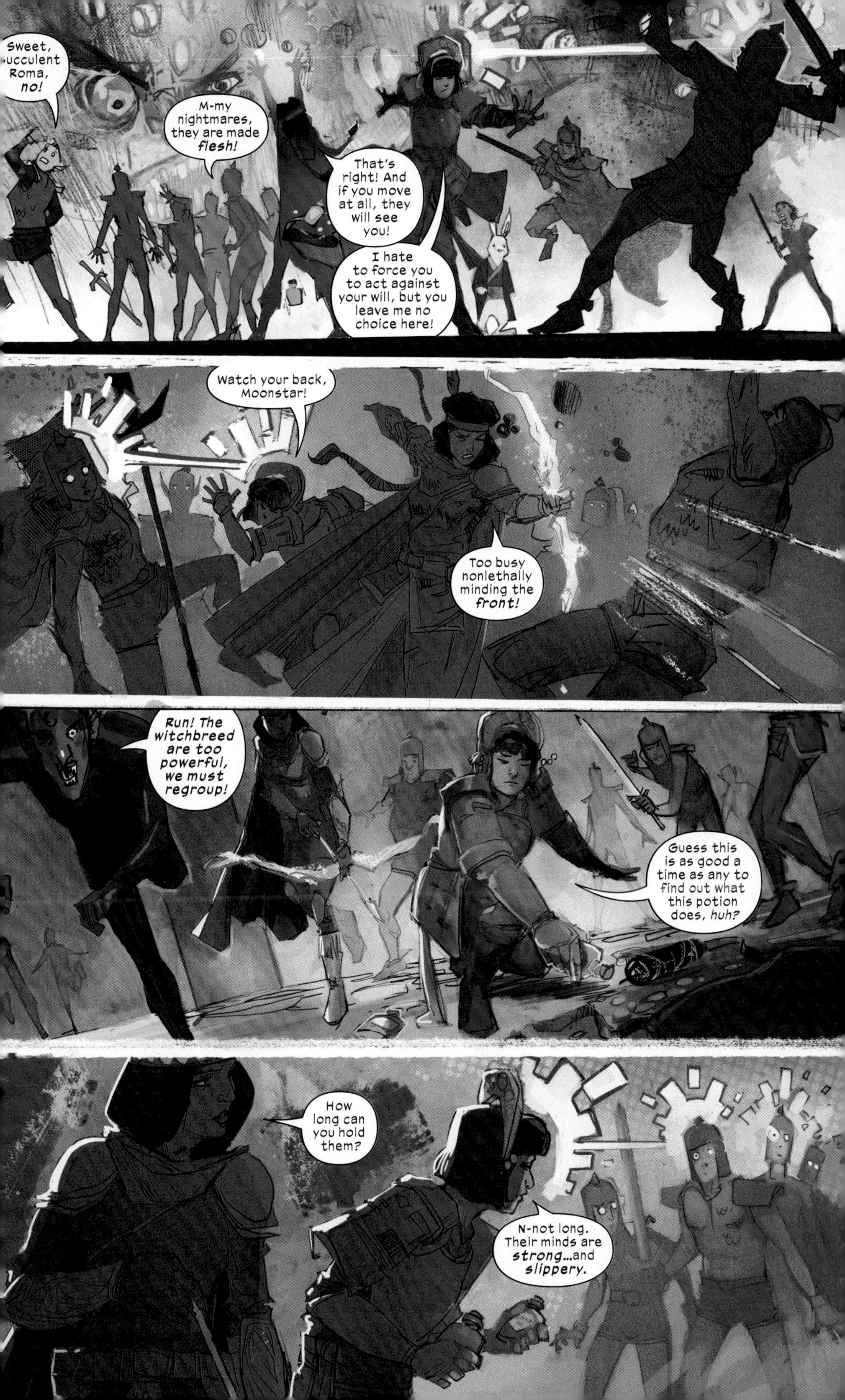

Sweet, succulent Roma, *no!*
M-my nightmares, they are made *flesh!*
That's right! And if you move at all, they will see you!
I hate to force you to act against your will, but you leave me no choice here!
Watch your back, Moonstar!
Too busy nonlethally minding the *front!*
Run! The witchbreed are too powerful, we must regroup!
Guess this is as good a time as any to find out what this potion does, *huh?*
How long can you hold them?
N-not long. Their minds are *strong*...and *slippery.*

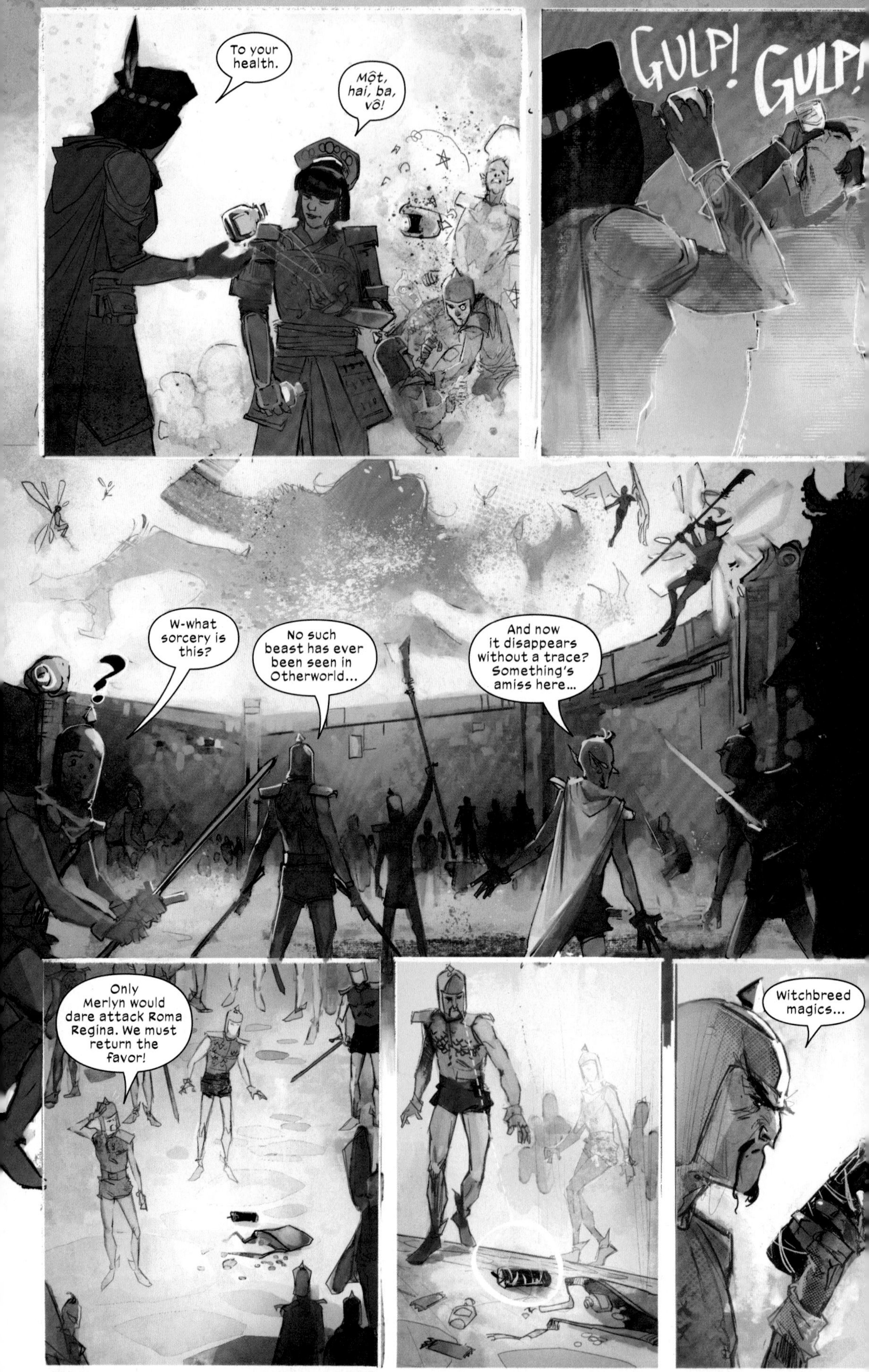
To your health.
Một, hai, ba, vô!
GULP! GULP!
W-what sorcery is this?
No such beast has ever been seen in Otherworld...
And now it disappears without a trace? Something's amiss here...
Only Merlyn would dare attack Roma Regina. We must return the favor!
Witchbreed magics...

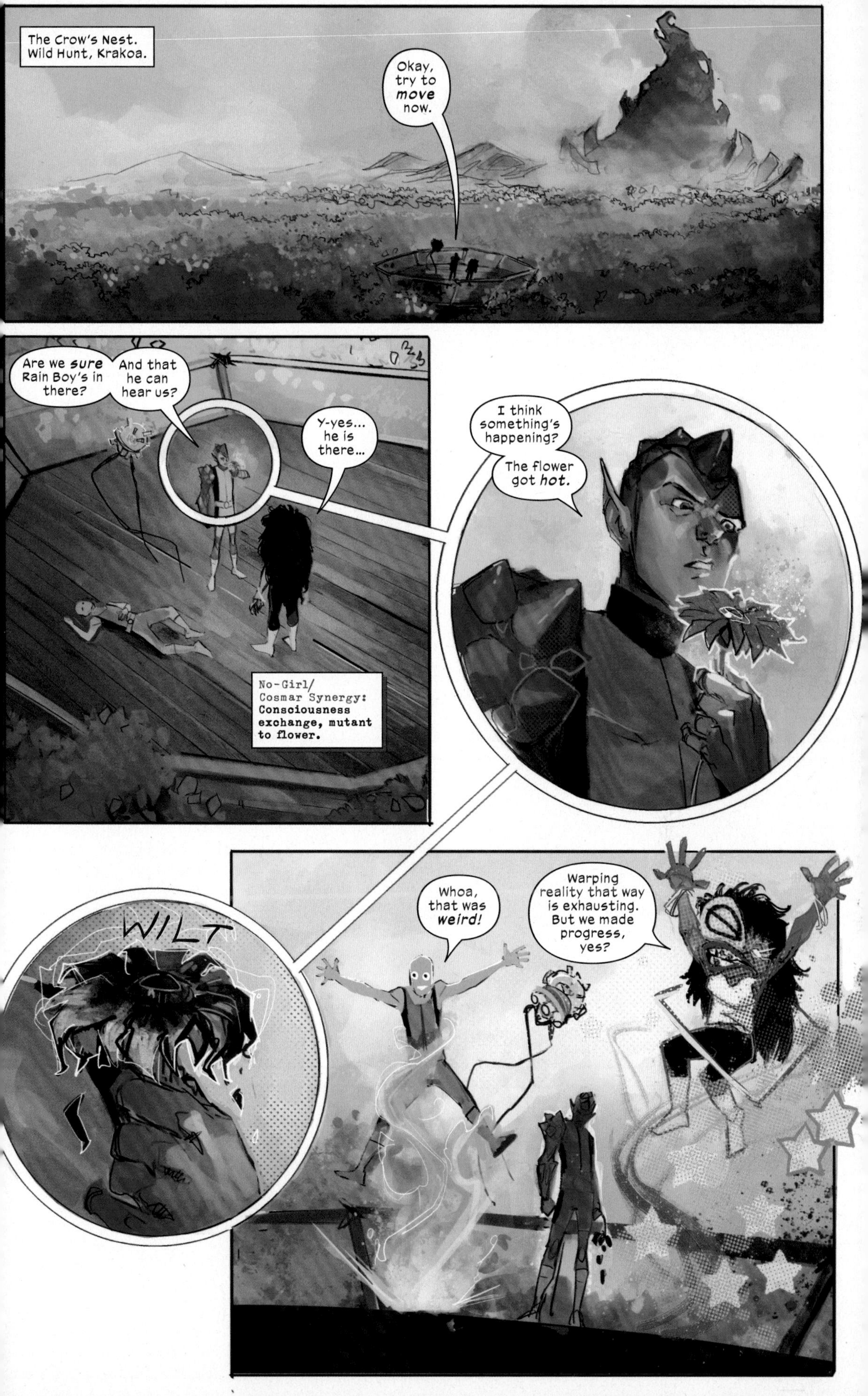
The Crow's Nest.
Wild Hunt, Krakoa.
Okay, try to *move* now.
Are we *sure* Rain Boy's in there?
And that he can hear us?
Y-yes... he is there...
I think something's happening?
The flower got *hot.*
No-Girl/ Cosmar Synergy: **Consciousness exchange, mutant to flower.**
WILT
Whoa, that was *weird!*
Warping reality that way is exhausting. But we made progress, yes?

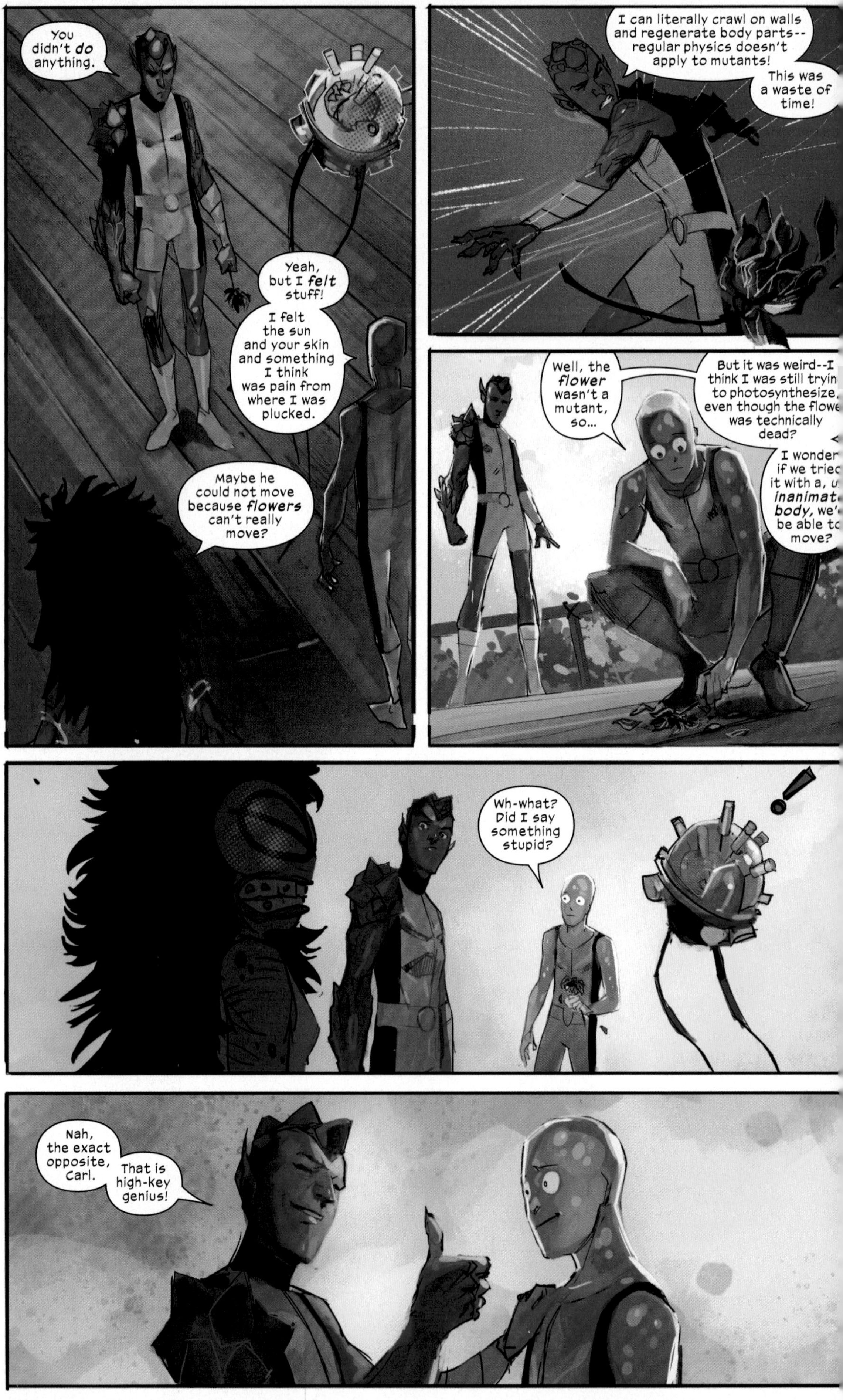
You didn't *do* anything.
Yeah, but I *felt* stuff!
I felt the sun and your skin and something I think was pain from where I was plucked.
Maybe he could not move because *flowers* can't really move?
I can literally crawl on walls and regenerate body parts--regular physics doesn't apply to mutants!
This was a waste of time!
Well, the *flower* wasn't a mutant, so...
But it was weird--I think I was still tryin to photosynthesize, even though the flowe was technically dead?
I wonder if we trie it with a, u *inanimat body,* we' be able t move?
Wh-what? Did I say something stupid?
!
Nah, the exact opposite, Carl.
That is high-key genius!

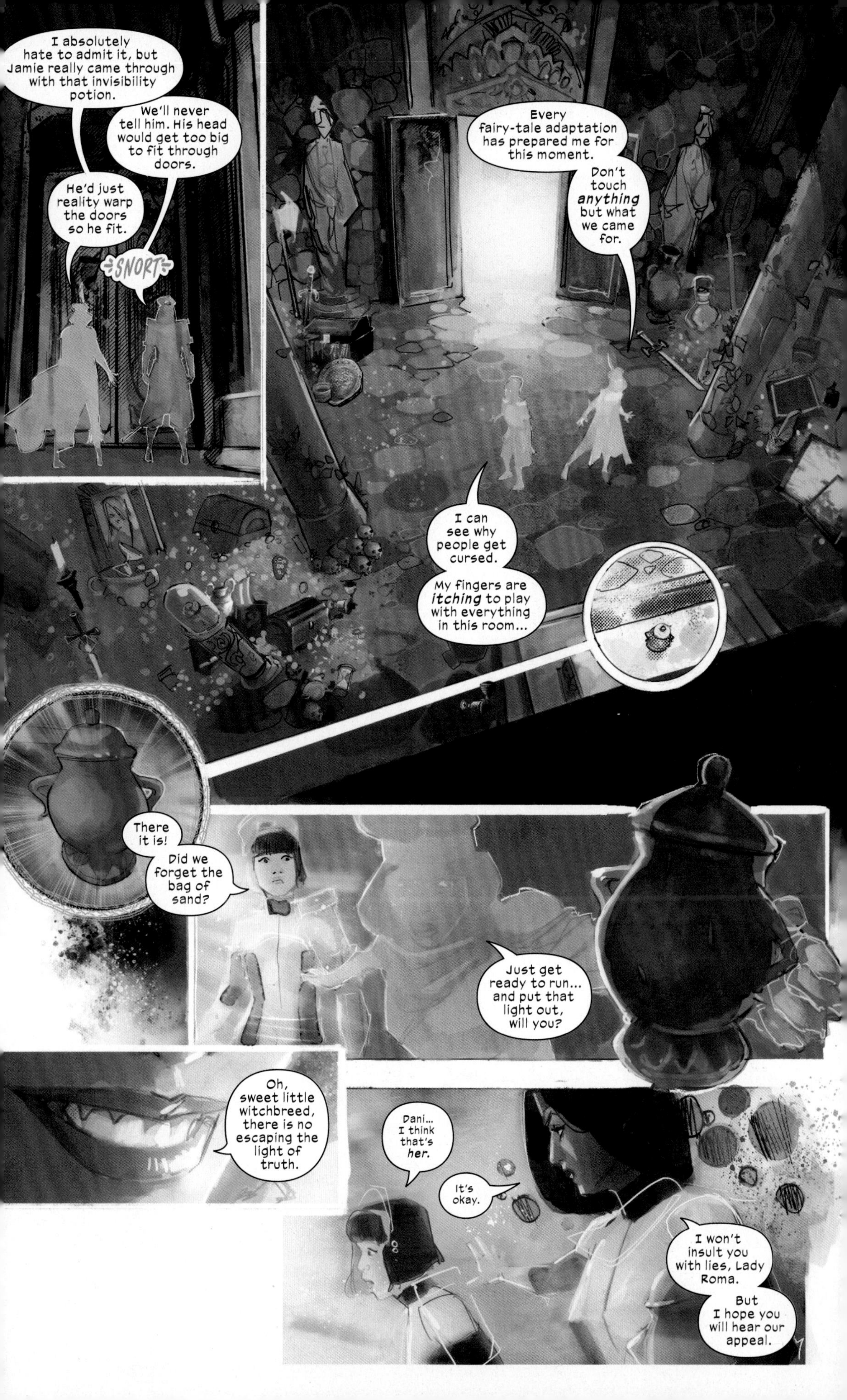

I absolutely hate to admit it, but Jamie really came through with that invisibility potion.
We'll never tell him. His head would get too big to fit through doors.
He'd just reality warp the doors so he fit.
SNORT
Every fairy-tale adaptation has prepared me for this moment.
Don't touch *anything* but what we came for.
I can see why people get cursed.
My fingers are *itching* to play with everything in this room...
There it is!
Did we forget the bag of sand?
Just get ready to run... and put that light out, will you?
Oh, sweet little witchbreed, there is no escaping the light of truth.
Dani... I think that's *her.*
It's okay.
I won't insult you with lies, Lady Roma.
But I hope you will hear our appeal.

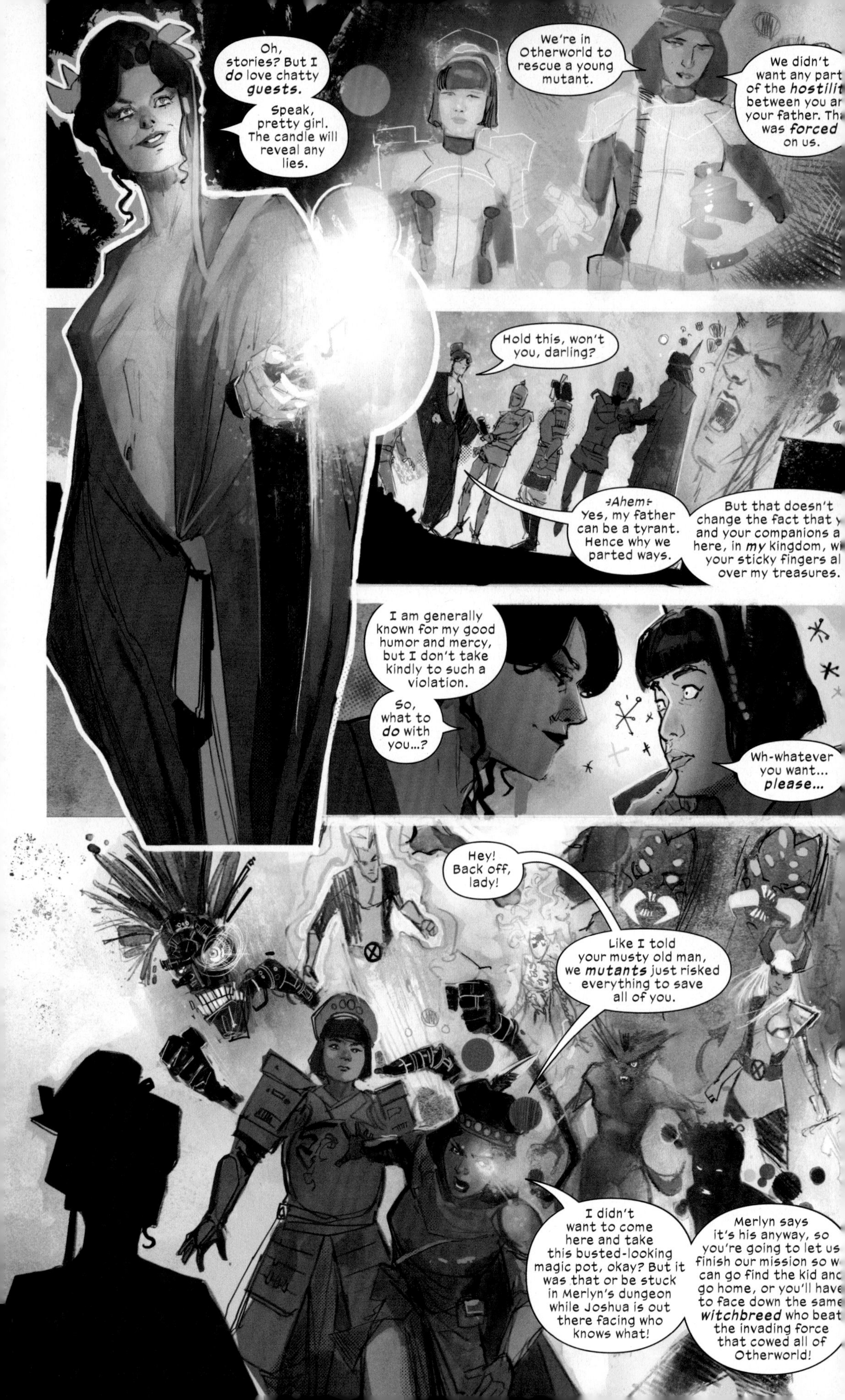
Oh, stories? But I do love chatty guests.
Speak, pretty girl. The candle will reveal any lies.
We're in Otherworld to rescue a young mutant.
We didn't want any part of the hostilit between you ar your father. Th was forced on us.
Hold this, won't you, darling?
=Ahem= Yes, my father can be a tyrant. Hence why we parted ways.
But that doesn't change the fact that y and your companions a here, in my kingdom, w your sticky fingers al over my treasures.
I am generally known for my good humor and mercy, but I don't take kindly to such a violation.
So, what to do with you...?
Wh-whatever you want... please...
Hey! Back off, lady!
Like I told your musty old man, we mutants just risked everything to save all of you.
I didn't want to come here and take this busted-looking magic pot, okay? But it was that or be stuck in Merlyn's dungeon while Joshua is out there facing who knows what!
Merlyn says it's his anyway, so you're going to let us finish our mission so w can go find the kid and go home, or you'll have to face down the same witchbreed who beat the invading force that cowed all of Otherworld!

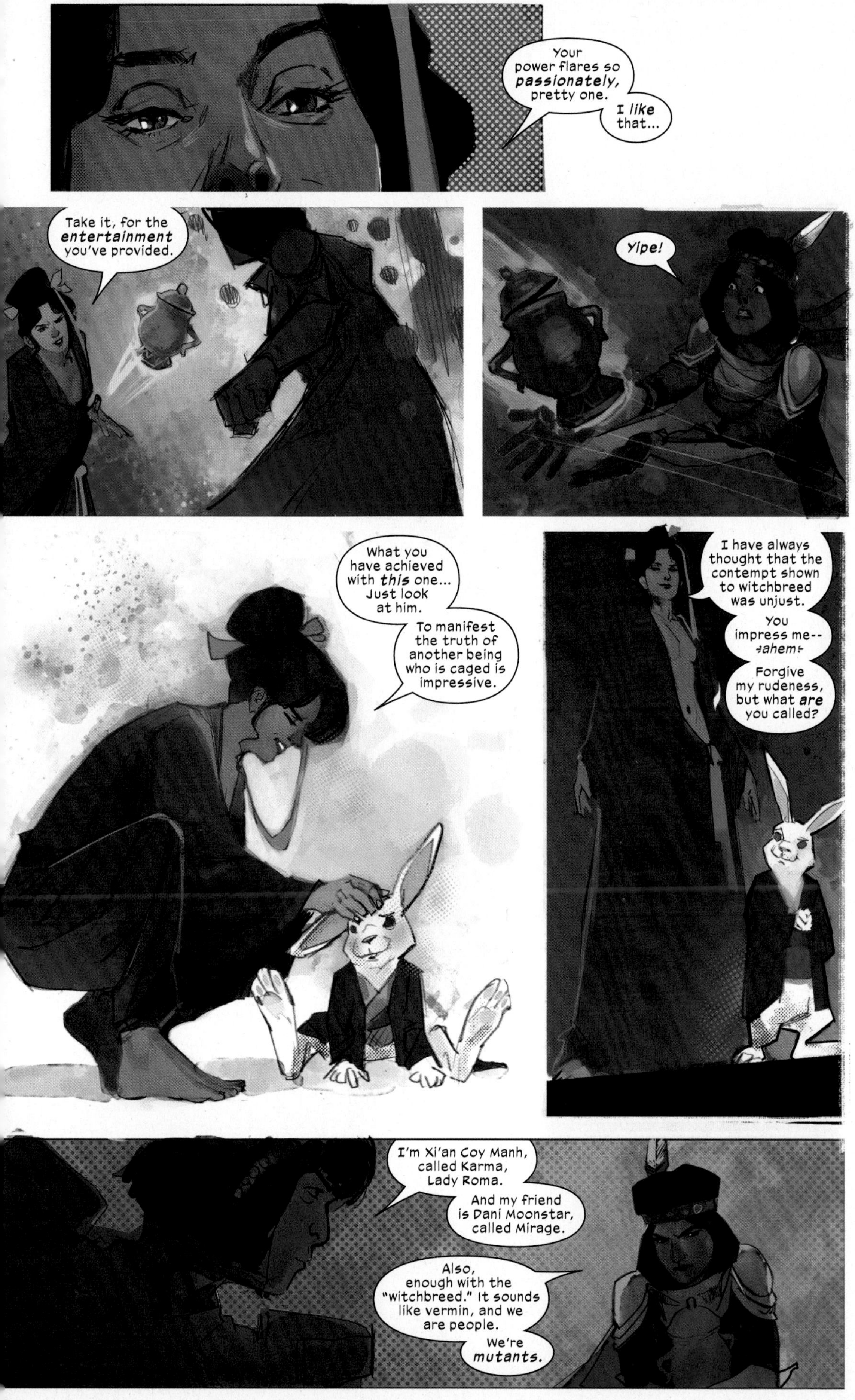
Your power flares so passionately, pretty one.
I like that...
Take it, for the entertainment you've provided.
Yipe!
What you have achieved with this one... Just look at him.
To manifest the truth of another being who is caged is impressive.
I have always thought that the contempt shown to witchbreed was unjust.
You impress me-- ‡ahem‡
Forgive my rudeness, but what are you called?
I'm Xi'an Coy Manh, called Karma, Lady Roma.
And my friend is Dani Moonstar, called Mirage.
Also, enough with the "witchbreed." It sounds like vermin, and we are people.
We're mutants.

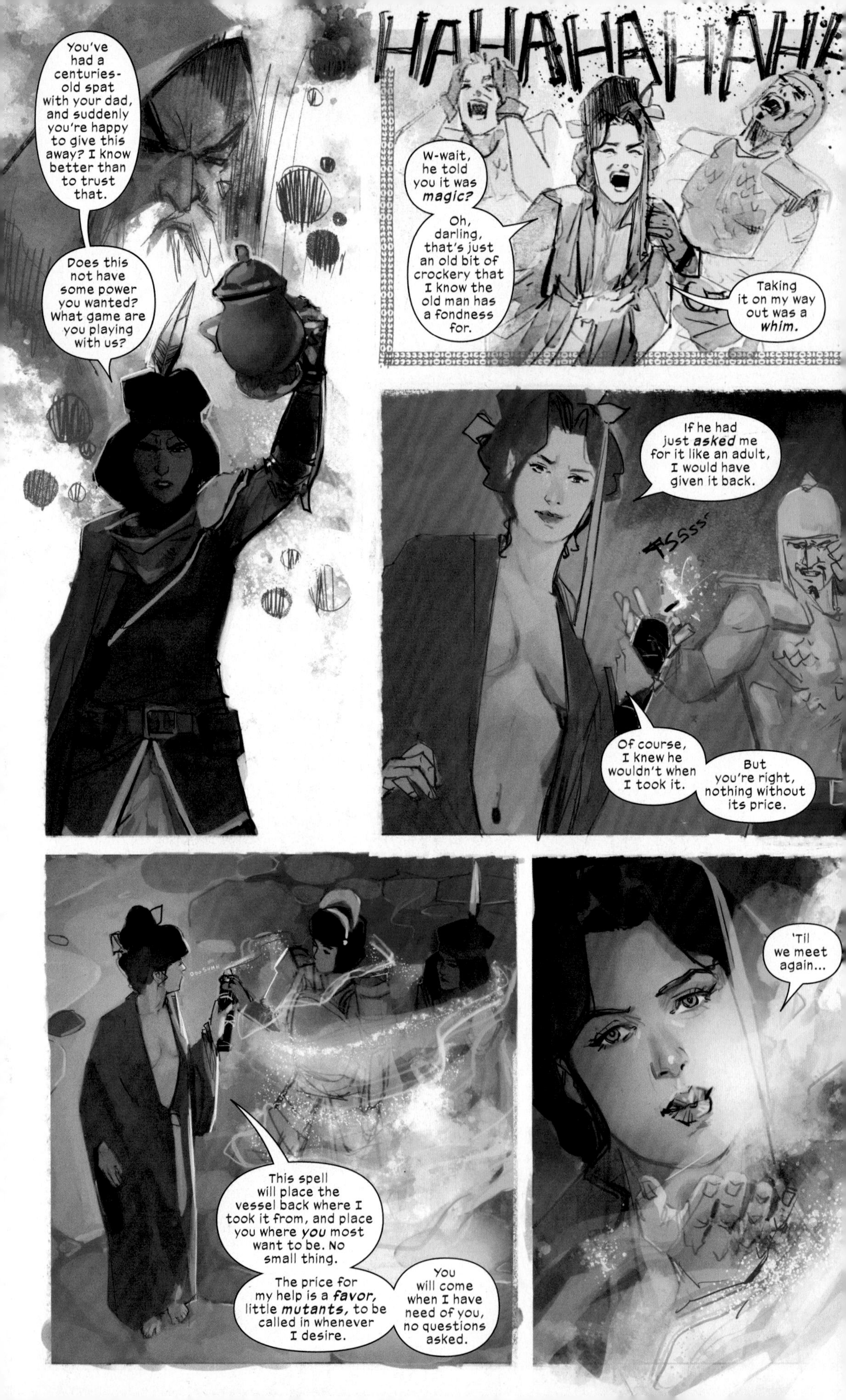
You've had a centuries-old spat with your dad, and suddenly you're happy to give this away? I know better than to trust that.
Does this not have some power you wanted? What game are you playing with us?
HAHAHAHAHAHA
W-wait, he told you it was *magic?*
Oh, darling, that's just an old bit of crockery that I know the old man has a fondness for.
Taking it on my way out was a *whim.*
If he had just *asked* me for it like an adult, I would have given it back.
TSSSS
Of course, I knew he wouldn't when I took it.
But you're right, nothing without its price.
This spell will place the vessel back where I took it from, and place you where *you* most want to be. No small thing.
The price for my help is a *favor,* little *mutants,* to be called in whenever I desire.
You will come when I have need of you, no questions asked.
'Til we meet again...

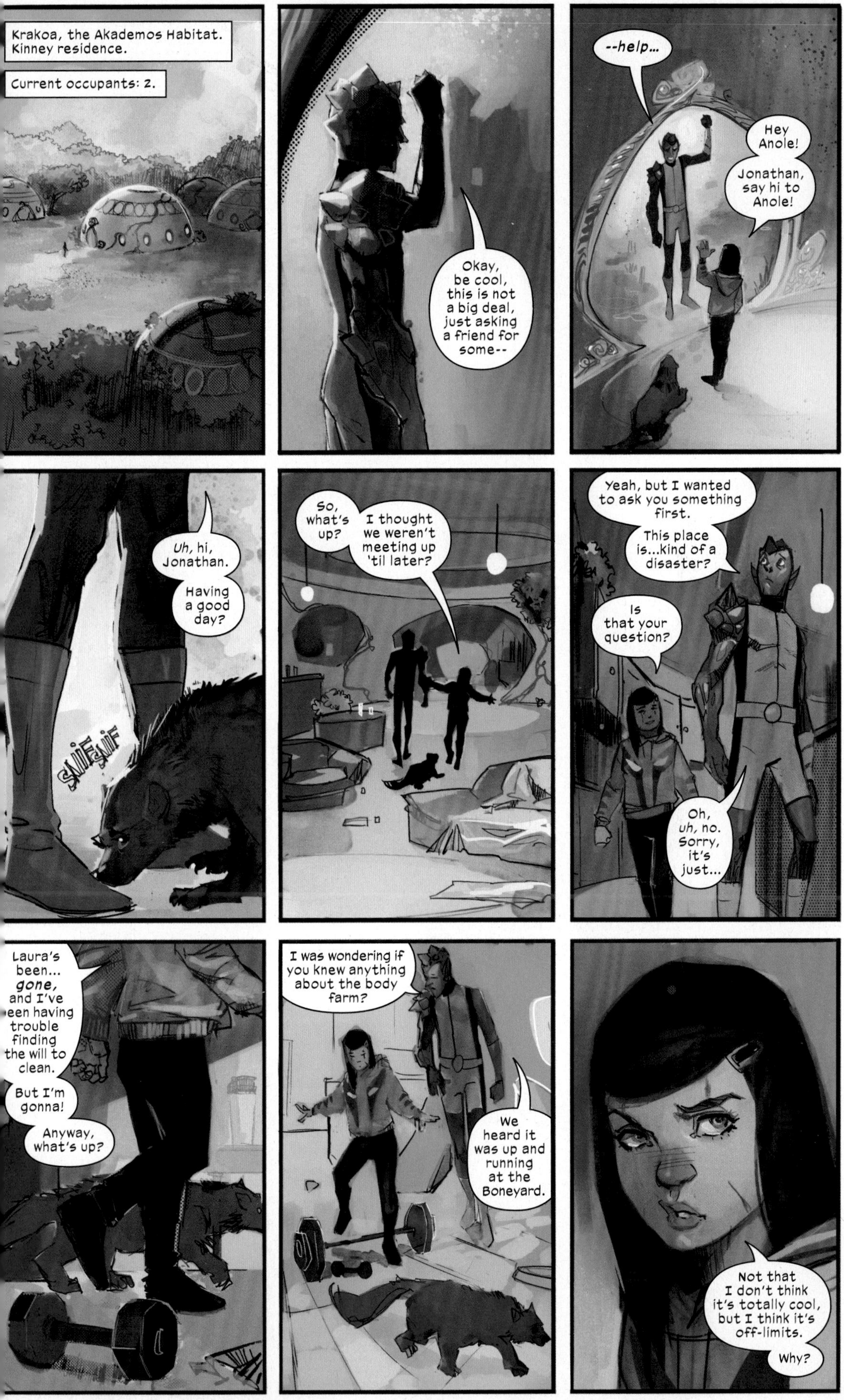

Krakoa, the Akademos Habitat. Kinney residence.
Current occupants: 2.
Okay, be cool, this is not a big deal, just asking a friend for some--
--help...
Hey Anole!
Jonathan, say hi to Anole!
Uh, hi, Jonathan.
Having a good day?
SNIFSNIF
So, what's up?
I thought we weren't meeting up 'til later?
Yeah, but I wanted to ask you something first.
This place is...kind of a disaster?
Is that your question?
Oh, uh, no. Sorry, it's just...
Laura's been... gone, and I've een having trouble finding the will to clean.
But I'm gonna!
Anyway, what's up?
I was wondering if you knew anything about the body farm?
We heard it was up and running at the Boneyard.
Not that I don't think it's totally cool, but I think it's off-limits.
Why?

TL;DR, we've been experimenting with trading consciousness some more.

We managed a flower, but it was kind of weak because they don't move.

But we think if we use a formerly mobile vessel, we'd be able to really control things!

And you want to use other people's bodies without asking them?

Why not just get a husk?

Husks are for resurrection-- they wouldn't let us have one.

Besides, you saw what happened with Cosmar at the party. What we need isn't a priority to *them.**

*In New Mutants #15! --AB

Okay, this is a *really* bad idea.

First, it feels weird to take someone's body without them knowing, and, *also*, it could go *wrong*...

Oh, so it's fine for X-Factor to toss the bodies around and watch them *rot* but not okay for us to include them in trying to *be better*?

You don't get what it's like! Having your body make people recoil when they see you or look at you with pity-- even *here!*

Yeah, but--

NO. No "but," not when *you* can pass for a human girl.

Not that we *want* to be human, but maybe we want to be beautiful. And that isn't immoral.

Just because I can hide my claws doesn't mean I don't know what it feels like to have my body be out of my control.

I-it's not the *same*, Gabby.

Also, uh, the people who made you think that you aren't beautiful are idiots. I love the way you look-- all of you.

I know that isn't comforting right now, but that's what we're *here* for. To be *ourselves*, to not have to care what *they* think.

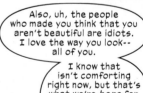

...yeah okay.

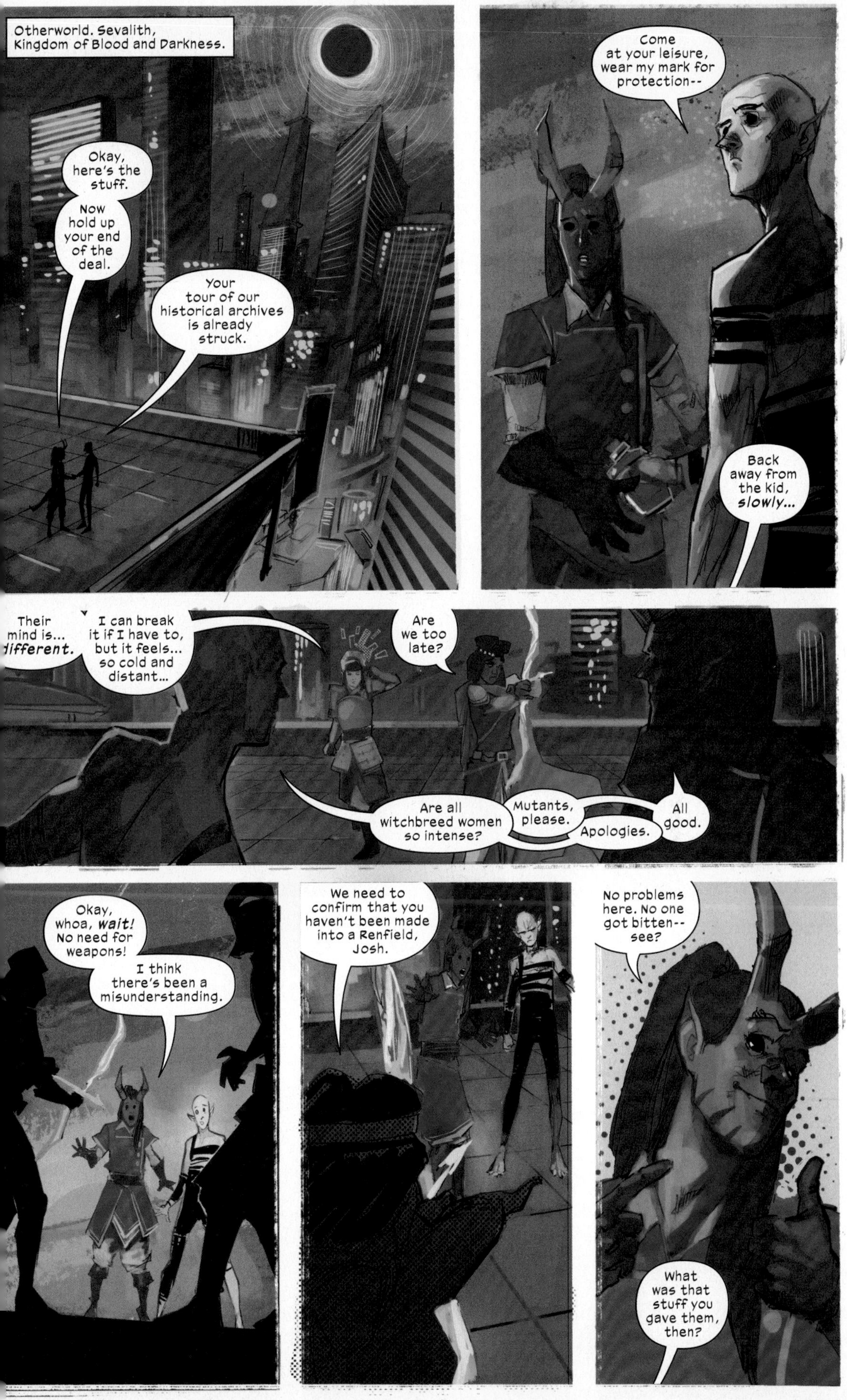
Otherworld. Sevalith, Kingdom of Blood and Darkness.
Okay, here's the stuff.
Now hold up your end of the deal.
Your tour of our historical archives is already struck.
Come at your leisure, wear my mark for protection--
Back away from the kid, slowly...
Their mind is... different.
I can break it if I have to, but it feels... so cold and distant...
Are we too late?
Are all witchbreed women so intense?
Mutants, please.
Apologies.
All good.
Okay, whoa, wait! No need for weapons!
I think there's been a misunderstanding.
We need to confirm that you haven't been made into a Renfield, Josh.
No problems here. No one got bitten-- see?
What was that stuff you gave them, then?

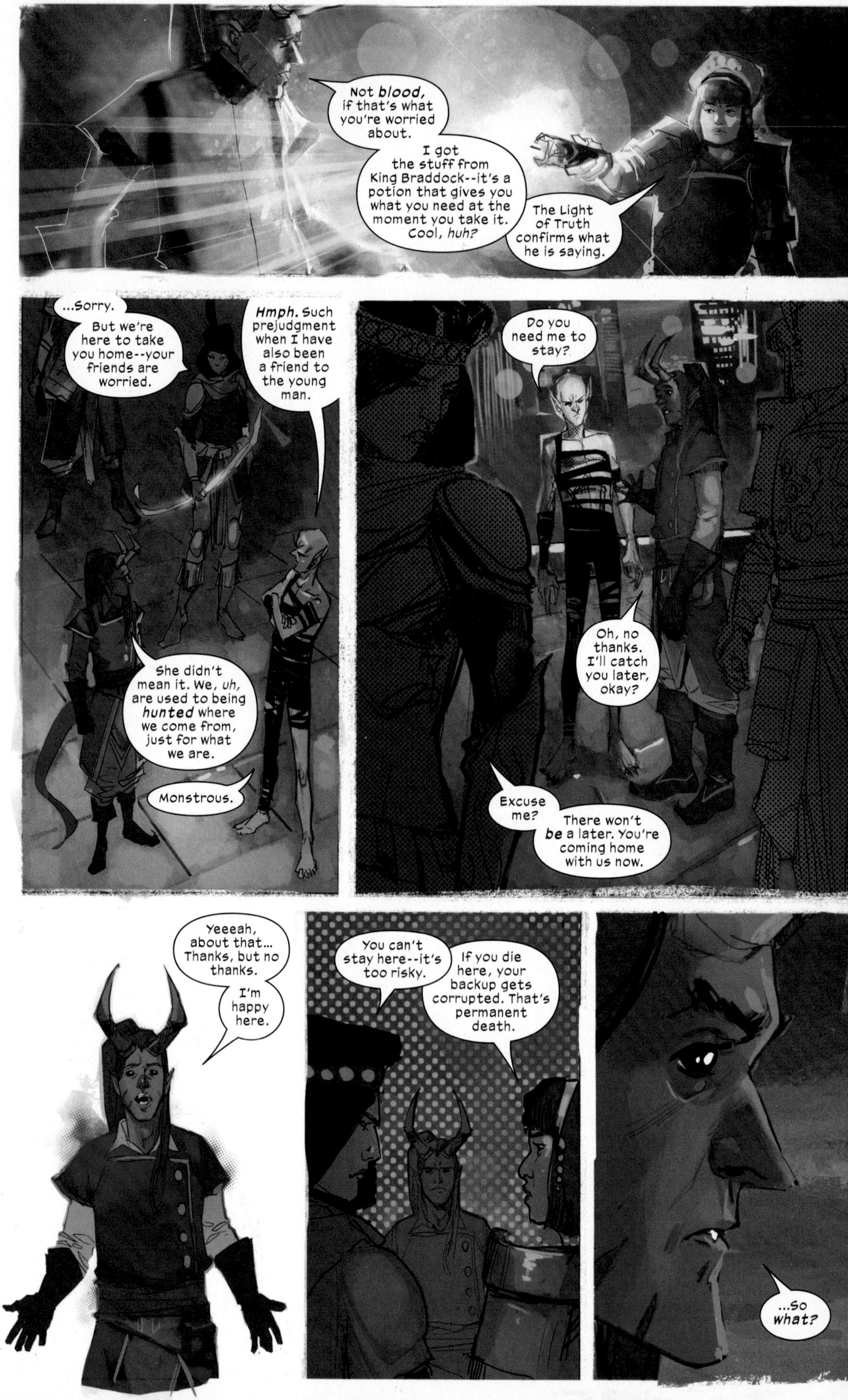

Not *blood,* if that's what you're worried about.
I got the stuff from King Braddock--it's a potion that gives you what you need at the moment you take it. Cool, *huh?*
The Light of Truth confirms what he is saying.
...Sorry.
But we're here to take you home--your friends are worried.
Hmph. Such prejudgment when I have also been a friend to the young man.
She didn't mean it. We, *uh,* are used to being ***hunted*** where we come from, just for what we are.
Monstrous.
Do you need me to stay?
Oh, no thanks. I'll catch you later, okay?
Excuse me?
There won't ***be*** a later. You're coming home with us now.
Yeeeah, about that... Thanks, but no thanks.
I'm happy here.
You can't stay here--it's too risky.
If you die here, your backup gets corrupted. That's permanent death.
...So ***what?***

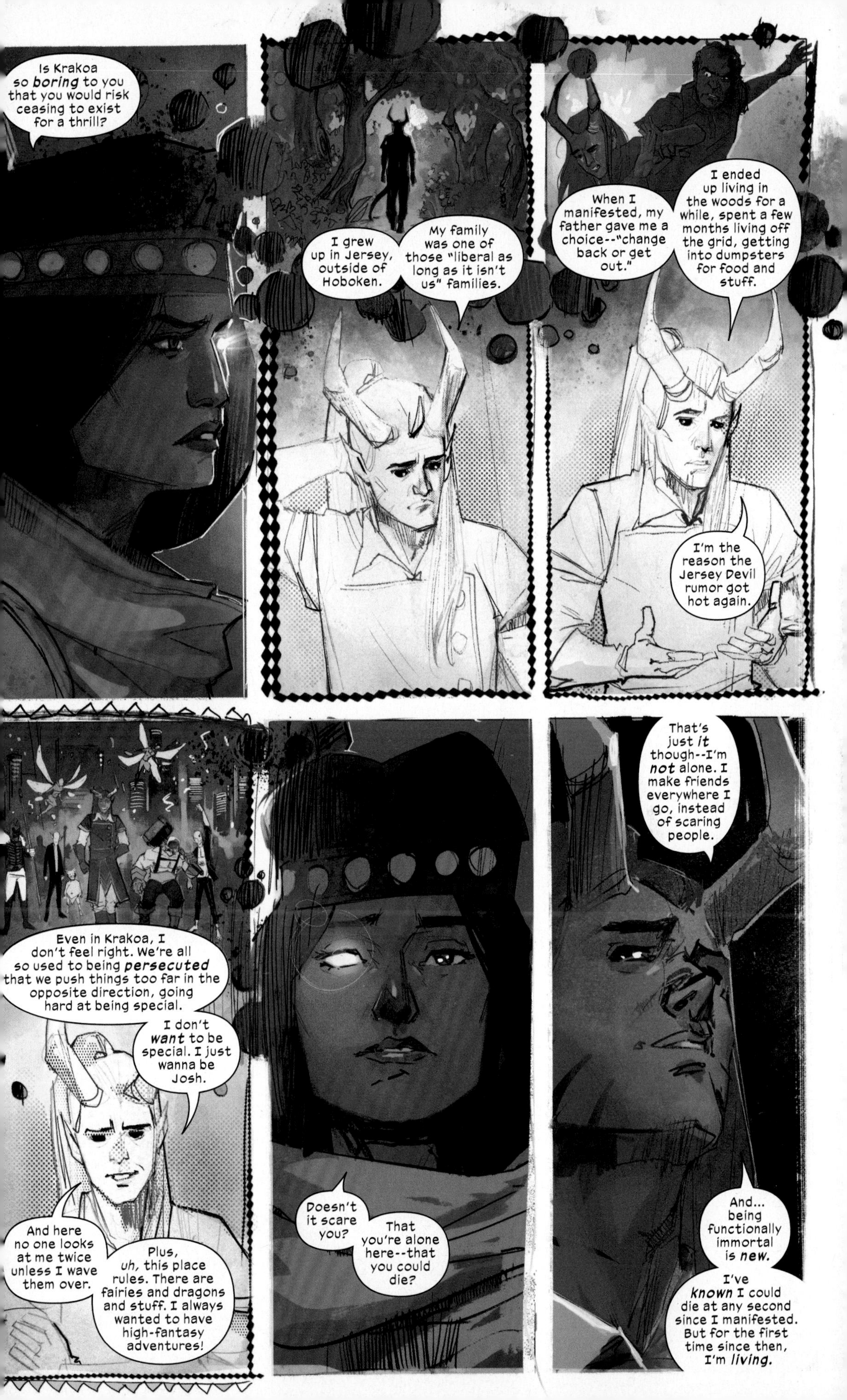

Is Krakoa so boring to you that you would risk ceasing to exist for a thrill?
I grew up in Jersey, outside of Hoboken.
My family was one of those "liberal as long as it isn't us" families.
When I manifested, my father gave me a choice--"change back or get out."
I ended up living in the woods for a while, spent a few months living off the grid, getting into dumpsters for food and stuff.
I'm the reason the Jersey Devil rumor got hot again.
Even in Krakoa, I don't feel right. We're all so used to being persecuted that we push things too far in the opposite direction, going hard at being special.
I don't want to be special. I just wanna be Josh.
And here no one looks at me twice unless I wave them over.
Plus, uh, this place rules. There are fairies and dragons and stuff. I always wanted to have high-fantasy adventures!
Doesn't it scare you?
That you're alone here--that you could die?
That's just it though--I'm not alone. I make friends everywhere I go, instead of scaring people.
And... being functionally immortal is new.
I've known I could die at any second since I manifested. But for the first time since then, I'm living.

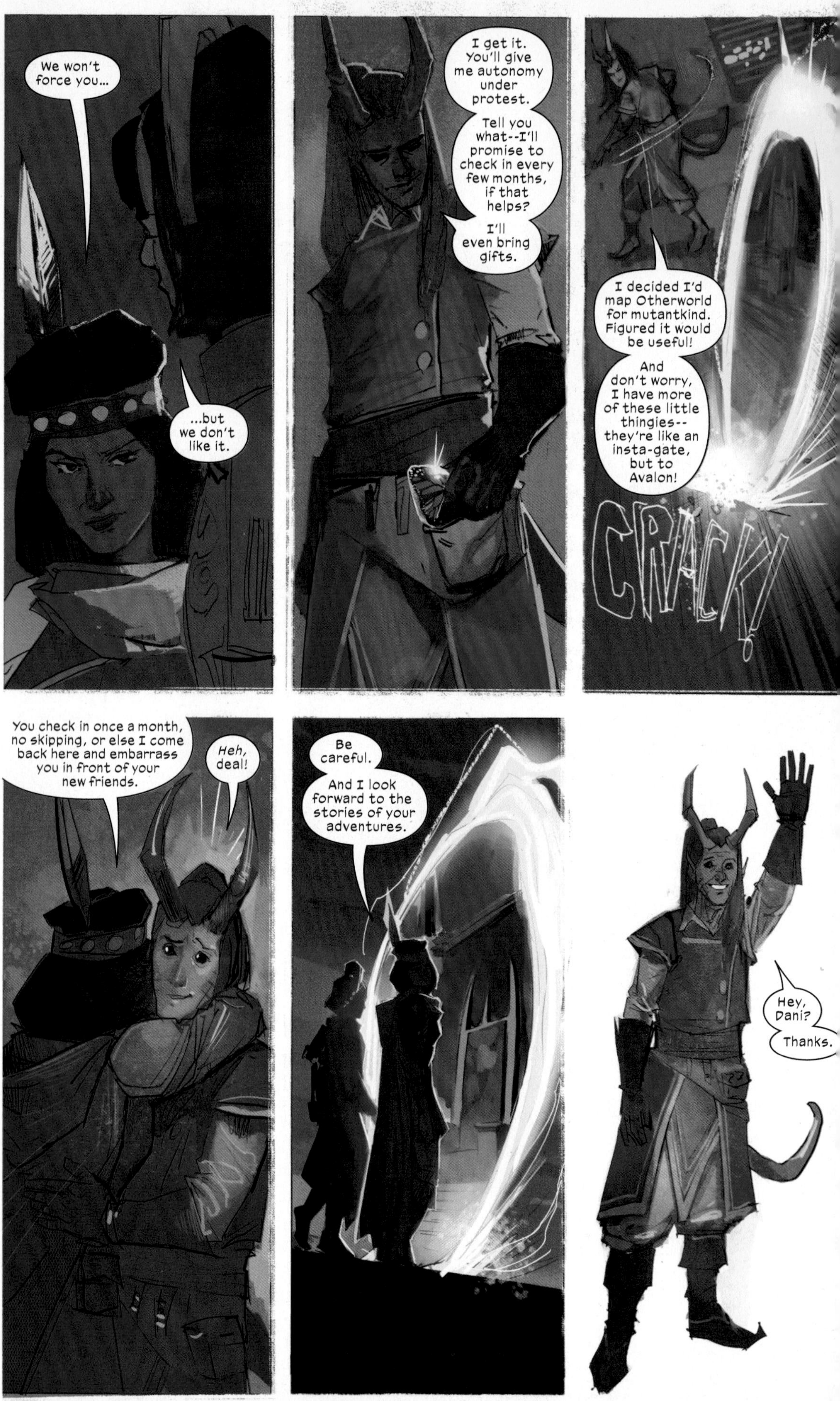

We won't force you...
...but we don't like it.
I get it. You'll give me autonomy under protest.
Tell you what--I'll promise to check in every few months, if that helps?
I'll even bring gifts.
I decided I'd map Otherworld for mutantkind. Figured it would be useful!
And don't worry, I have more of these little thingies--they're like an insta-gate, but to Avalon!
CRACK!
You check in once a month, no skipping, or else I come back here and embarrass you in front of your new friends.
Heh, deal!
Be careful.
And I look forward to the stories of your adventures.
Hey, Dani?
Thanks.

WARPATH JOURNAL, ENTRY 003

Write down all the compliments you can remember that you've received.

I have gotten many compliments over my life, so recounting them all isn't useful here. But some that I go back to in my mind are the following:

Domino tells me I fill out my uniform well. It's a vain joy, but I would be lying if I said it didn't make me feel good.

Wolverine once told me that of all the people who threw him in a Fastball Special, I was the most mindful of his body, and that I could "toss him any time."

Silver Samurai once told me he enjoys my knifework.

Write about something that is frustrating to you.

I don't like the idea of talking out of school, so to speak, but, this space may be useful as a tool to examine my reactions.

Lately, Warlock has taken to avoiding Cypher, and instead is following others around, imitating the way we move, look and sometimes speak.

I understand that he is not mocking us -- while he has a well-developed sense of humor, it is mostly at his own expense. He isn't the kind of being that finds fun in cruelty. It reminds me of a child trying to find their own identity through play, which isn't a bad thing, but something about his behavior irks me.

If I wasn't currently training groups of mutants (of various ages) without the bothersome feeling, I would say it is because I don't do well with certain stages of learning/self-exploration, but that isn't it.

I am a person of action -- I confront things that need confronting and deal with them head on -- but I haven't here, and that bothers me almost more than Warlock. His sincerity and confusion are too much to look at sometimes, and I don't know if confrontation is what he needs right now.

So I am not able to act, just observe. Which is...very frustrating.

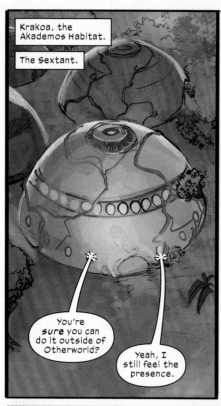

Krakoa, the Akademos Habitat.

The Sextant.

You're *sure* you can do it outside of Otherworld?

Yeah, I still feel the presence.

We don't know if your theory is right.

Yes, I'm manifesting some sort of psychic entity, but there is no way to be sure if it is connected to you, let alone that it is your brother.

You absorbed him so thoroughly, I don't know that I could connect with him through that.

But if it is...are you *sure* this is what you want?

Do you trust me?

You have to ask?

What you've been through... it weighs heavy.

You have done what you needed to do to survive.

Yes, I have. But Krakoa is about *more* than just surviving, isn't it?

≠sigh≠ What makes you think it's him?

When we were children, Tran and I were obsessed with fairy tales.

They were a way to escape the pain we experienced and to explain the things we feared.

His favorite was about the rabbit on the moon.

I think the concept that there was a place that was safe and magical... close enough to see but too far to be intruded on by anyone...

He connected deeply to that idea.

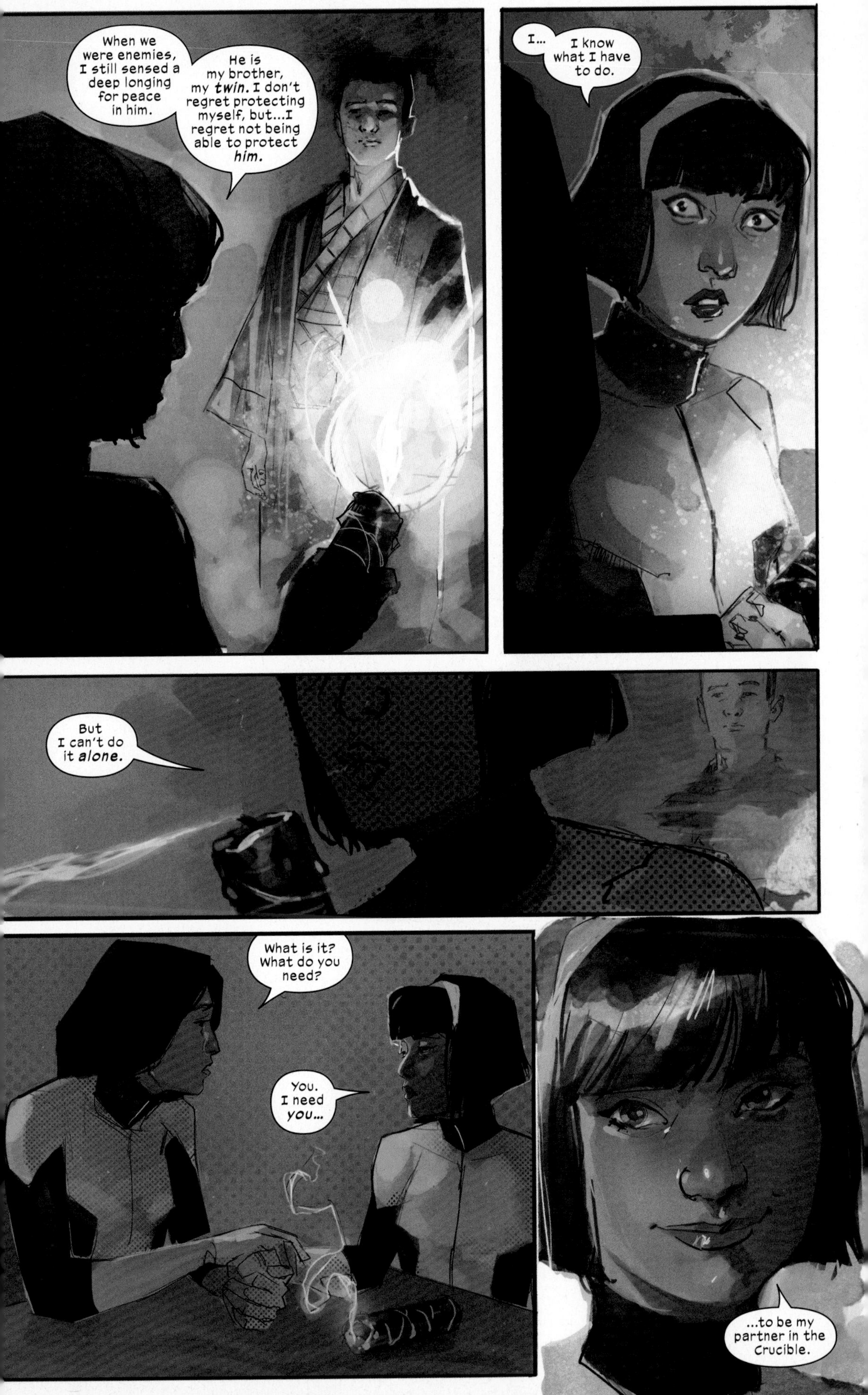
When we were enemies, I still sensed a deep longing for peace in him.
He is my brother, my *twin.* I don't regret protecting myself, but...I regret not being able to protect *him.*
I...
I know what I have to do.
But I can't do it *alone.*
What is it? What do you need?
You. I need *you...*
...to be my partner in the Crucible.

[reign_of_x]

[kra_]
[koa_]

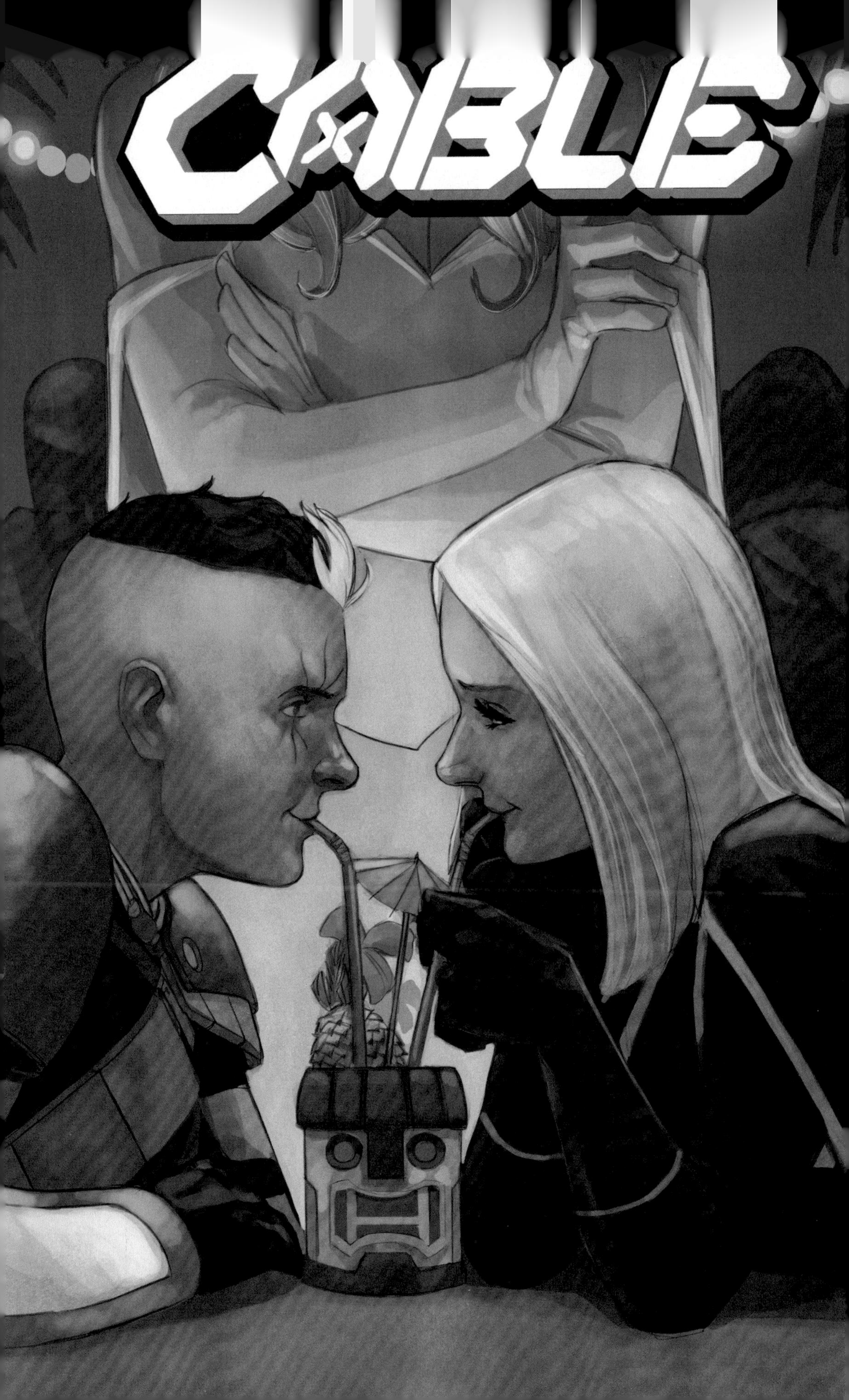
CABLE

[ca__[0.9]
[ble_[0.9]

Cable? Everybody was scared of
the old man...nobody is scared
of the kid.

-- ANONYMOUS PATRON AT
THE GREEN LAGOON

[ca__[0.X]
[ble_[0.X]

[ca__[0.9].....]
[ble_[0.9].....]

[Cable_alpha.]

We detected her off the coast of Krakoa 25 minutes ago.

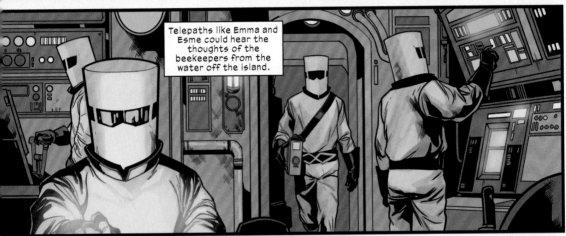

Telepaths like Emma and Esme could hear the thoughts of the beekeepers from the water off the island.

REACTOR ROOM

Usually we just ignore them, but today they came within 100 meters, so we decided to have some *fun*.

Hey! That's a no-go zone.

You're a no-go zone.

Don't worry-- our reactor inspection went great!

'Sup, guys.
How's your head?
Wha--
KLONK
UGHNN!
Alert! Alert! Power levels are dropping!
Heh.
KLIK
TORPEDO LAUNCH

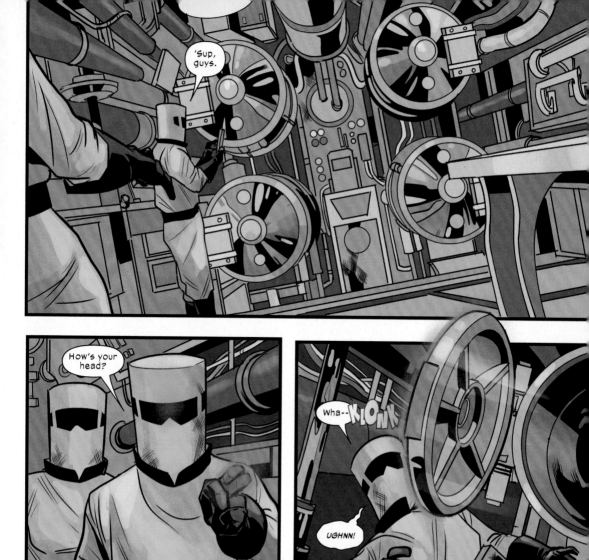

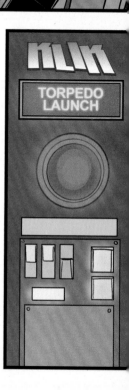

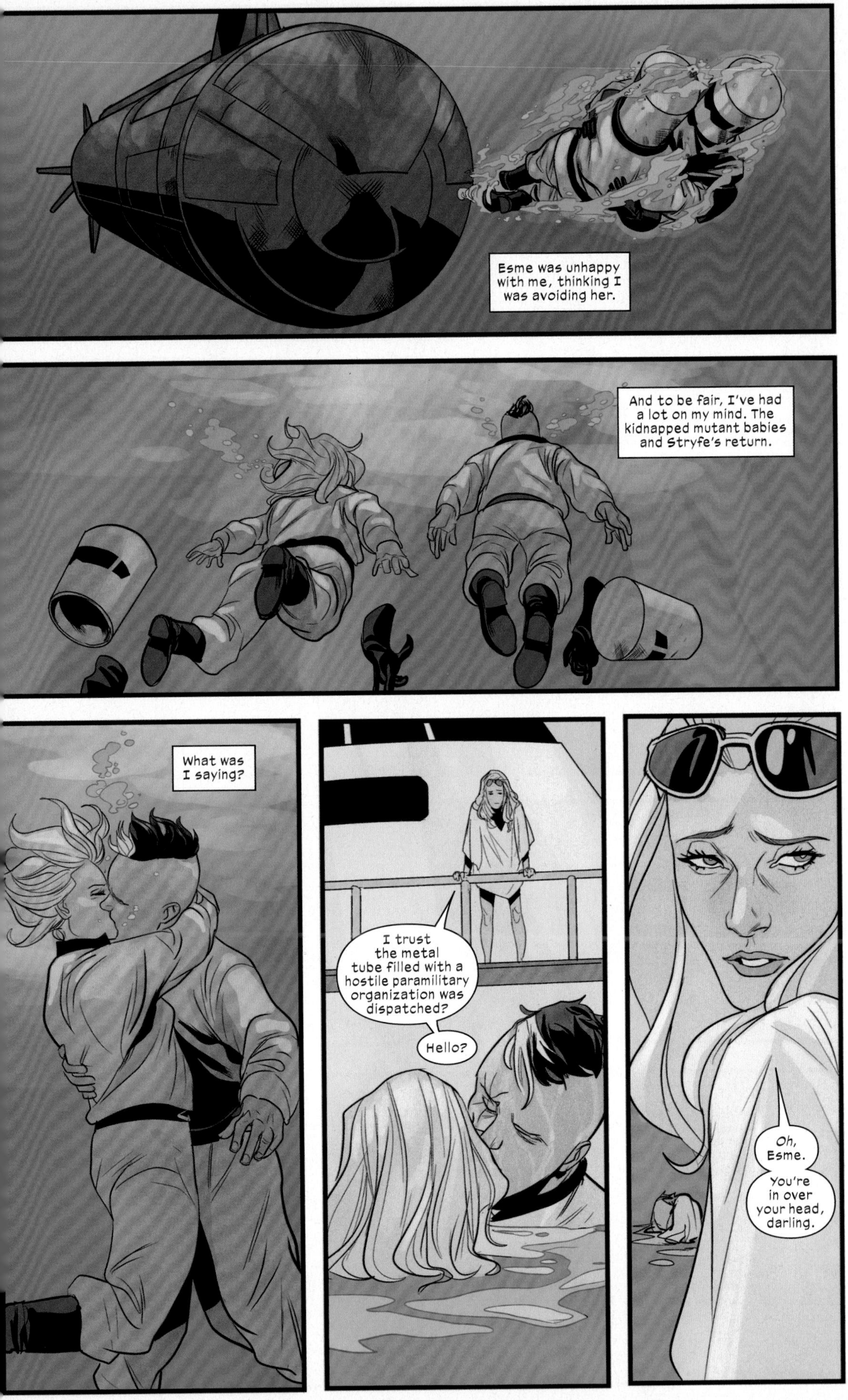
Esme was unhappy with me, thinking I was avoiding her.
And to be fair, I've had a lot on my mind. The kidnapped mutant babies and Stryfe's return.
What was I saying?
I trust the metal tube filled with a hostile paramilitary organization was dispatched?
Hello?
Oh, Esme.
You're in over your head, darling.

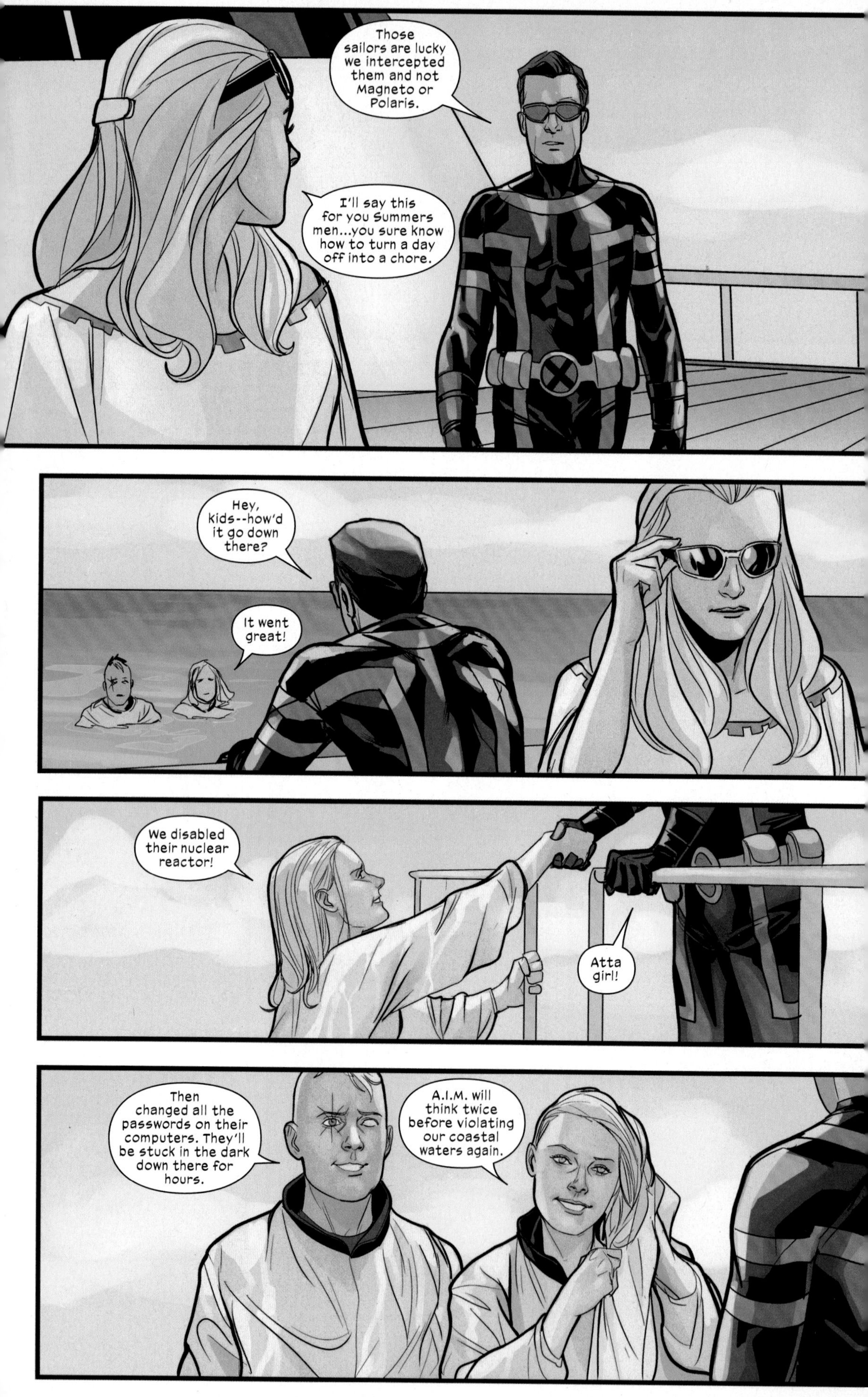

Those sailors are lucky we intercepted them and not Magneto or Polaris.
I'll say this for you Summers men...you sure know how to turn a day off into a chore.
Hey, kids--how'd it go down there?
It went great!
We disabled their nuclear reactor!
Atta girl!
Then changed all the passwords on their computers. They'll be stuck in the dark down there for hours.
A.I.M. will think twice before violating our coastal waters again.

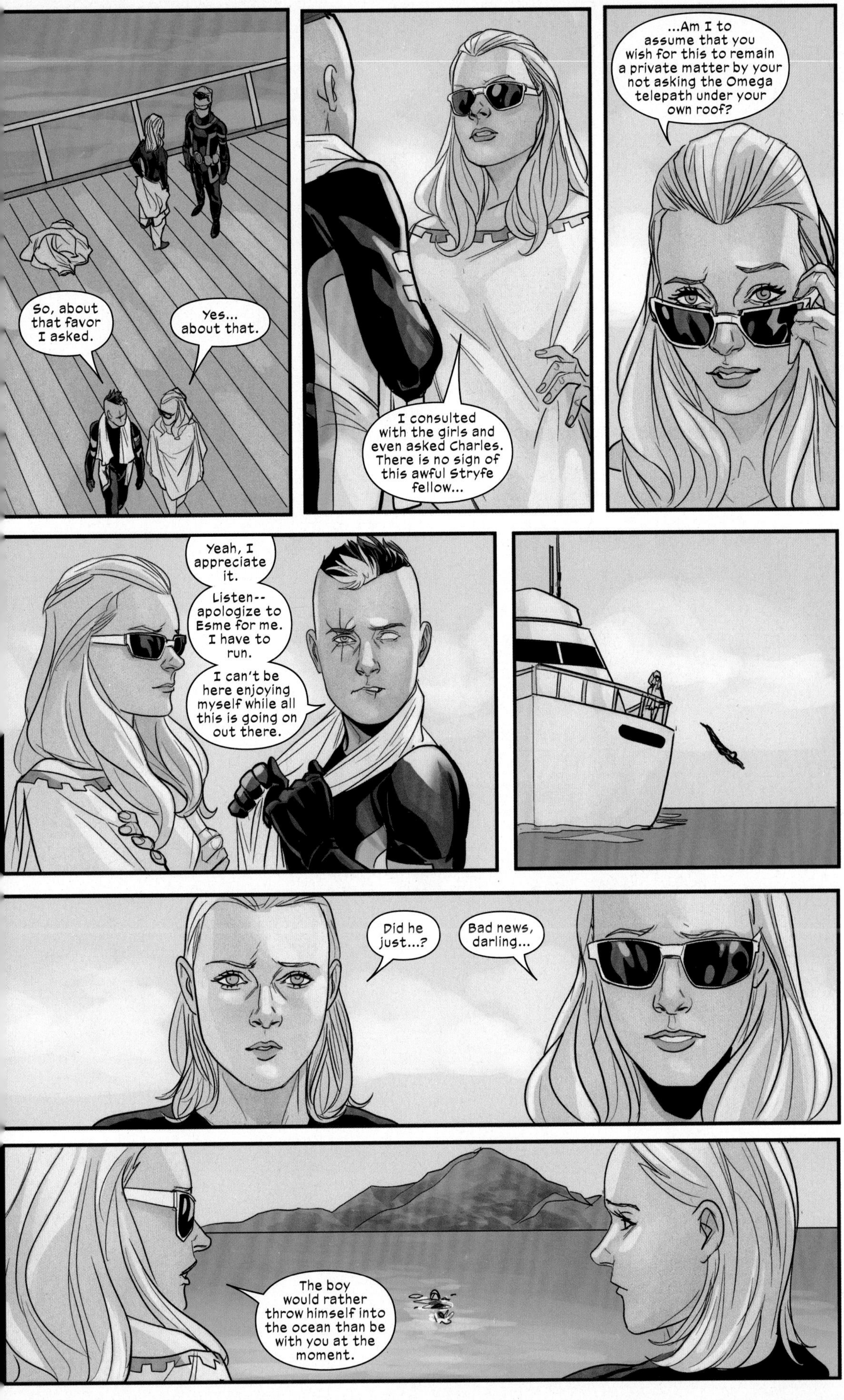
So, about that favor I asked.
Yes... about that.
I consulted with the girls and even asked Charles. There is no sign of this awful Stryfe fellow...
...Am I to assume that you wish for this to remain a private matter by your not asking the Omega telepath under your own roof?
Yeah, I appreciate it.
Listen-- apologize to Esme for me. I have to run.
I can't be here enjoying myself while all this is going on out there.
Did he just...?
Bad news, darling...
The boy would rather throw himself into the ocean than be with you at the moment.

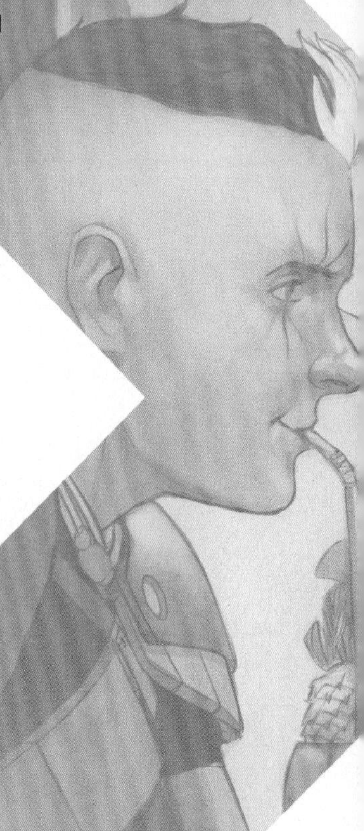

HEAVY WEIGHT

CABLE has been on the hunt for justice -- taking down the Order of X, a group kidnapping mutant babies and discovering that Stryfe, the enemy -- and clone -- of his older self, is alive and well.

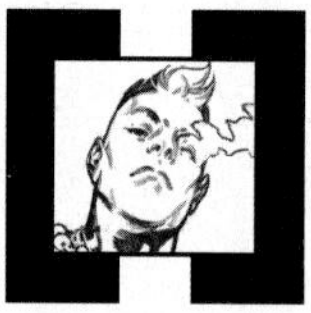

Cable

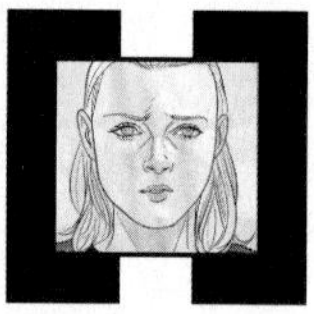

Esme Cuckoo

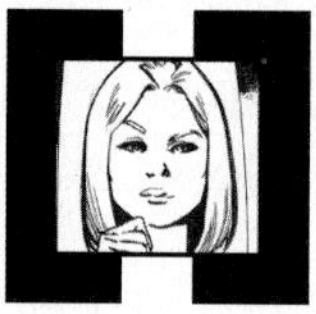

Emma Frost

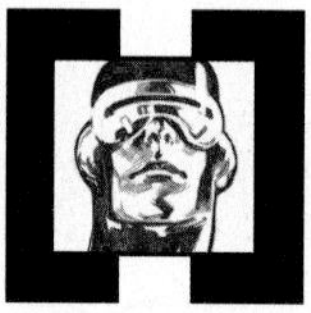

Cyclops

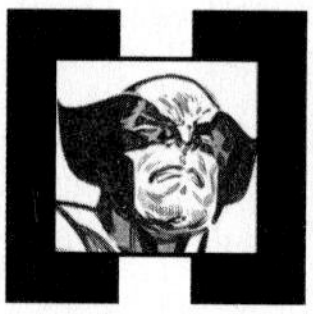

Wolverine

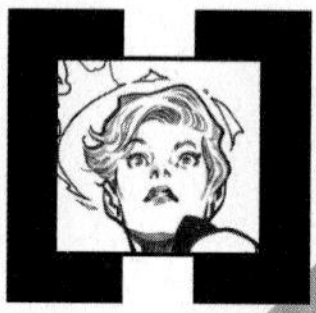

Rachel Summers

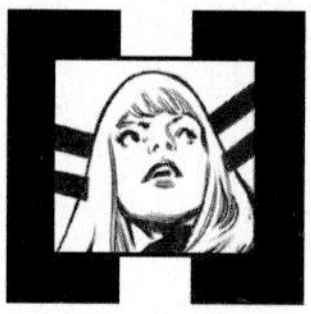

Magik

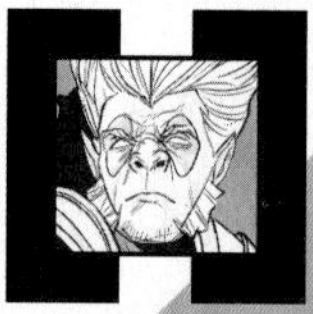

Wildside

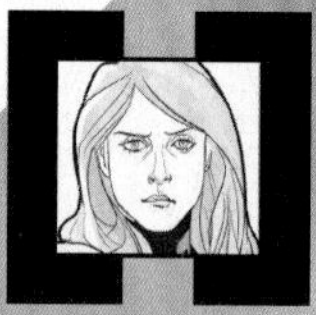

Hope Summers

[00_Reign]
[00___ofX]

CABLE

[X_09]

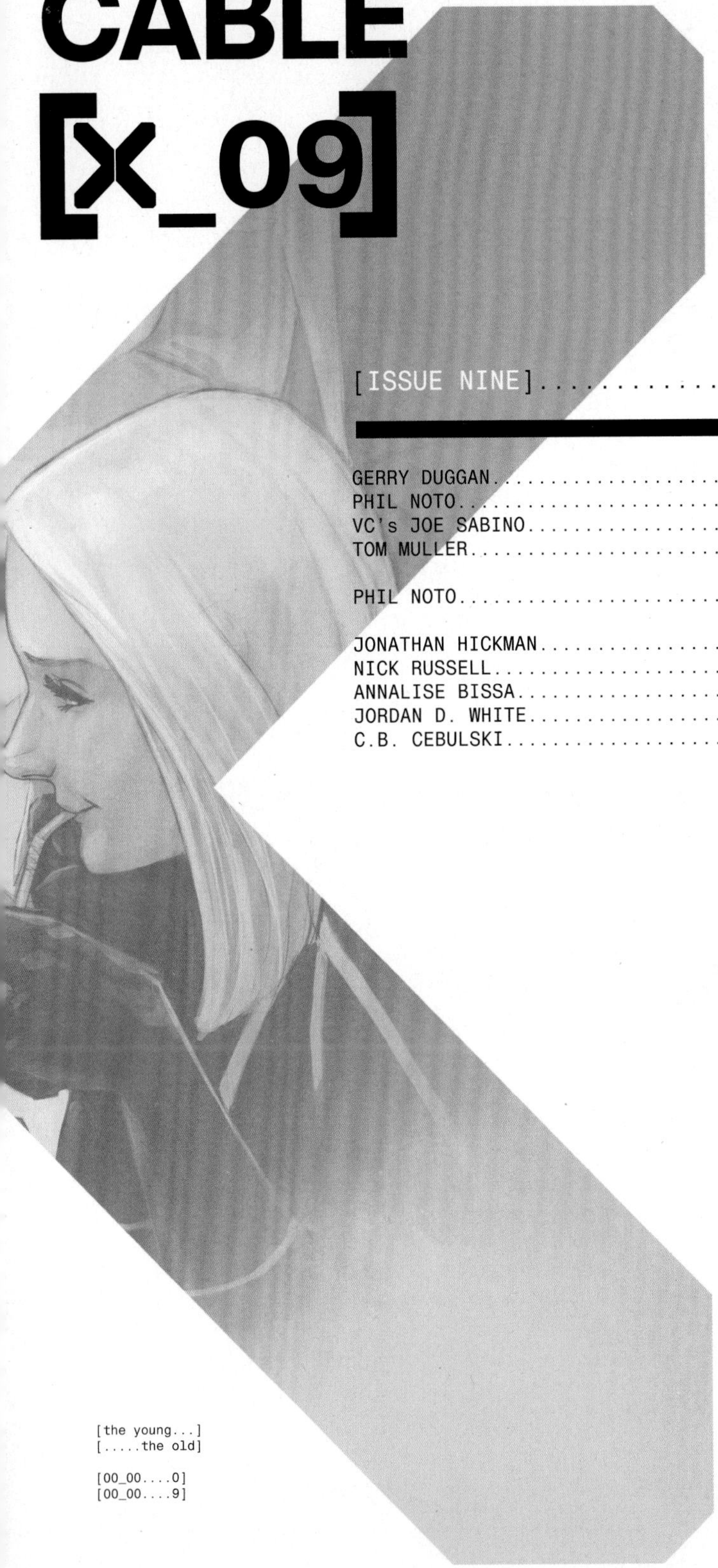

[ISSUE NINE].......................BARGAINING

GERRY DUGGAN...................................[WRITER]
PHIL NOTO......................................[ARTIST]
VC's JOE SABINO..............................[LETTERER]
TOM MULLER.....................................[DESIGN]

PHIL NOTO...............................[COVER ARTIST]

JONATHAN HICKMAN...........................[HEAD OF X]
NICK RUSSELL..............................[PRODUCTION]
ANNALISE BISSA......................[ASSOCIATE EDITOR]
JORDAN D. WHITE...............................[EDITOR]
C.B. CEBULSKI.......................[EDITOR IN CHIEF]

[the young...]
[.....the old]

[00_00....0]
[00_00....9]

[XX___past]
[00_______]

[00_______]

[future_XX]

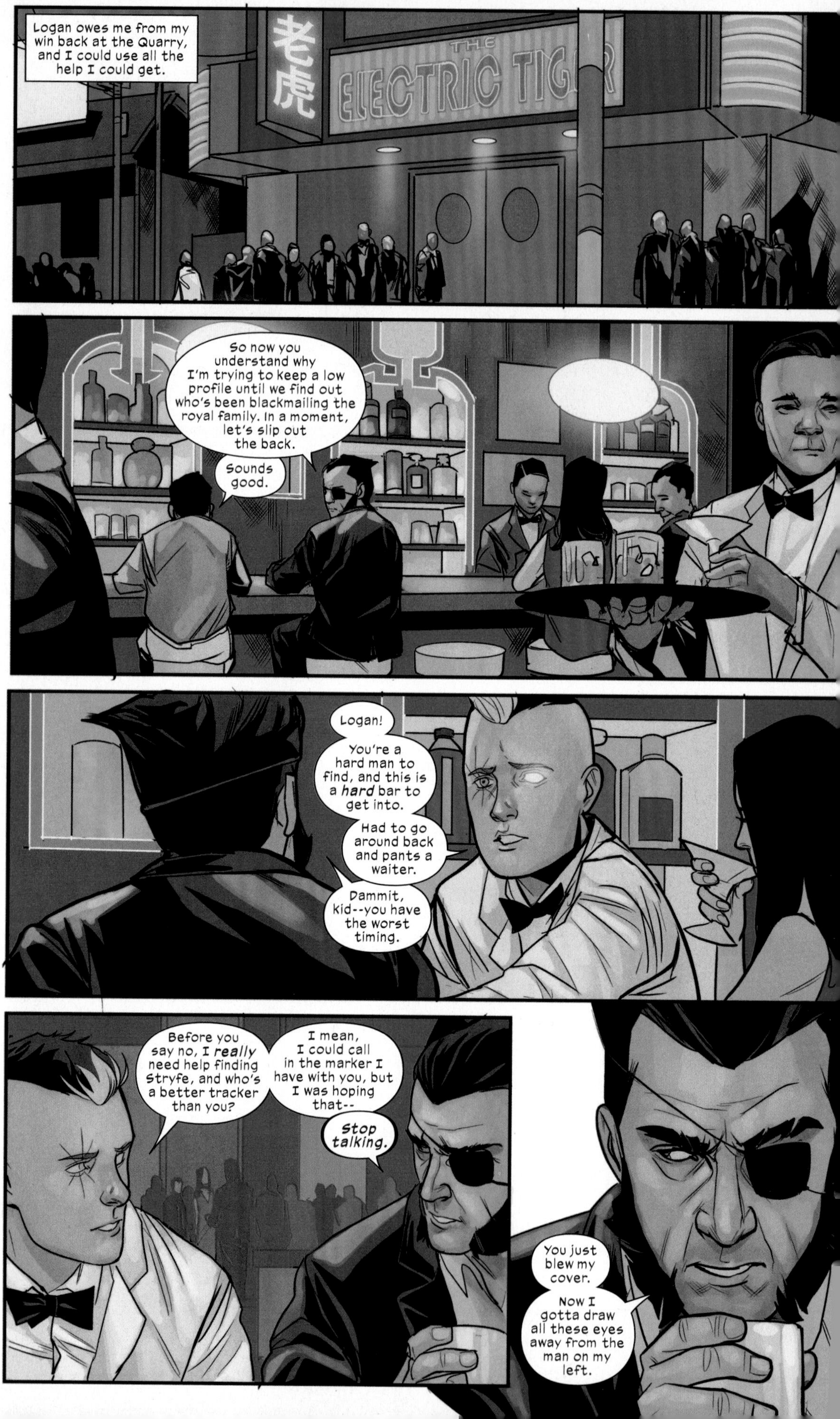

Logan owes me from my win back at the Quarry, and I could use all the help I could get.
老虎
THE ELECTRIC TIG
So now you understand why I'm trying to keep a low profile until we find out who's been blackmailing the royal family. In a moment, let's slip out the back.
Sounds good.
Logan!
You're a hard man to find, and this is a *hard* bar to get into.
Had to go around back and pants a waiter.
Dammit, kid--you have the worst timing.
Before you say no, I *really* need help finding Stryfe, and who's a better tracker than you?
I mean, I could call in the marker I have with you, but I was hoping that--
Stop talking.
You just blew my cover.
Now I gotta draw all these eyes away from the man on my left.

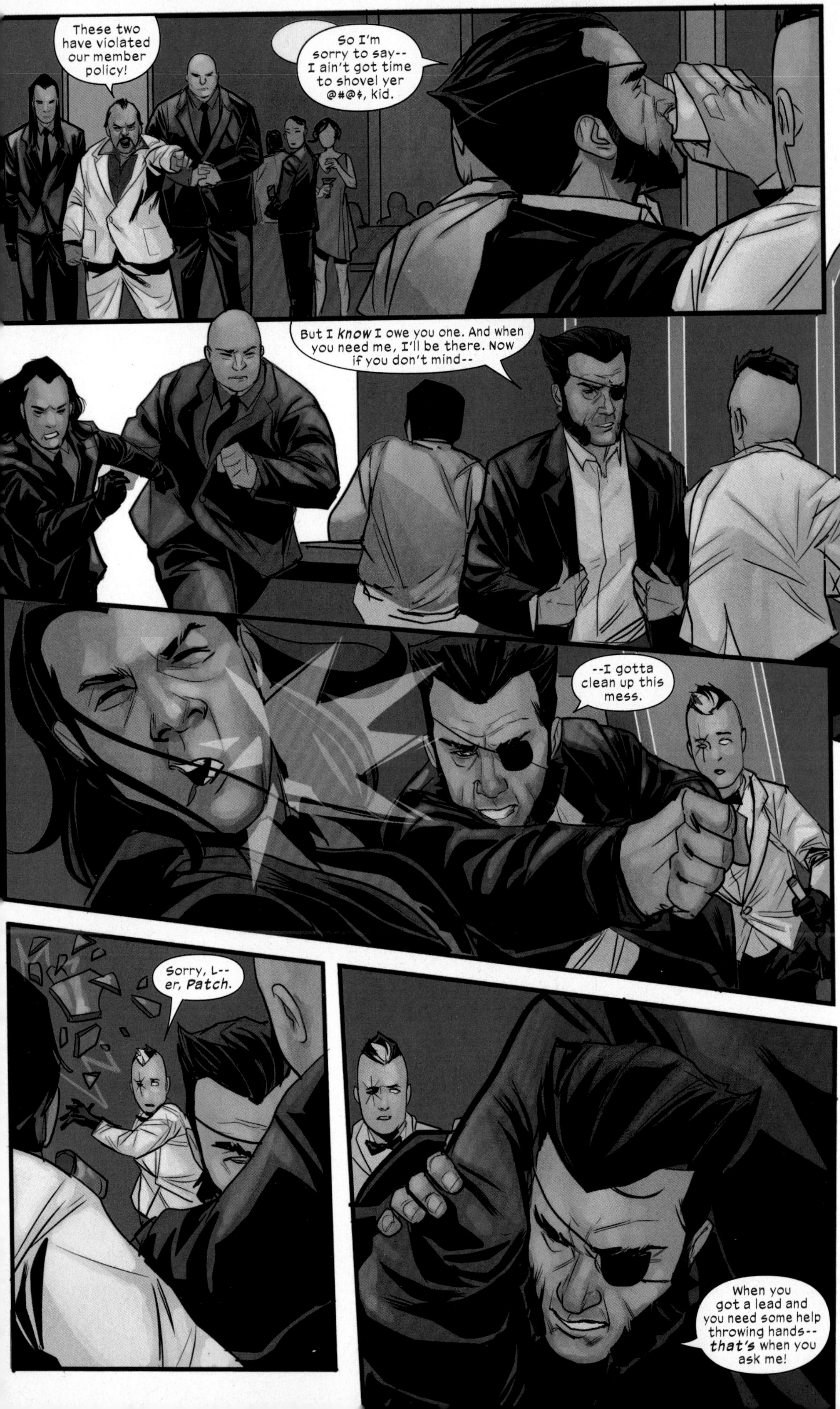
These two have violated our member policy!
So I'm sorry to say-- I ain't got time to shovel yer @#@$, kid.
But I know I owe you one. And when you need me, I'll be there. Now if you don't mind--
--I gotta clean up this mess.
Sorry, L-- er, Patch.
When you got a lead and you need some help throwing hands-- that's when you ask me!

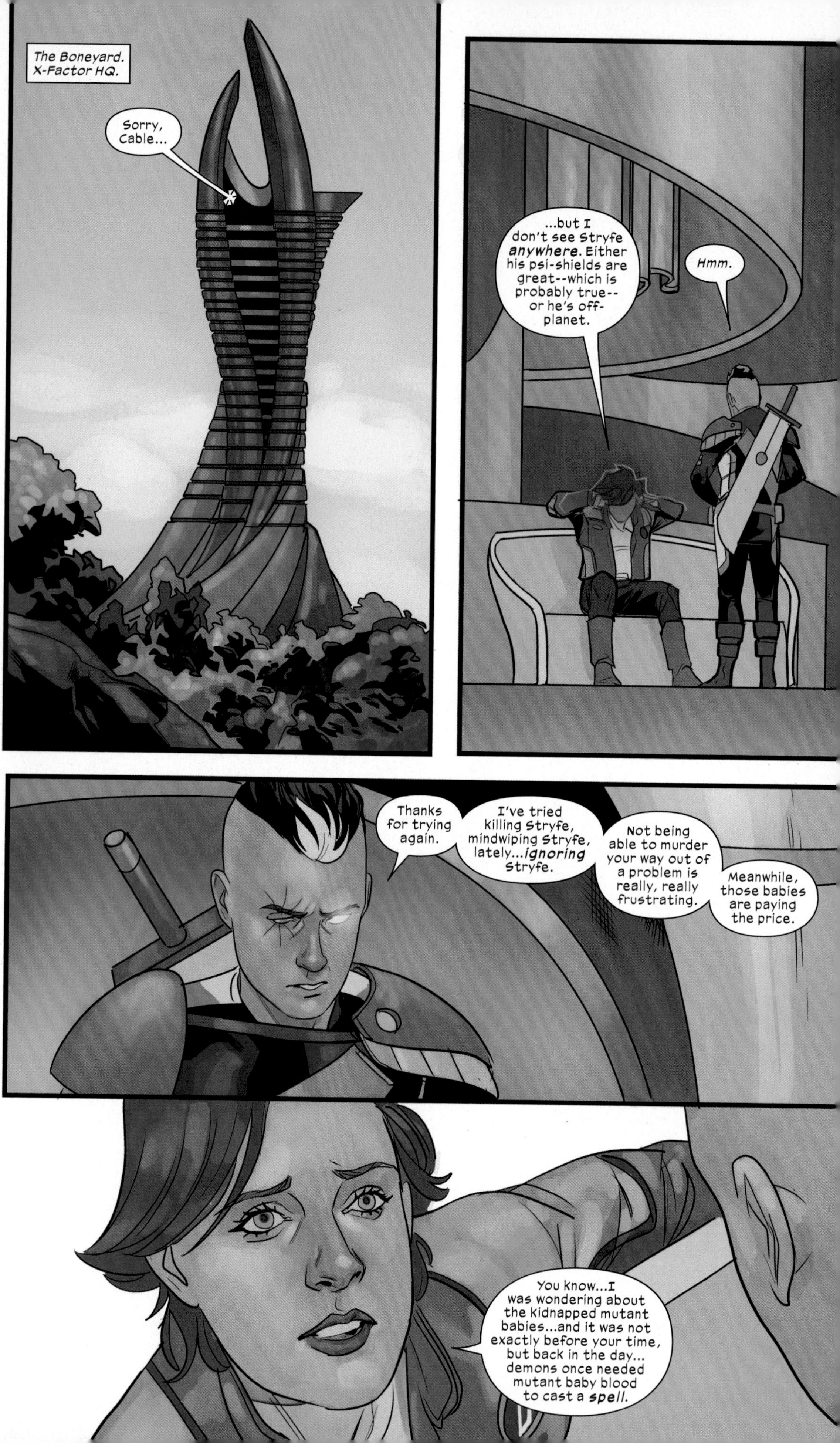
The Boneyard. X-Factor HQ.
Sorry, Cable...
...but I don't see Stryfe *anywhere*. Either his psi-shields are great--which is probably true--or he's off-planet.
Hmm.
Thanks for trying again.
I've tried killing Stryfe, mindwiping Stryfe, lately...*ignoring* Stryfe.
Not being able to murder your way out of a problem is really, really frustrating.
Meanwhile, those babies are paying the price.
You know...I was wondering about the kidnapped mutant babies...and it was not exactly before your time, but back in the day... demons once needed mutant baby blood to cast a *spell*.

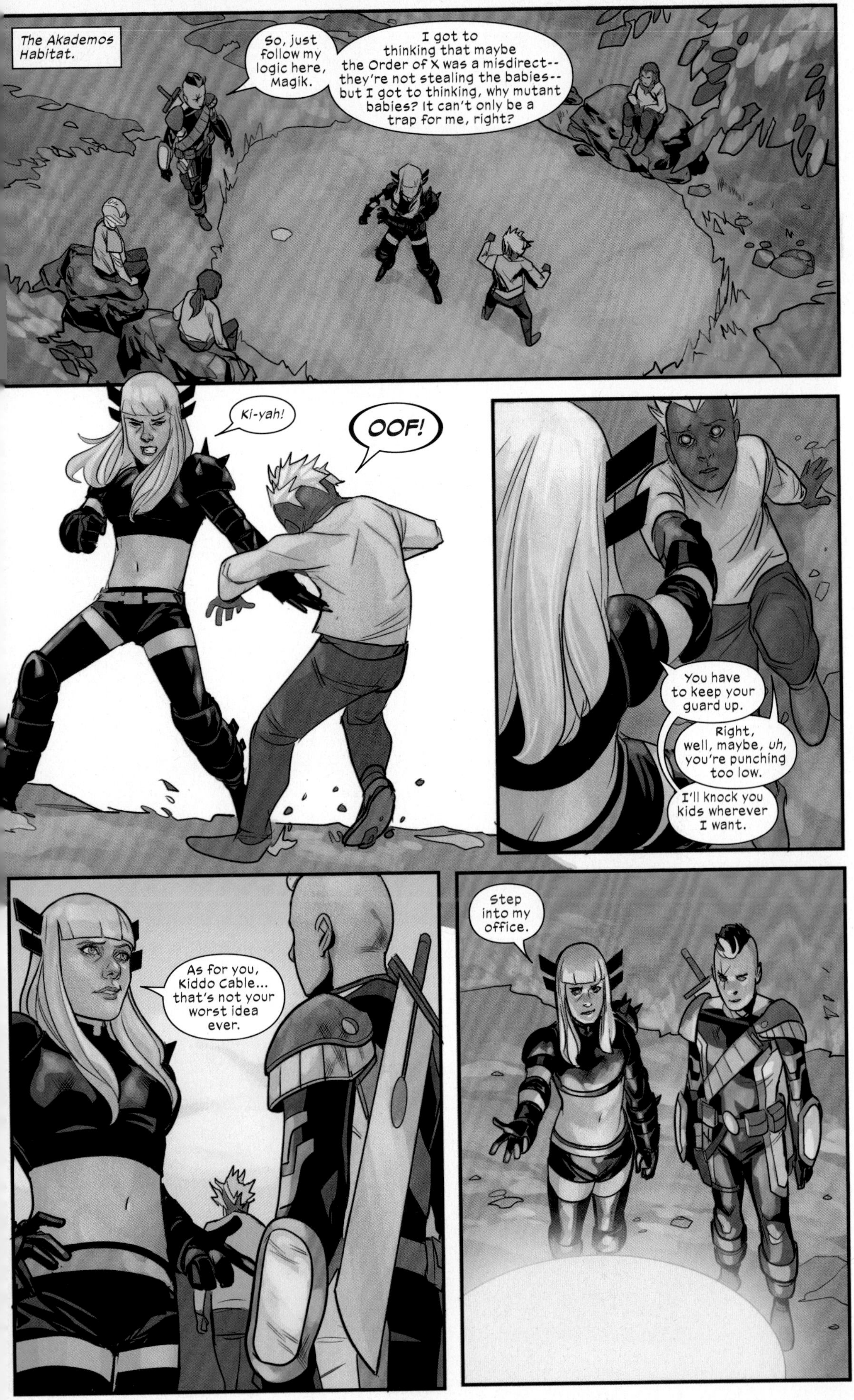
The Akademos Habitat.
So, just follow my logic here, Magik.
I got to thinking that maybe the Order of X was a misdirect-- they're not stealing the babies-- but I got to thinking, why mutant babies? It can't only be a trap for me, right?
Ki-yah!
OOF!
You have to keep your guard up.
Right, well, maybe, *uh*, you're punching too low.
I'll knock you kids wherever I want.
As for you, Kiddo Cable... that's not your worst idea ever.
Step into my office.

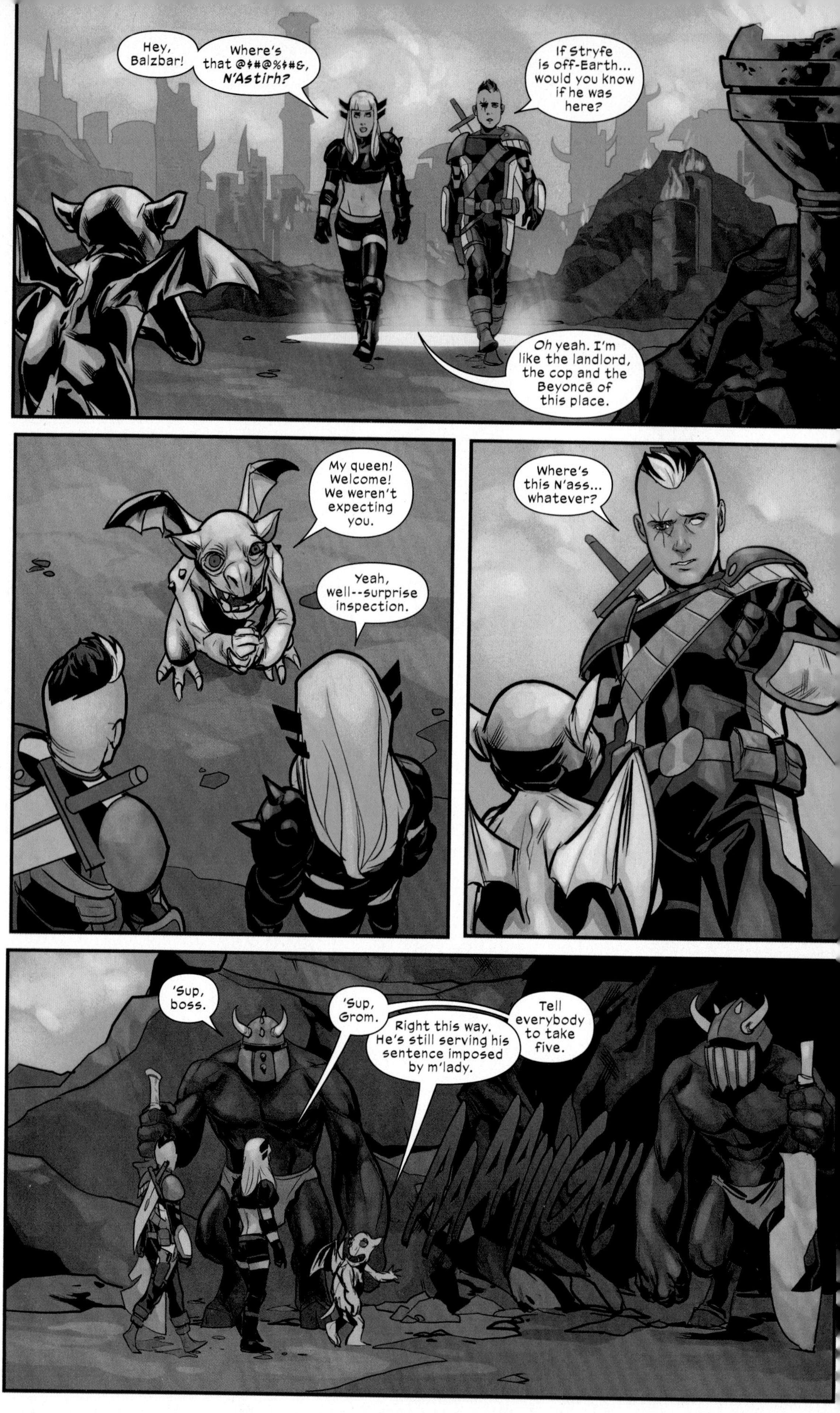

Hey, Balzbar!
Where's that @$#@%$#&, *N'Astirh?*
If Stryfe is off-Earth... would you know if he was here?
Oh yeah. I'm like the landlord, the cop and the Beyoncé of this place.
My queen! Welcome! We weren't expecting you.
Yeah, well--surprise inspection.
Where's this N'ass... whatever?
'Sup, boss.
'Sup, Grom.
Right this way. He's still serving his sentence imposed by m'lady.
Tell everybody to take five.

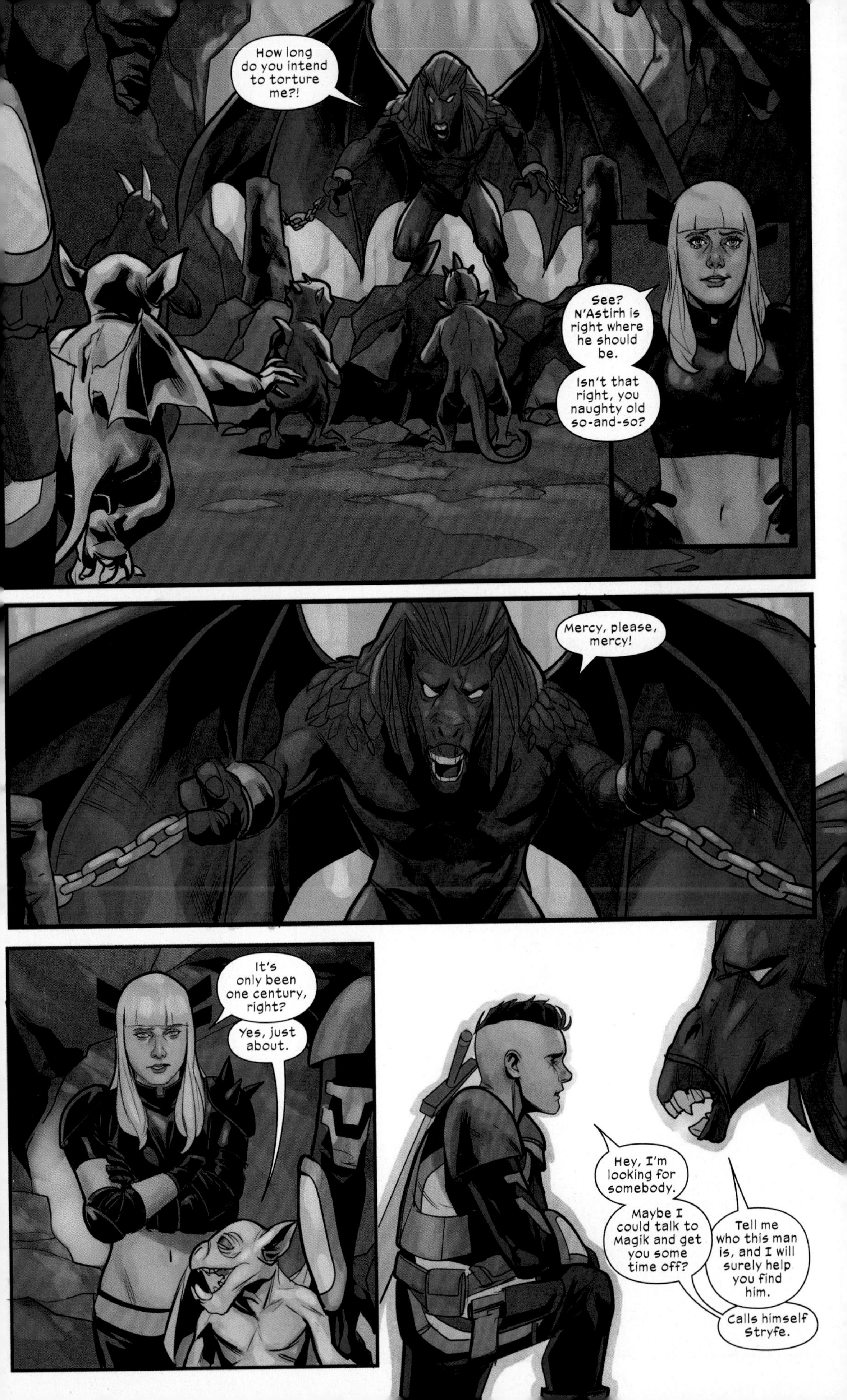

How long do you intend to torture me?!
See? N'Astirh is right where he should be.
Isn't that right, you naughty old so-and-so?
Mercy, please, mercy!
It's only been one century, right?
Yes, just about.
Hey, I'm looking for somebody.
Maybe I could talk to Magik and get you some time off?
Tell me who this man is, and I will surely help you find him.
Calls himself Stryfe.

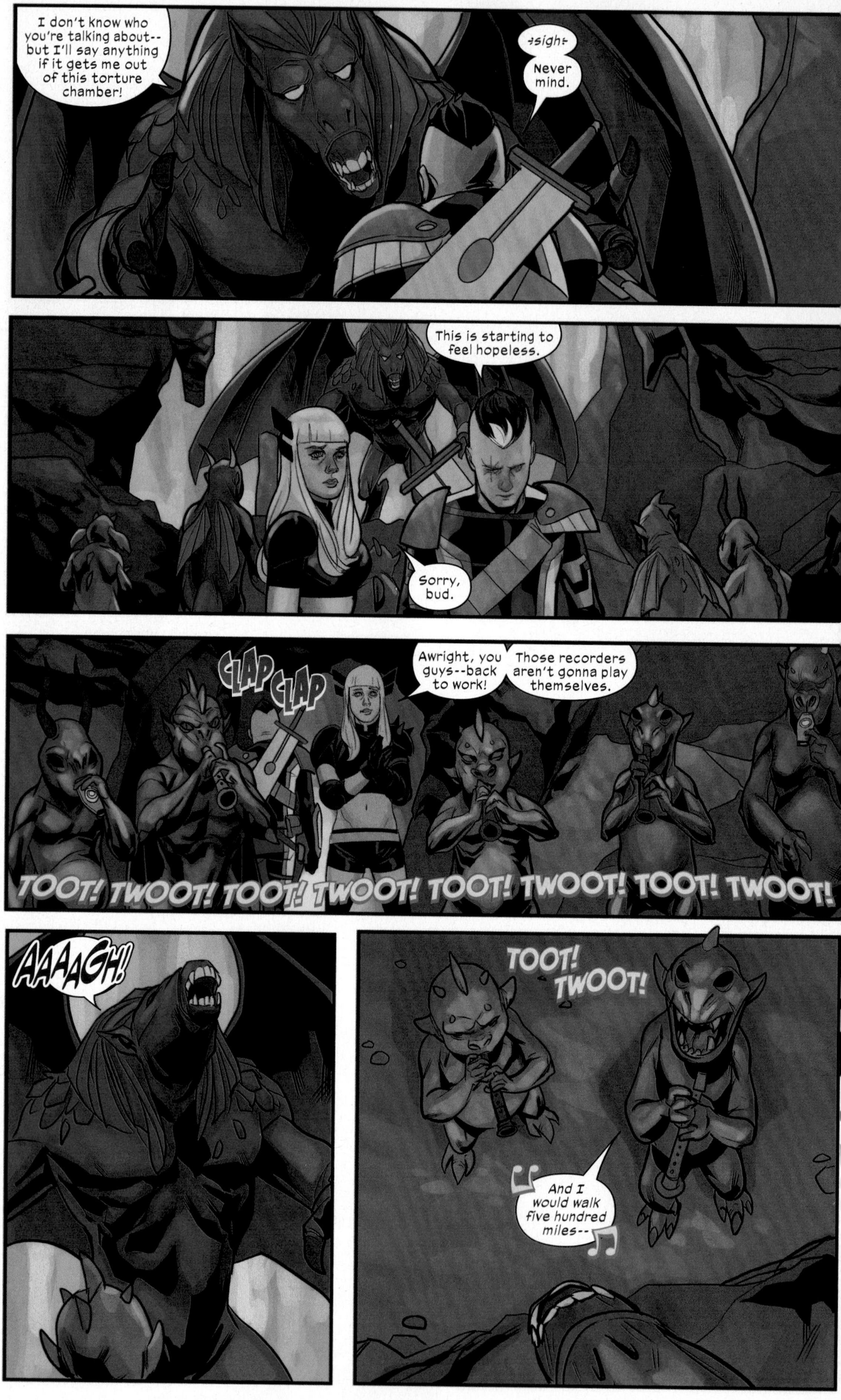
I don't know who you're talking about--but I'll say anything if it gets me out of this torture chamber!
-sigh-
Never mind.
This is starting to feel hopeless.
Sorry, bud.
CLAP CLAP
Awright, you guys--back to work!
Those recorders aren't gonna play themselves.
TOOT! TWOOT! TOOT! TWOOT! TOOT! TWOOT! TOOT! TWOOT!
AAAAGH!
TOOT! TWOOT!
And I would walk five hundred miles--

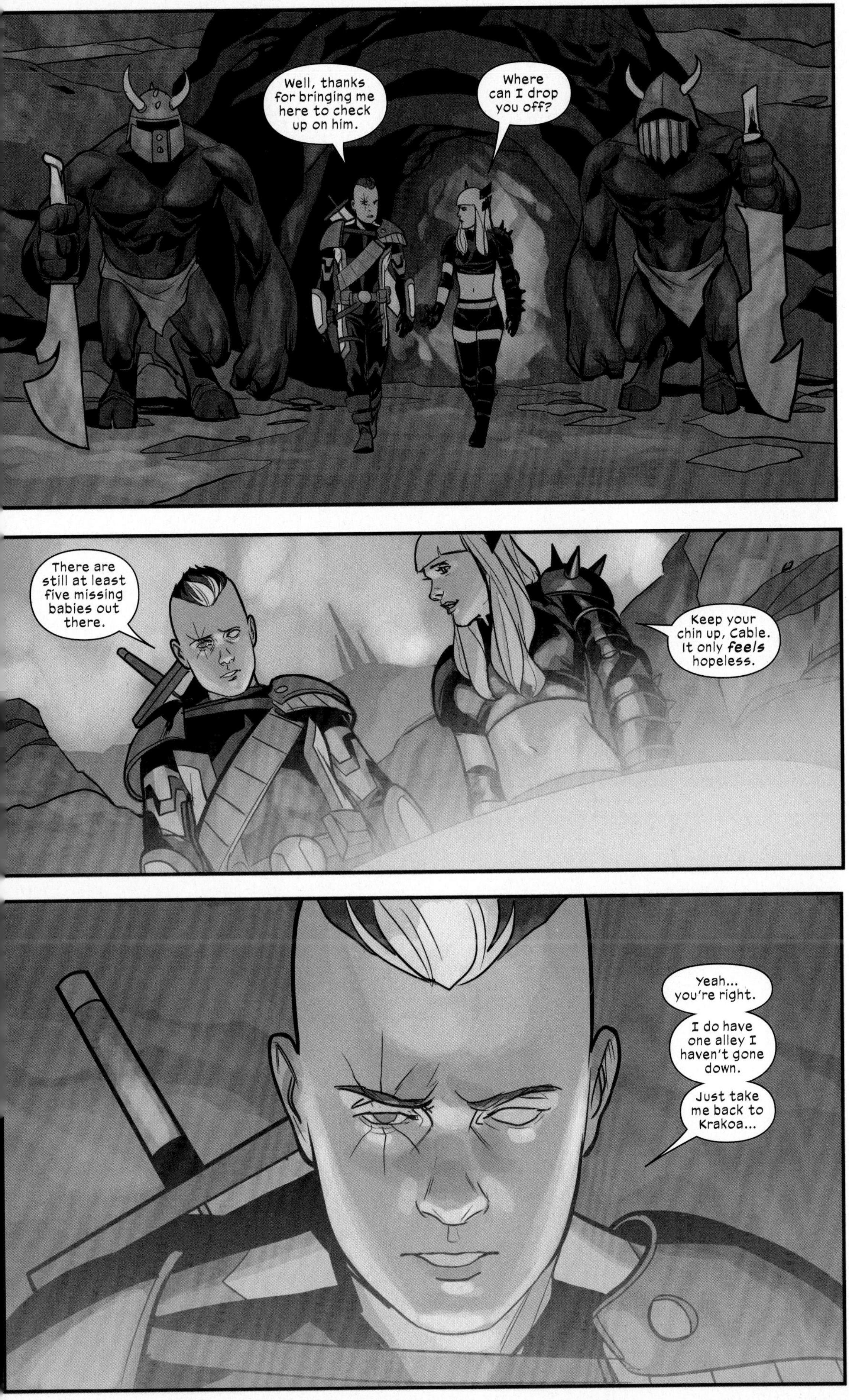
Well, thanks for bringing me here to check up on him.
Where can I drop you off?
There are still at least five missing babies out there.
Keep your chin up, Cable. It only *feels* hopeless.
Yeah... you're right.
I do have one alley I haven't gone down.
Just take me back to Krakoa...

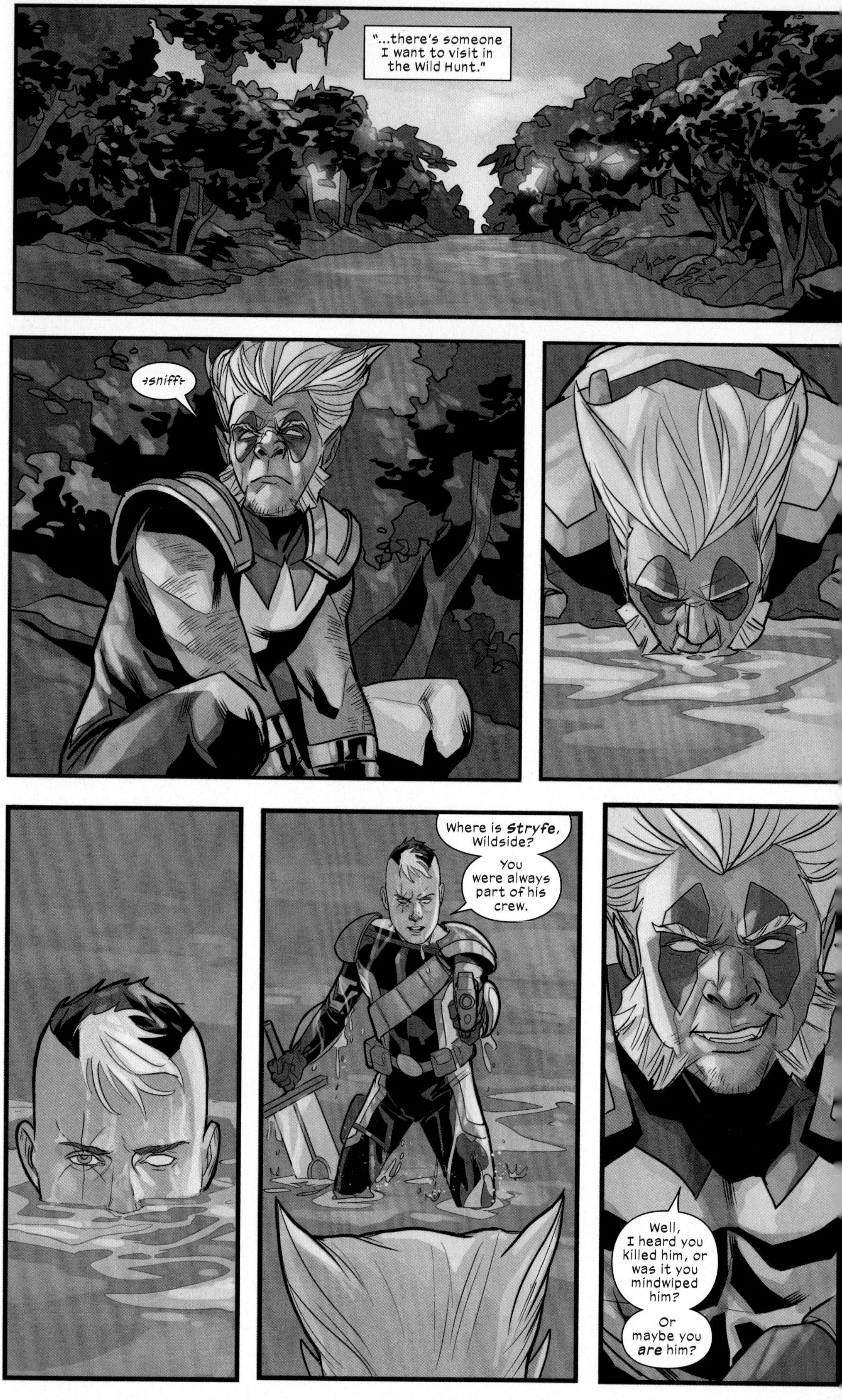
"...there's someone I want to visit in the Wild Hunt."
=sniff=
Where is Stryfe, Wildside?
You were always part of his crew.
Well, I heard you killed him, or was it you mindwiped him?
Or maybe you are him?

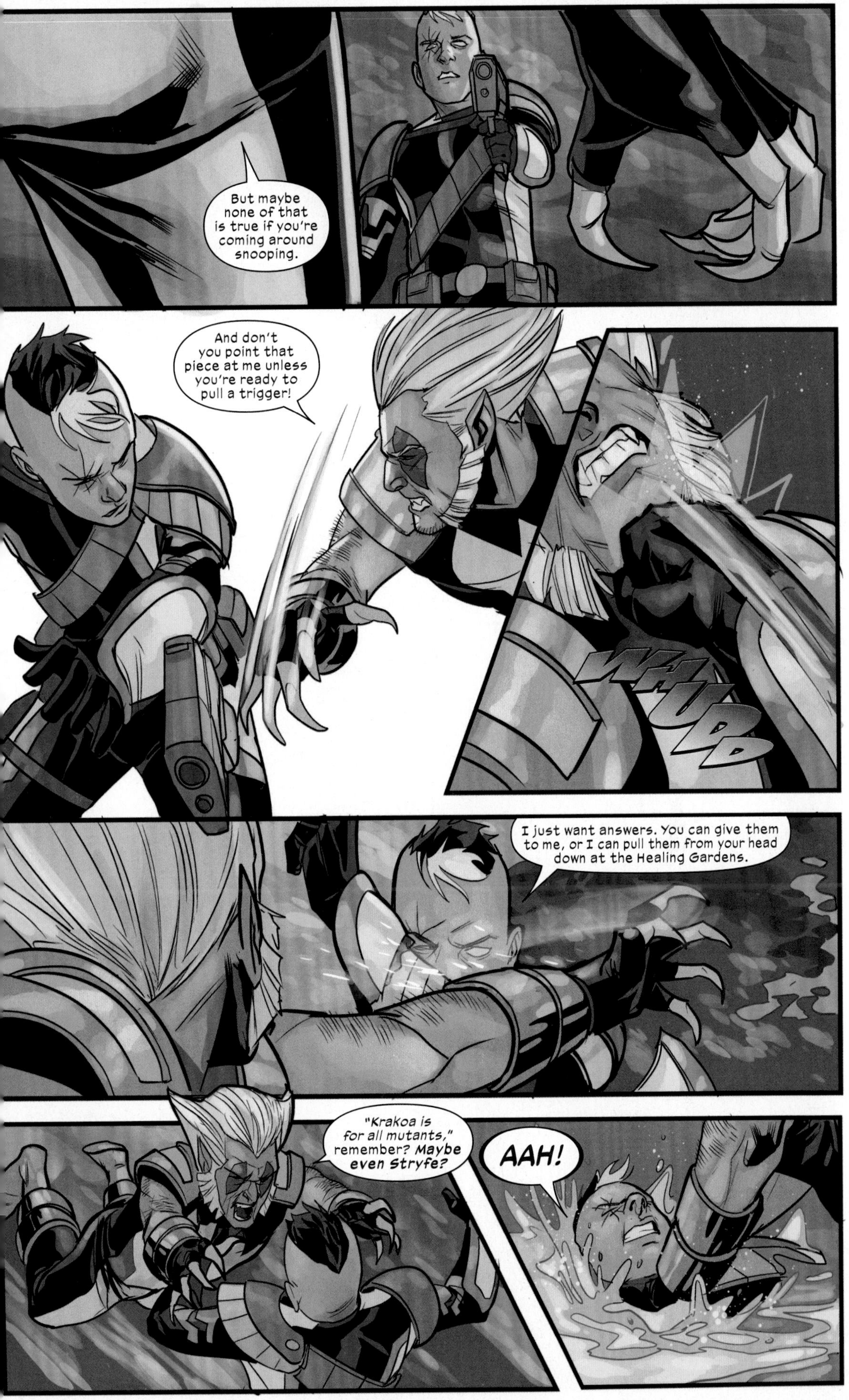
But maybe none of that is true if you're coming around snooping.
And don't you point that piece at me unless you're ready to pull a trigger!
WHUDD
I just want answers. You can give them to me, or I can pull them from your head down at the Healing Gardens.
"Krakoa is for all mutants," remember? Maybe even Stryfe?
AAH!

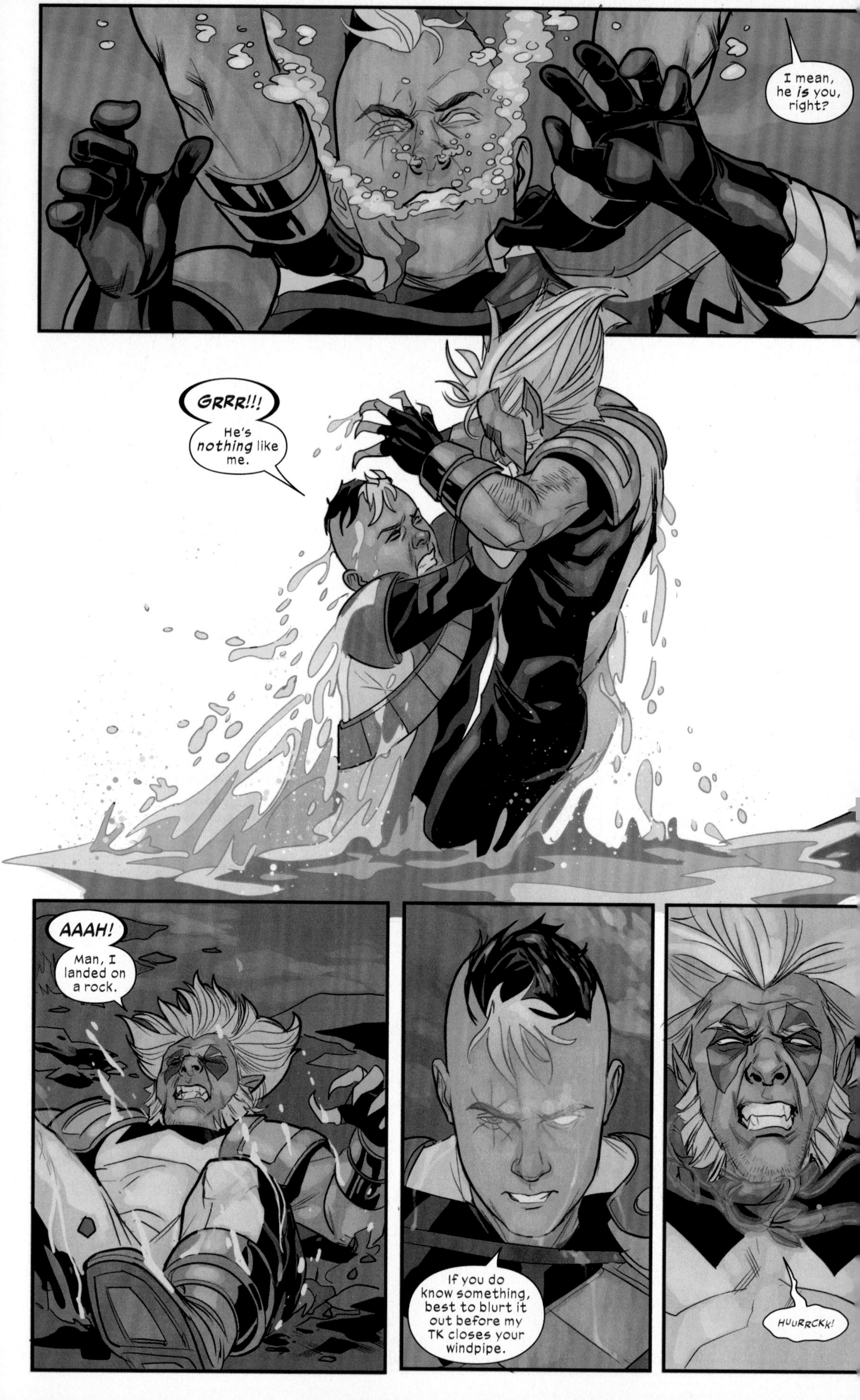

I mean, he *is* you, right?
GRRR!!!
He's *nothing* like me.
AAAH!
Man, I landed on a rock.
If you do know something, best to blurt it out before my TK closes your windpipe.
HUURRCKK!

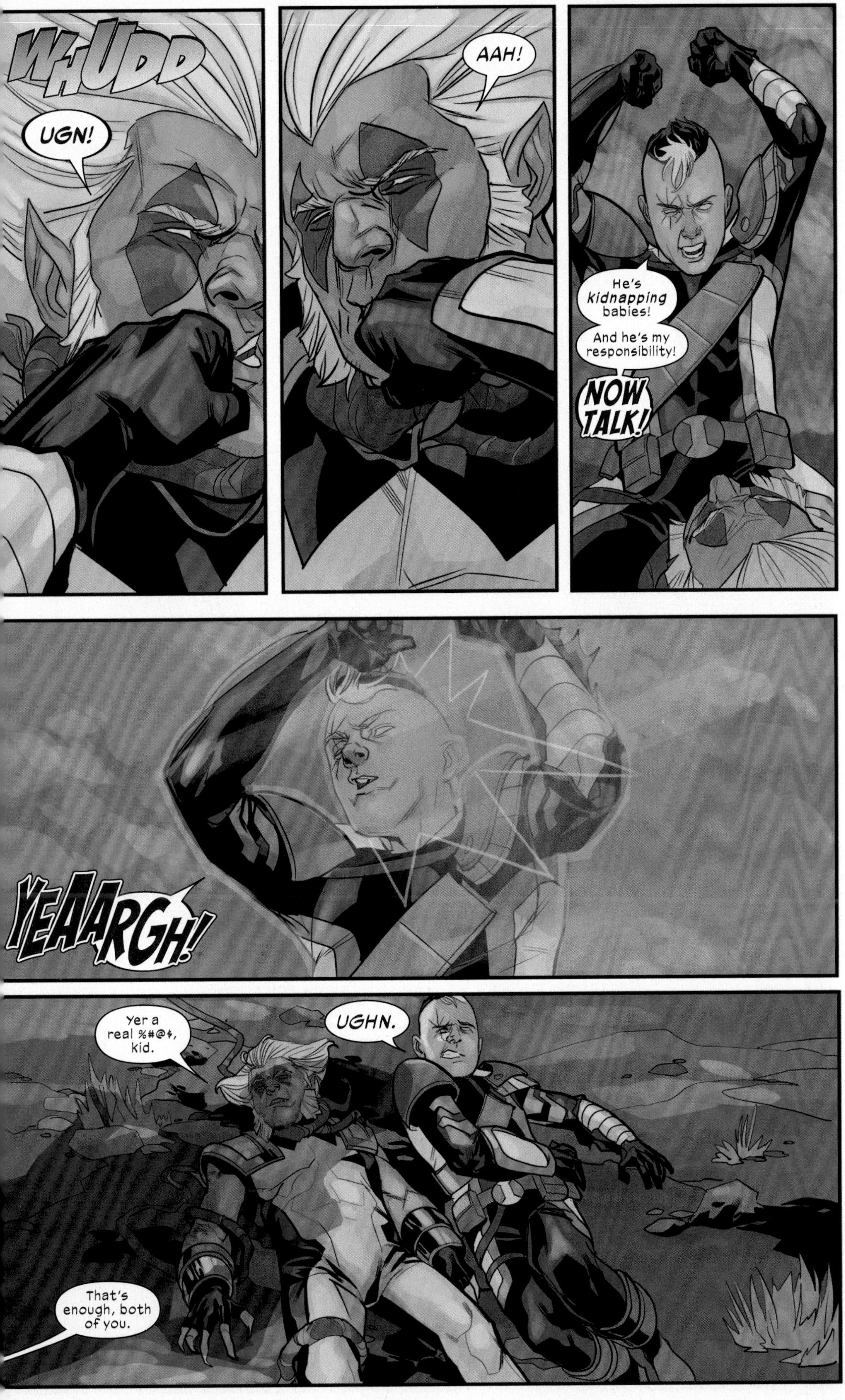
WHUDD
UGN!
AAH!
He's kidnapping babies!
And he's my responsibility!
NOW TALK!
YEAARGH!
Yer a real %#@$, kid.
UGHN.
That's enough, both of you.

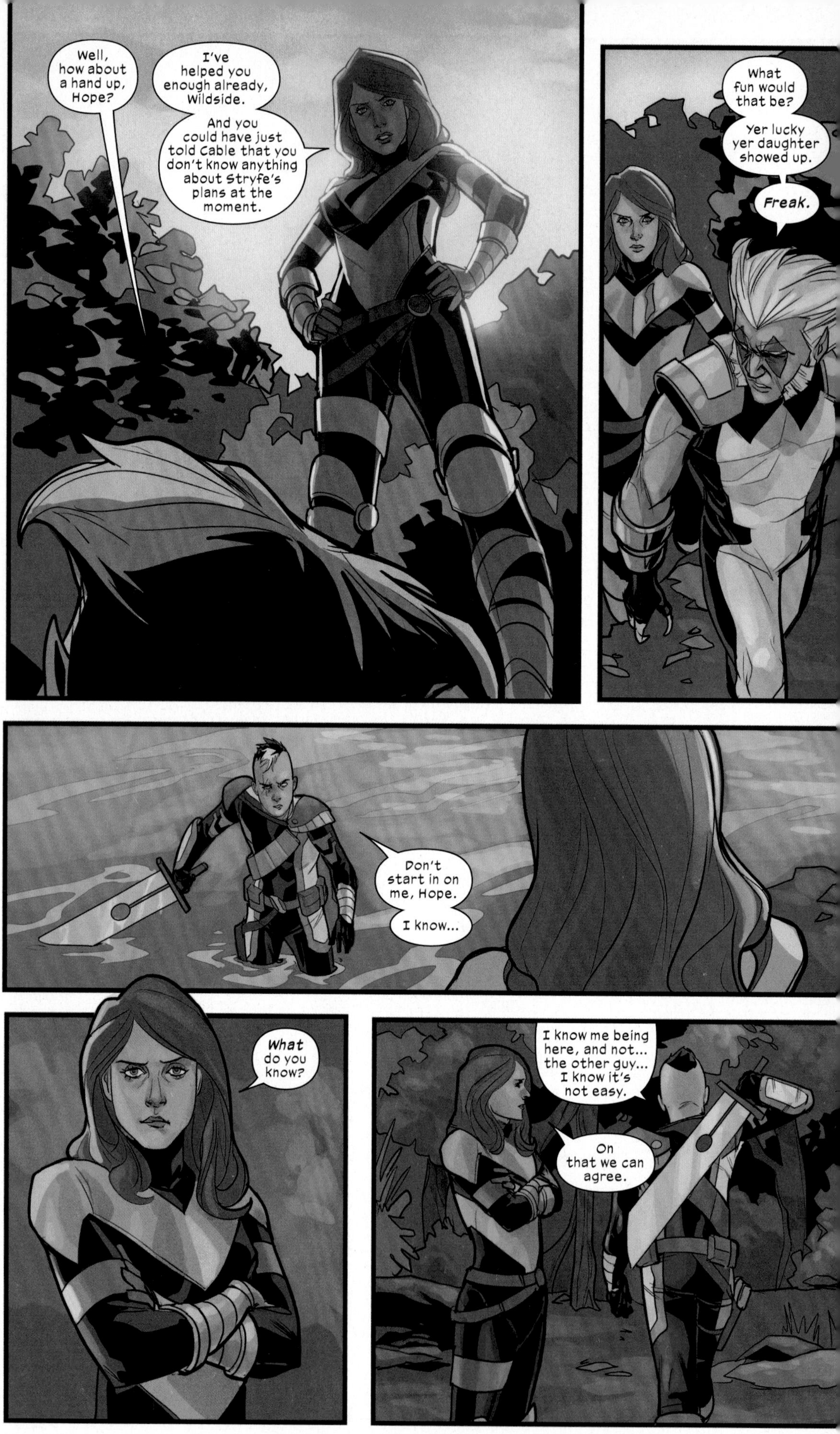
Well, how about a hand up, Hope?
I've helped you enough already, Wildside.
And you could have just told Cable that you don't know anything about Stryfe's plans at the moment.
What fun would that be?
Yer lucky yer daughter showed up.
Freak.
Don't start in on me, Hope.
I know...
What do you know?
I know me being here, and not... the other guy... I know it's not easy.
On that we can agree.

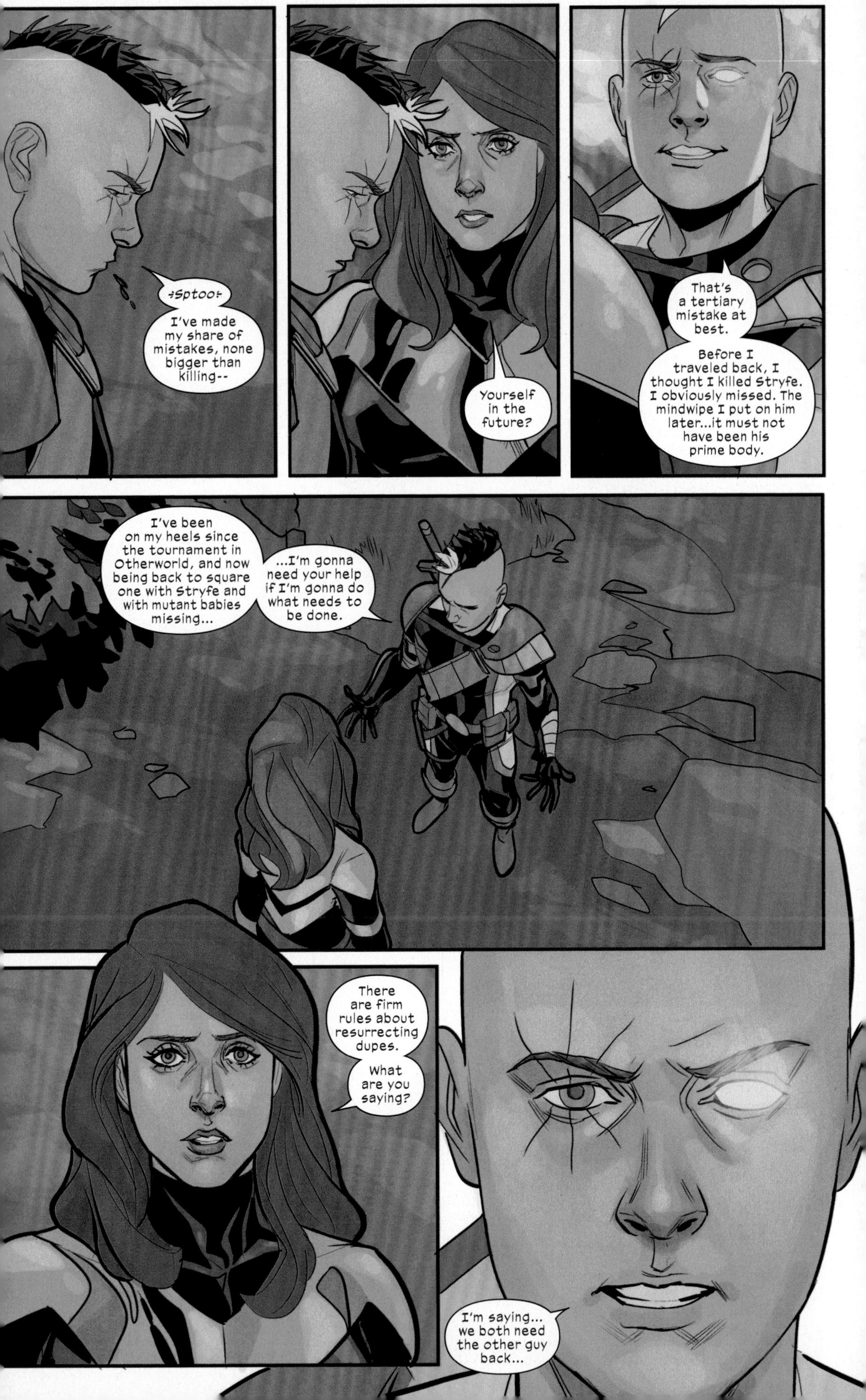
-Sptoo-
I've made my share of mistakes, none bigger than killing--
Yourself in the future?
That's a tertiary mistake at best.
Before I traveled back, I thought I killed Stryfe. I obviously missed. The mindwipe I put on him later...it must not have been his prime body.
I've been on my heels since the tournament in Otherworld, and now being back to square one with Stryfe and with mutant babies missing...
...I'm gonna need your help if I'm gonna do what needs to be done.
There are firm rules about resurrecting dupes.
What are you saying?
I'm saying... we both need the other guy back...

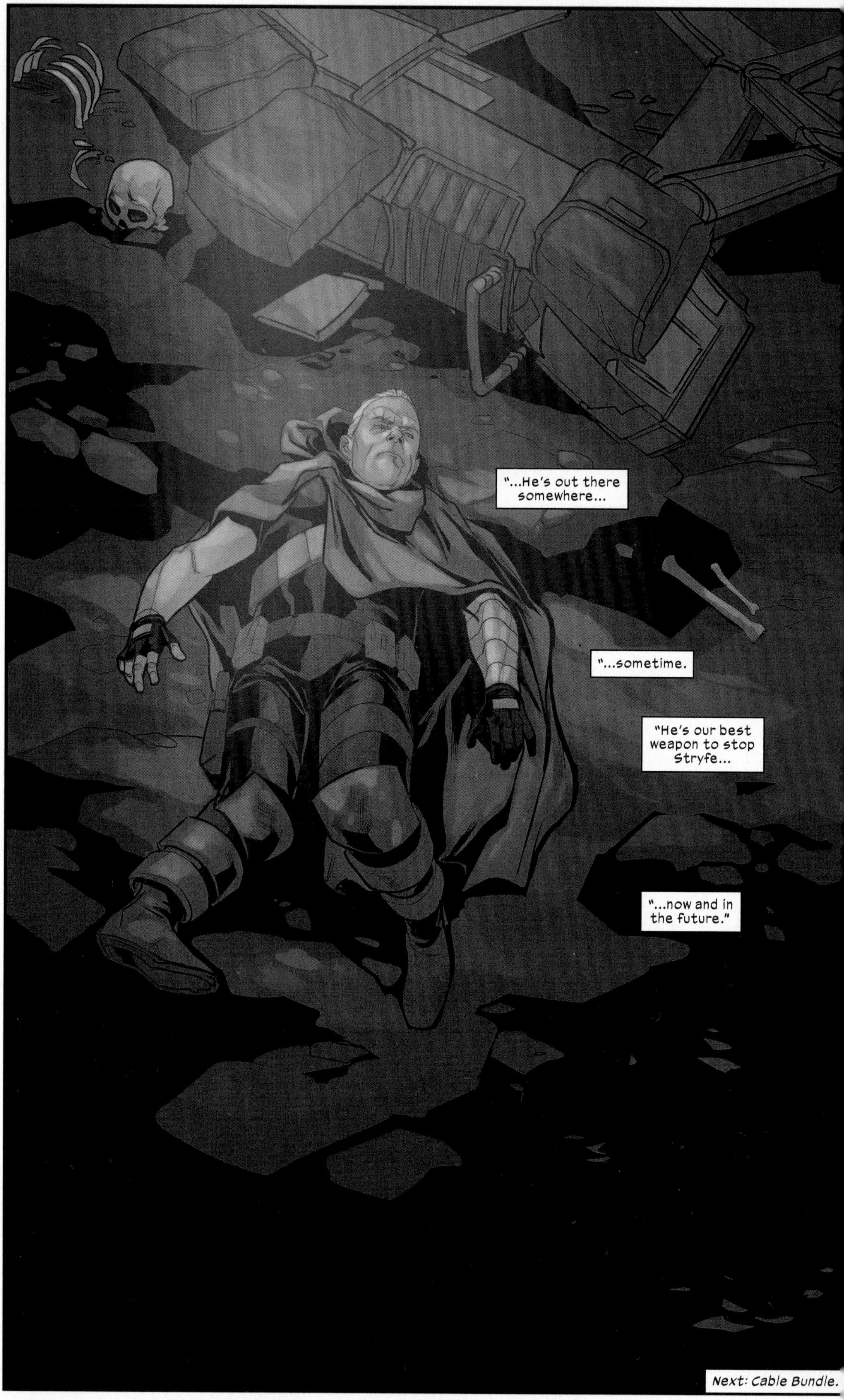
"...He's out there somewhere...
"...sometime.
"He's our best weapon to stop Stryfe...
"...now and in the future."
Next: Cable Bundle.

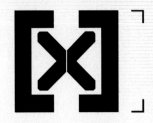

Re: Duplicates

When the resurrection process was solidified one of the first questions that came up was that of duplicates. It was decided that it would undermine the validity of the protocols if multiple versions of the same person were to be produced. This decision was then extended out to the concept of duplicates in general, that other forms -- clones, versions from alternate dimensions, or time-travelling doubles -- would also not be eligible for resurrection. Or perhaps, to put a finer point on it, only one of the duplicates would be eligible.

(Exceptions were made in cases where "duplication" is an extension of mutant gifts -- e.g. the Stepford Cuckoos being able to be resurrected back to their five selves or Madrox Prime being able to be resurrected even if one or more of his dupes have survived.)

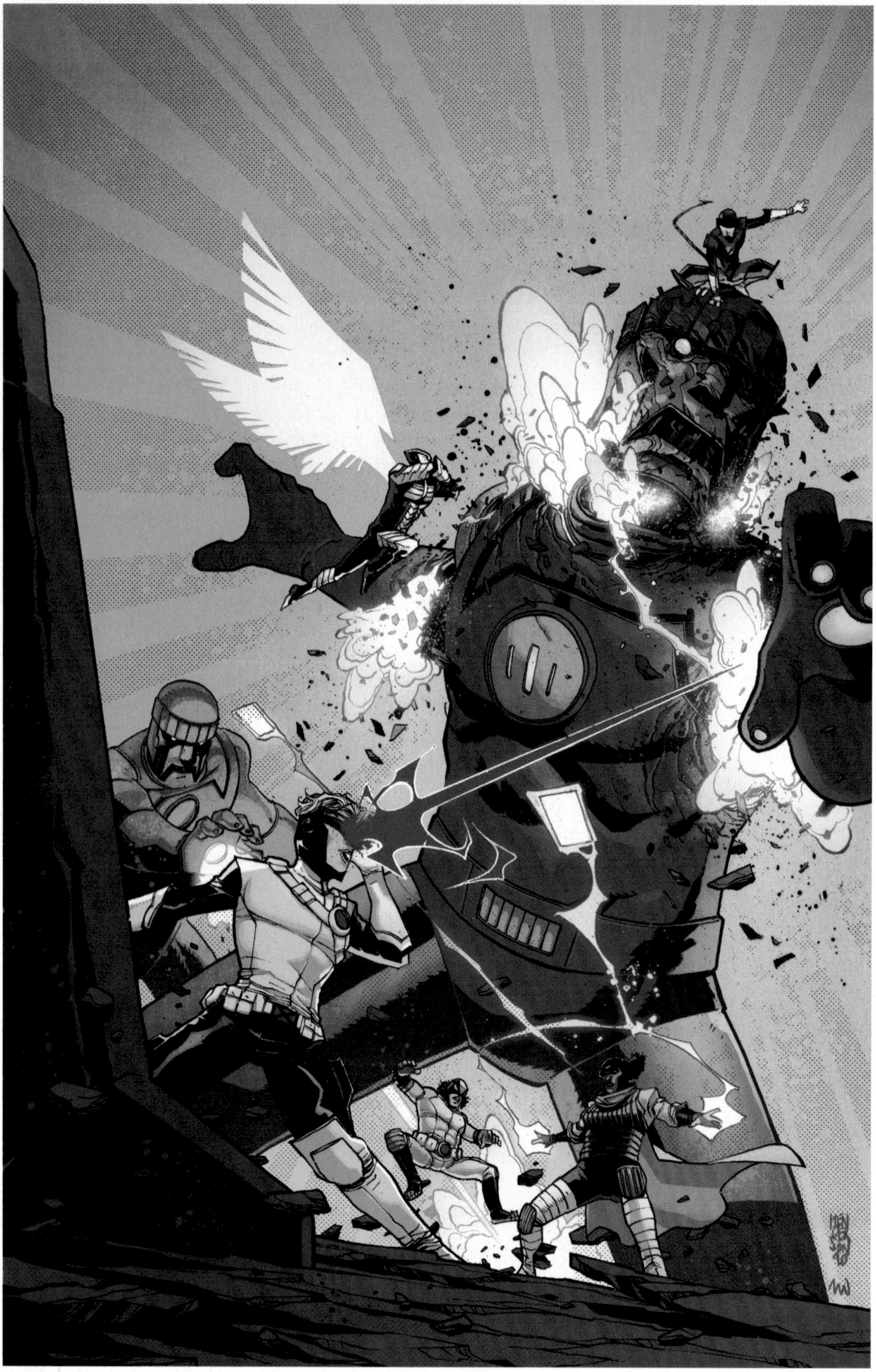

Children of the Atom #2 Variant

by Mike Henderson
& Nolan Woodard

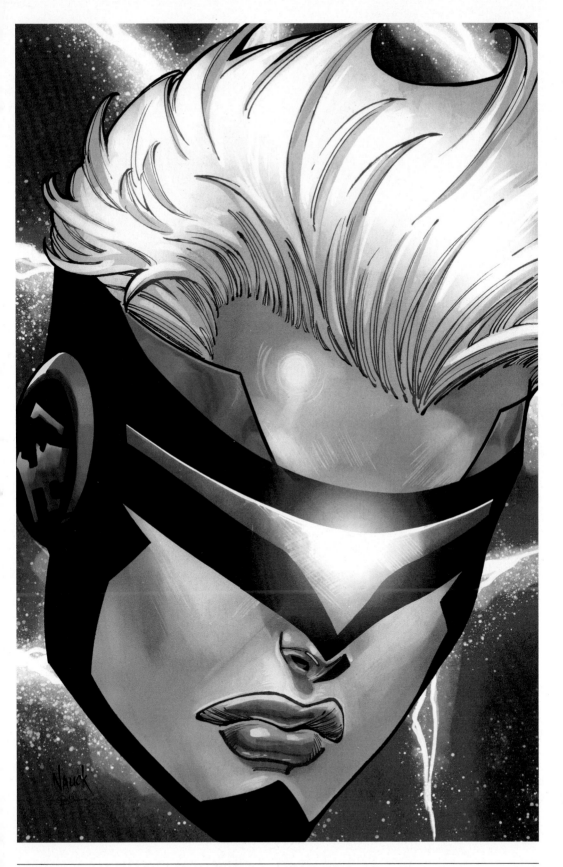

Children of the Atom #2 Headshot Variant by Todd Nauck
& Rachelle Rosenberg

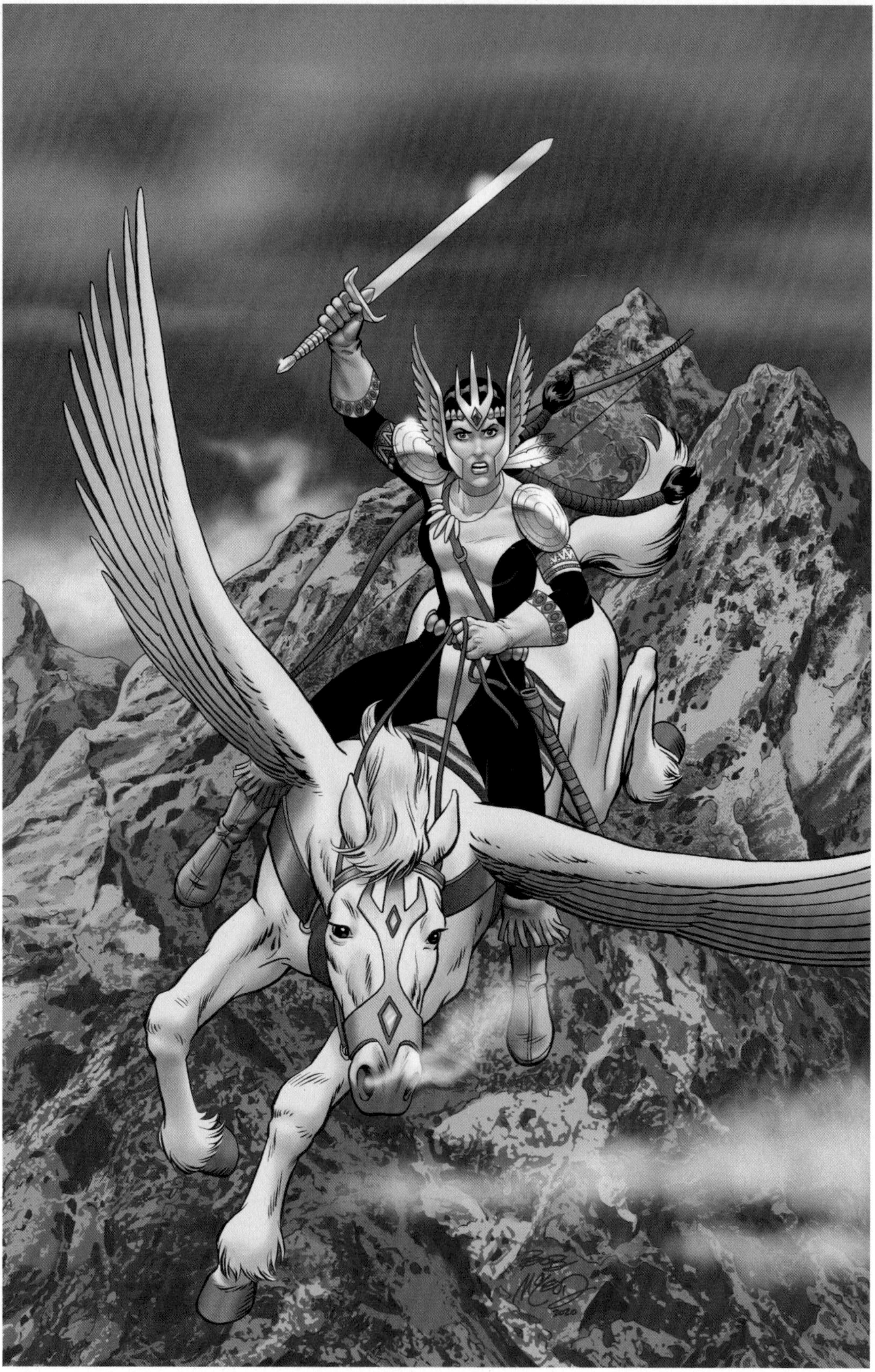

New Mutants #17 Variant by Bob McLeod

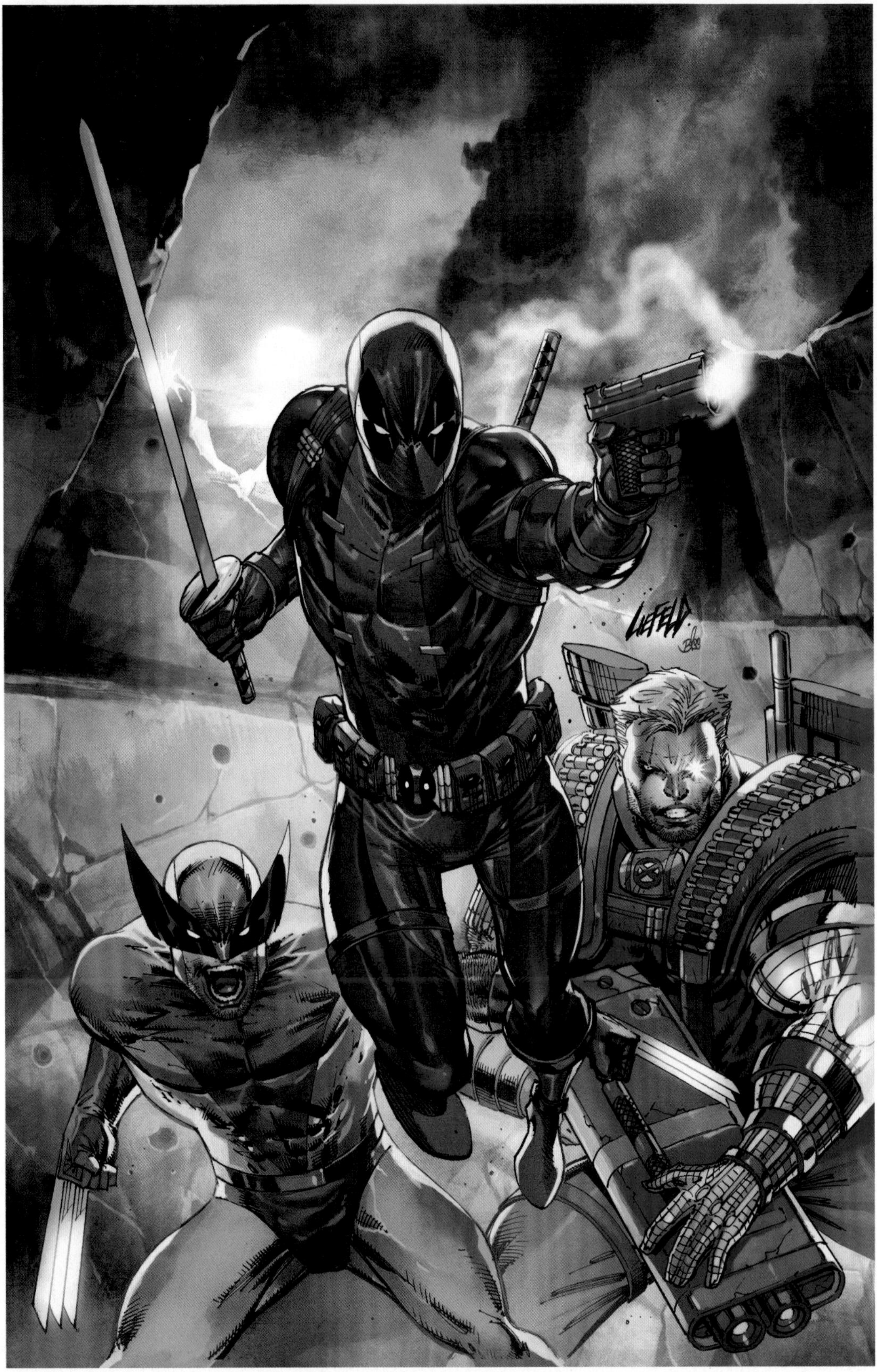
LIEFELD

X-Force #18 Deadpool 30th Anniversary Variant by Rob Liefeld

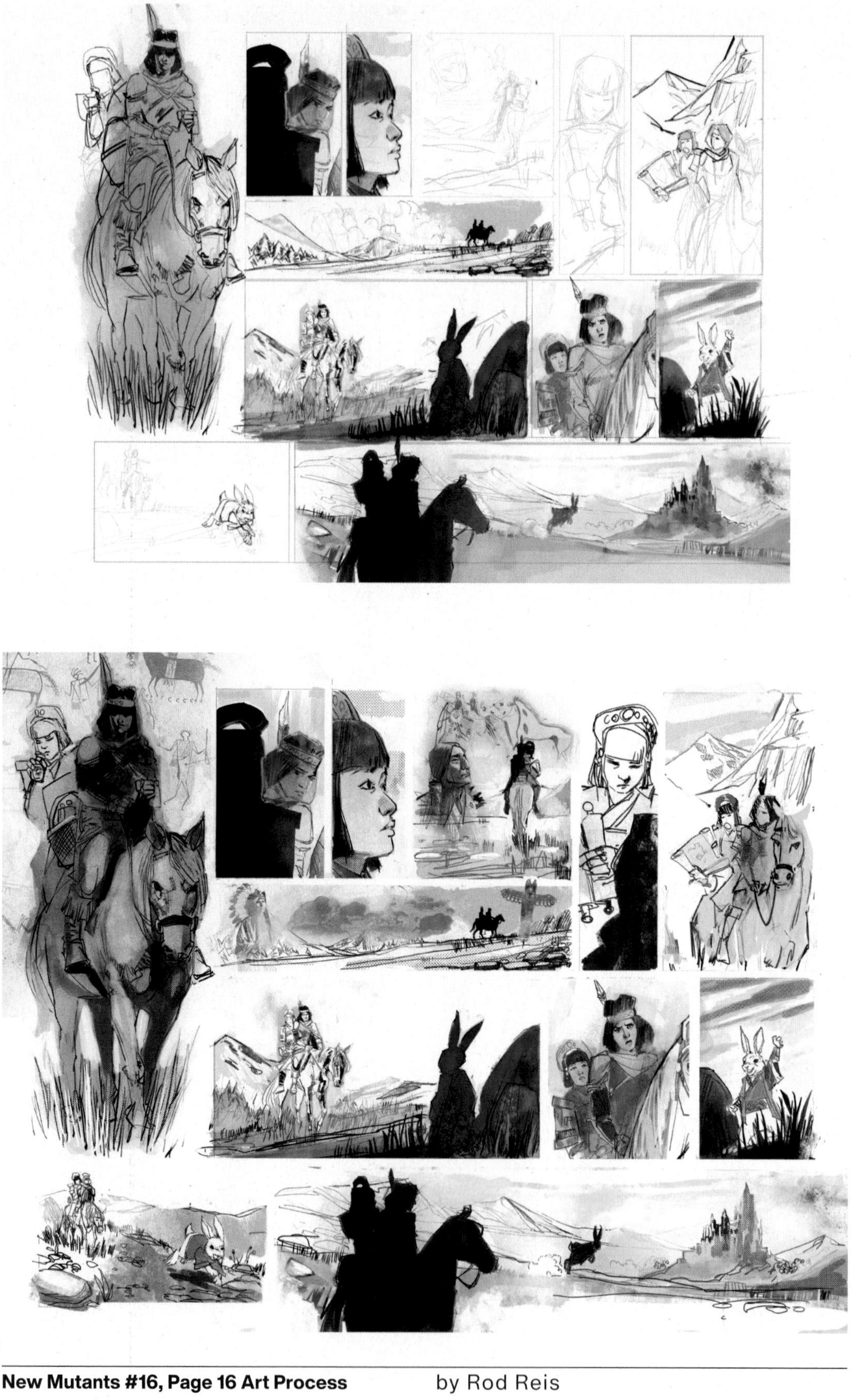

New Mutants #16, Page 16 Art Process by Rod Reis

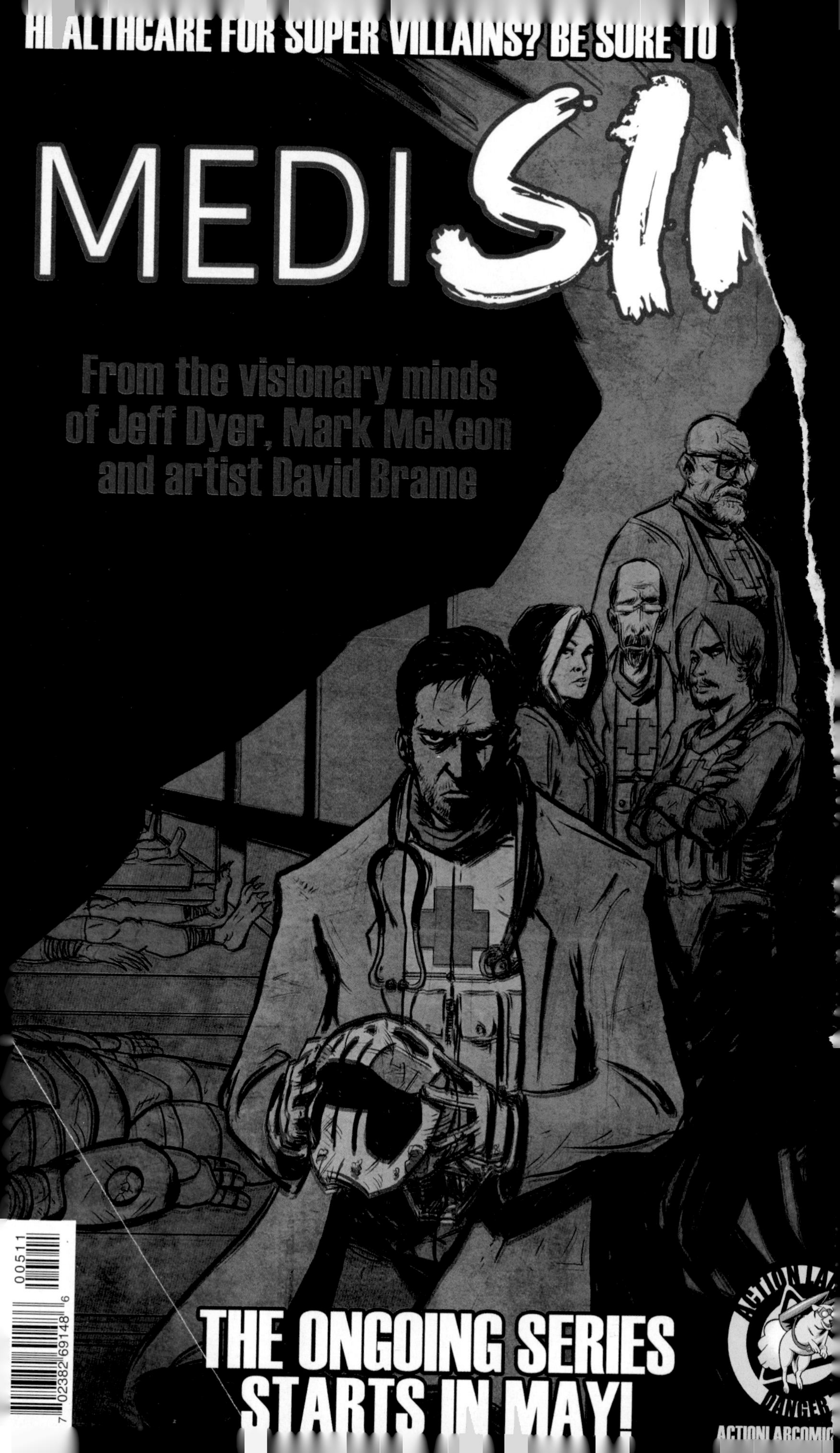
H ALTHCARE FOR SUPER VILLAINS? BE SURE TO
MEDI
From the visionary minds of Jeff Dyer, Mark McKeon and artist David Brame
THE ONGOING SERIES STARTS IN MAY!

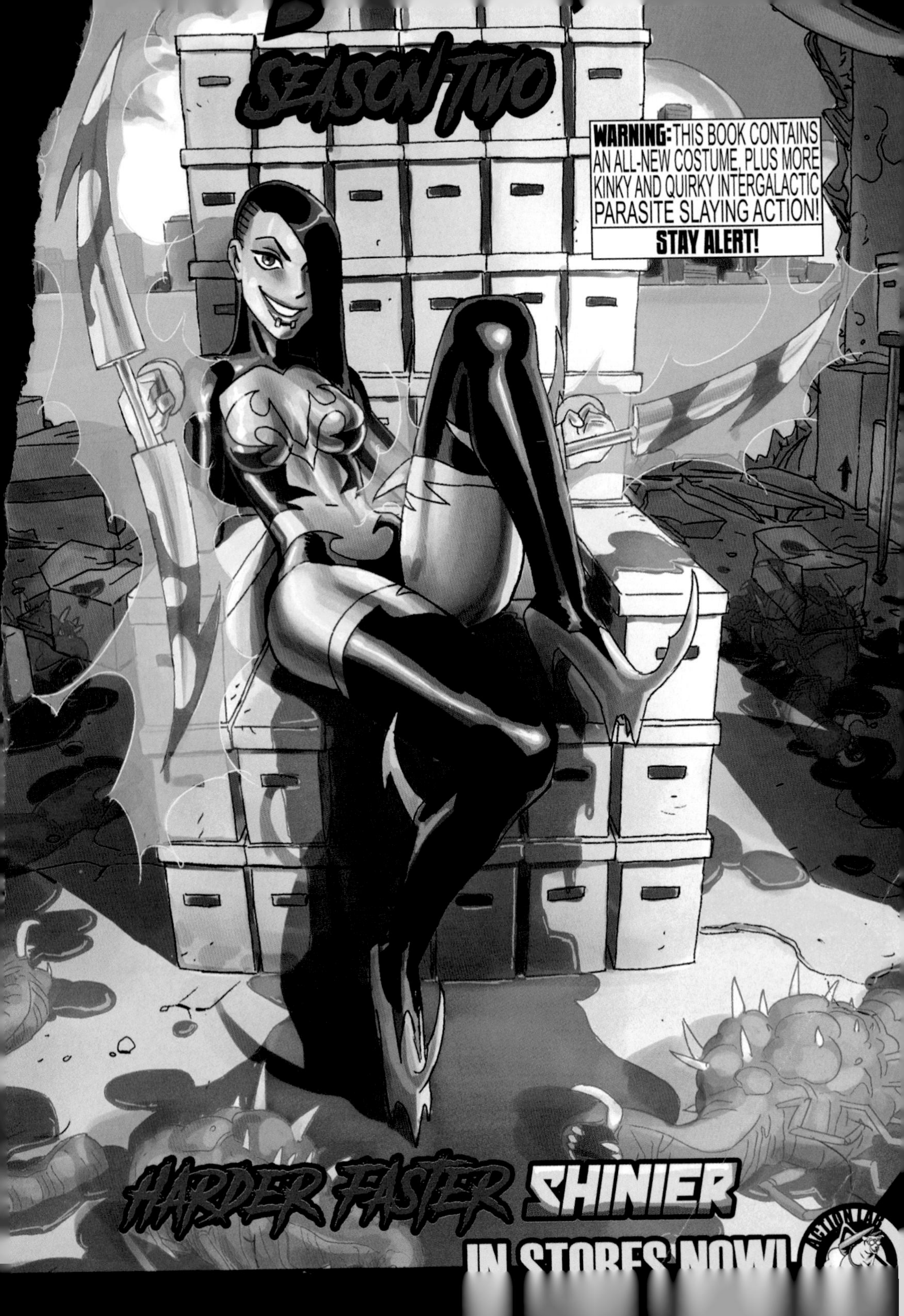
SEASON TWO
WARNING: THIS BOOK CONTAINS AN ALL-NEW COSTUME, PLUS MORE KINKY AND QUIRKY INTERGALACTIC PARASITE SLAYING ACTION!
STAY ALERT!
HARDER FASTER SHINIER
IN STORES NOW!

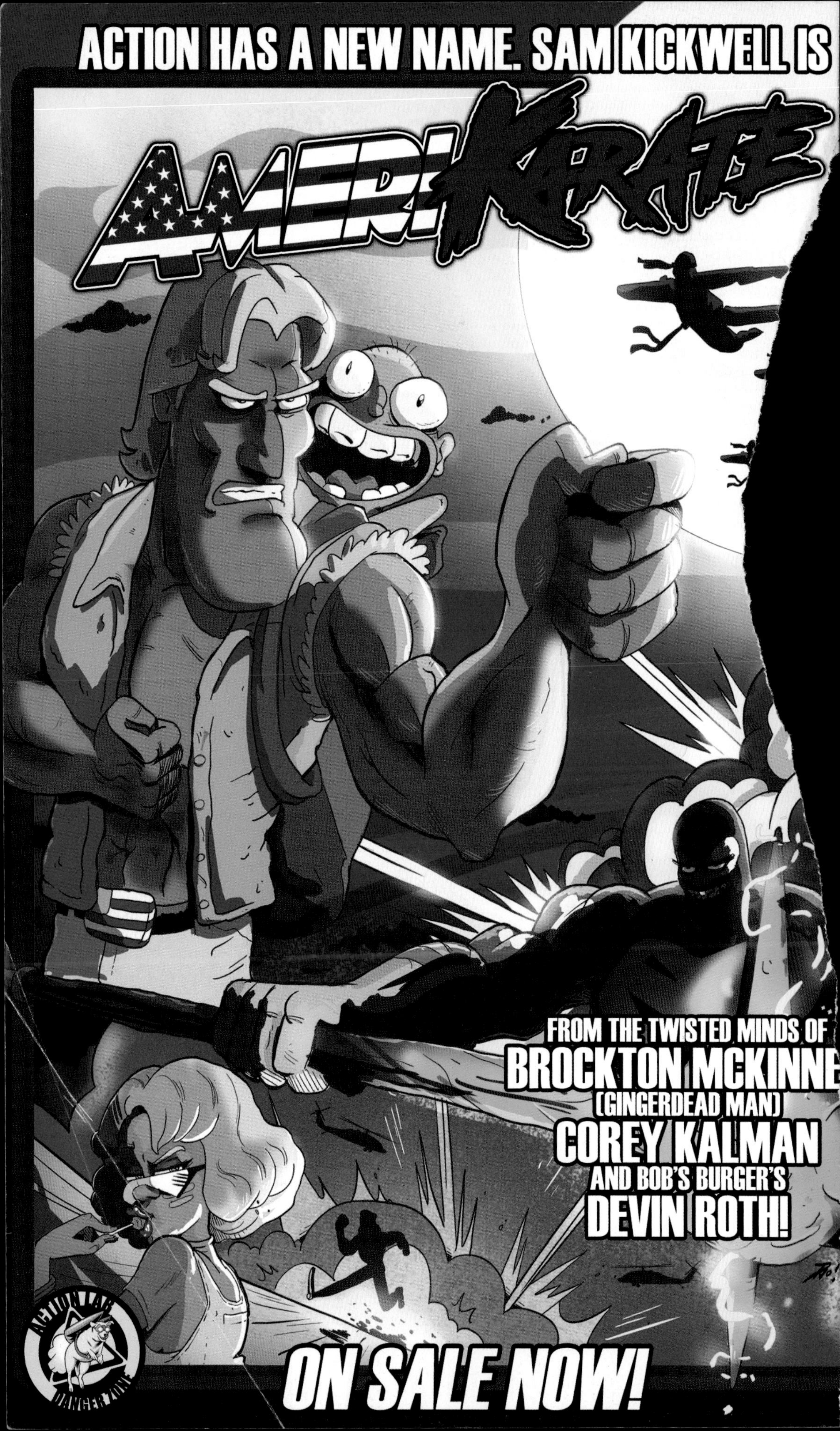
ACTION HAS A NEW NAME. SAM KICKWELL IS
AMERIKARATE
FROM THE TWISTED MINDS OF
BROCKTON MCKINNE
(GINGERDEAD MAN)
COREY KALMAN
AND BOB'S BURGER'S
DEVIN ROTH!
ACTION LAB
DANGER ZONE
ON SALE NOW!

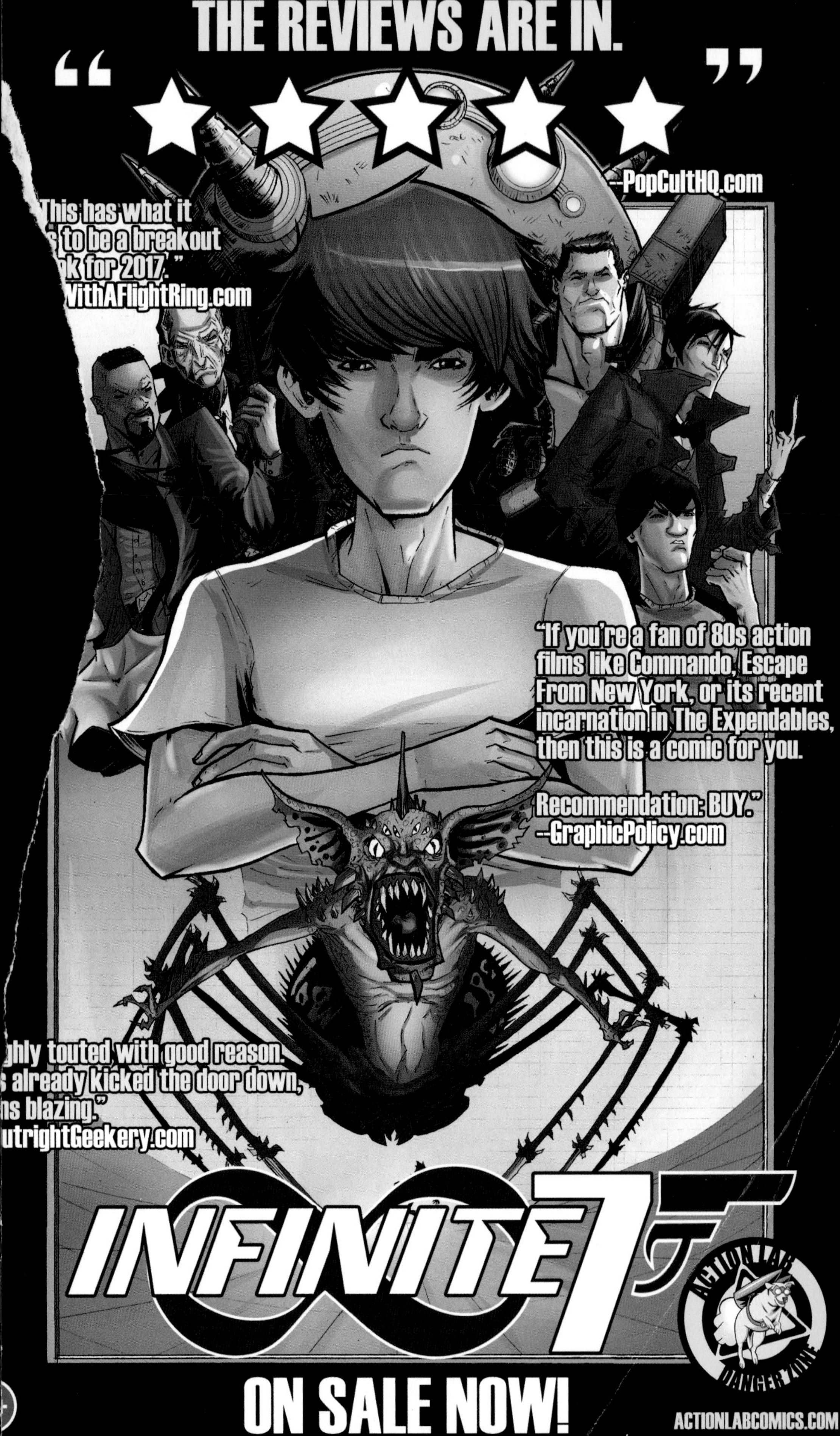
THE REVIEWS ARE IN.
--PopCultHQ.com
This has what it
s to be a breakout
ok for 2017."
WithAFlightRing.com
"If you're a fan of 80s action films like Commando, Escape From New York, or its recent incarnation in The Expendables, then this is a comic for you.
Recommendation: BUY."
--GraphicPolicy.com
ghly touted with good reason.
s already kicked the door down,
ns blazing."
utrightGeekery.com
INFINITE 7
ACTION LAB
DANGER ZONE
ON SALE NOW!
ACTIONLABCOMICS.COM